Don't Laugh

Keeping the Joneses Up, Vol. I

Sacha Jones

Umbilical Books

Copyright © 2016, 2024 Sacha Jones

First published in 2016 as *The Grass Was Always Browner* by Finch Publishing Pty Limited.

Sacha Jones asserts her moral right to be identified as the author of this work.

All rights reserved. No part of this publication may be reproduced or transmitted in any form or by any means, electronic or mechanical, including photocopying, recording or information storage and retrieval systems, without permission in writing from the copyright holder.

Published by Umbilical Books
Contact: umbilicalbooks@gmail.com

A catalogue record for this book is available from the National Library of New Zealand.

ISBN 978-0-473-70962-4 (Paperback)
ISBN 978-0-473-70963-1 (EPUB)

Cover design: Nicole Davies

Contents

Prologue	1
1. What's in a name?	3
2. The girl with the long second toe	14
3. Keeping the Joneses up	31
4. Pink milk blues	50
5. Green eyes, brown socks	66
6. Of mice, men, money and mayhem	86
7. Too many teeth	101
8. The toughest girl in school	113
9. Sentimental Saturday	140
10. Running off to join the ballet	156
11. An absentminded professor en pointe	174
12. My brilliant year	197
13. Welcome to Wagga Wagga	217
14. Laxatives to London	240
Epilogue	269
Acknowledgments	273
About the Author	275
Other Books by the Author	277

Prologue

The Grass Was Always Browner

When I grew up, the grass was always greener somewhere else. To be fair, the grass where I lived was brown most of the year round and covered in biting bindis to boot, it being Australia where everything bites, even the grass. Also, I have green eyes and it stands to reason green eyes are going to want to see green more than other colour eyes. It didn't help that I was the only member of my family of five with green eyes.

I think the final straw for me growing up was that the suburb of Sydney I grew up in was called French's Forest but was clearly no forest. Forests are lush, green, shady places with frolicking critters and chirruping birds. Where we lived was the bush: brash, brittle and barking – and brown. Our critters had about as much frolic as a blowfly; our *birds* – and I use the term loosely because our airborne creatures were more like medium-sized dogs with wings – wouldn't have chirruped if you'd paid them. Chirruping was strictly for sissies as far as *our* birds were concerned. 'Mwa-ha-ha-haaaa,' laughed these brash beasts of the bush from their dawn perch on the neighbourhood's hoists, reminding those of us trying to make our homes in the fake forest just what a bunch of sad and sorry fools we were.

As for our trees, with their perpetually peeling, skyscraper trunks, uncoordinated limbs and dry, brittle leaves the colour of an old bruise, they were about as lush as Lent. An ant was lucky to find shade under those loose and lanky limbs – an Australian ant, which is naturally about ten times the size of a regular ant, forget about it. No. Where we lived was no forest; it should have been called French's Bush. I don't know who French was, but in my book he (or she, but probably he) has a lot to answer for.

You can change a fair bit about yourself growing up but not, as it turns out, the name of your suburb or the colour of your eyes (or suburb). I know that *now*. But growing up I didn't quite. Growing up in the fake forest, I felt I couldn't breathe and had to find a way out to greener and more truthfully named pastures or die trying. And so I did. This is my, somewhat unlikely, laughable if you dare, story.

But a quick word of warning to any other green-eyed prisoners of the fake forest out there who might be inclined to want to follow in my footsteps: *don't*. That particular portal of peculiarity is closed. And even if it wasn't, I wouldn't recommend it. Because once out of the fake forest you might just find, as I did, that you're not entirely out of the woods. So what I say instead is: find your own way out. Or stay put. Laxatives are not for everyone.

Chapter 1

What's in a name?

If things were called what they were supposed to be called and people were born where they were supposed to be born, I would have been called Sacha and born in Russia – ideally in a proper forest. Alas, being born in Australia to non-Russian parents, I was *not* called Sacha or born in, or anywhere near, a proper forest, as already established. I was called Sally and born in the bush.

Sacha is a Russian Greek French Slavic name meaning, in all those languages, brave defender of mankind. Sally is a name in English only that means precisely nothing; or worse than nothing. It is a nickname for another equally dull name, Sarah, as well as an abbreviation of salamander – a less dull name for a human, granted, but one that is shared with a small lizard. Not even a *large* lizard. It's also a verb. One can sally forth, for goodness sake! In short, *Sally* barely knows who, what or where she is, and this was my first problem growing up, even before I realised I was living in a fake forest in which the grass, and everything else, bit.

Added to this first problem, as if that were possible, was the unhappy coincidence that the Henderson's Labrador who lived three doors down answered to the very name. When 'Sally, come *here!*' rang out in our neighbourhood, I'd come here in a hurry only to find my parents enjoying a quiet cocktail on the veranda, somewhat surprised to see me here, there or anywhere. My name was so meaningless my parents sometimes forgot I even existed. I envied that dog; having a meaningless name must be so much less demoralising for a dog.

'Why did you call me Sally?' I pressed my mother from an early age, having an uneasy feeling that the Henderson's dog had had something to do with it. My mother's reply of 'I just liked the name,' was entirely too vague, not to mention improbable, to reassure me.

My second given name is Charlotte. Growing up I didn't mind Charlotte nearly as much as I minded Sally, in part because it was Mum's mother's name and she was not a dog – or a small lizard. Indeed, I didn't know any dogs (or small lizards) called Charlotte, though there was one spider, but she was a very special spider, so I didn't have any objection to that. Also I quite *liked* Nana, as we called the original Charlotte; our only living grandparent, at least as far as we had been led to believe. Dad's mother, as it turned out, was also alive and living quite nearby, but that fact was kept from us until she was dead and we were all grown up. But I liked Nana not only because I knew that she was alive, but because I'd heard tell of how she used to ride her horse bareback and side-saddle through the waves of

Bondi beach when she was a girl, which sounded pretty impressive to me.

But the trouble with Charlotte was that it was not my first name and nobody called me by it, unless I was being 'too clever for my own good' or 'always wanting the last word'. At these times, which were not altogether infrequent when I was growing up, Dad would look to Mum, provided Nana wasn't present, and say: 'She's not called Charlotte for nothing,' which took some of the charm off that name for me too, even if it did mean I was at least called Charlotte for *something*, which was better than for nothing – or for a dog or a small lizard.

Still, when Dad said 'she's not called Charlotte for nothing' I wanted to protest, 'But I'm *not* called Charlotte, remember? I'm called Sally.' I didn't think my parents should be able to have it both ways. I didn't protest, however, as I was already in trouble for being too clever for my own good, but I probably should have done because I was right.

But what I really wanted was my very own name, not a verb or a dog or a lizard, and one preferably with a Russian inflexion. Was that too much to ask? Apparently it was.

'Marinka' was the name I came up with when I was eight or nine and tried to get people to call me by instead of Sally. But for some reason it never caught on. It's not as easy as it sounds getting people to call you by an entirely different name, at least not in the fake forest, which is ironic, I think.

It was not until much later on that I figured out you can make Sacha, a perfectly decent Russian-sounding, mostly human name – if one usually given to boys – by squashing my first two names together and removing most of the letters. It's a pity I didn't work this out sooner, because as it turns out it is even harder to get people to call you by a completely different name after 40 years than it is after eight or nine. But at least I worked it out before I wrote this book. Who wants to read a book about a girl called Sally? I'll leave that as a rhetorical question.

*　*　*

It is probably best not to get me started on Jones. Indeed, if truth be told, despite the Henderson's dog, small lizards and verbs, I think I might have been happy with *Sally* if my last name had not been the most common and least Russian-sounding name in all of Australia, if not the world. And I confess I abandoned Jones at the first opportunity. In fact I may even have rushed into marriage with someone not called Jones for that very reason. Why I came back to Jones is a little more complicated, although the fact that I didn't marry a Russian is probably part of the story.

Another part of the story is that Jones was not exactly Dad's name, for Dad was a bit of a name-changer too. Jones was the name Dad chose, or modified, for reasons that are a little unclear but had something to do with him losing all faith in his mother and father, as well as him wanting to reject the pretentiousness of the family brand that his original name symbolised for him. Growing up I clashed with Dad somewhat, though not only because he changed his name from a more distinctive one to the most ordinary name in the entire world. But I don't think this helped. Names are important. Today that choice and others he made make a bit more sense to me, as does the name Jones. Let me explain – briefly – why.

Dad was born Mark Lloyd-Jones, the son of Eric Lloyd-Jones, a Managing Director of the family business, David Jones. David Jones, the Welsh founder of Australia's first and, some would say finest department store and the oldest department store in the world to be still trading under its original name. When David set up his store in 1838 he had just been Jones, but somewhere along the line the 'Lloyd' was adopted by his descendants and 'Lloyd-Jones' became the name synonymous with the David Jones family brand. As an adult, Dad rejected the pompousness of this double-barrelled family brand, officially demoting his 'Lloyd' to the status of a middle name, a name he would, eventually, pass on to his son. The Lloyd would be lost to his daughters entirely.

Dad was born in 1920, the last of four children; an 'afterthought', he always said, as he was eight years younger than his next youngest sibling. He was born with a shiny silver spoon in his mouth to be sure, his father at the time being lauded in the papers as 'the Merchant Prince of Sydney'. But the shine soon wore off that silver spoon when his father, who Dad said had been pressured into the directorship when he was too young after *his* father was killed in a freak train accident involving an exploding boiler, decided, at the tender age of 38, and when Dad was only two, it was time to retire to concentrate on playing tennis. Although by all accounts Eric had been a successful manager of the family firm, overseeing its' shift of the basis of production from imported goods to locally manufactured goods, opening Australia's largest factory of its kind employing 1000 workers in the process, he felt he'd had enough of this success and left the job in the hands of his brother Charles, the man who went on to become 'Sir Charles Lloyd Jones', one of the most well-regarded Australians of all time, knighted for his services to retail and for his role as the founding Chairman of the Australian Broadcasting Corporation (ABC). Oh, well. Our loss was clearly the country's, and our cousins', gain.

For Sir Charles' tennis-mad younger brother and family did not fare *quite* so well, and that is putting things mildly. With four children still to raise, this rash decision of Eric's to take early retirement from one of the country's top jobs to play more tennis, was, by all accounts, not terribly well received by his wife, Kathleen Booth-Jones – *before* she married. That is what can happen when you're a Jones. You can be a Jones-Jones, as my other grandmother, the one we thought was dead, was. Or rather, she was a Booth-Jones-Lloyd-Jones, on account of everybody trying to jazz up their Jones; everybody except Dad, that is. But one good thing about being a Jones is that when we marry another Jones, because there are so many of us it doesn't necessarily mean we are marrying our first or even second cousins, though one of David Jones' sons did marry his first cousin, but that's another story (though it would explain a lot).

But cousins or not, Kathleen was not happy about this reckless move and threatened to leave Eric if he lost his money, causing endless bitter fights about money versus tennis that Dad remembered as the main feature of his early childhood, and that were likely some part of the cause of his lifelong stutter. In the end, Eric left Kathleen *before* he lost all his money and as a consequence, Dad, who, under pressure, chose to go with his father, never saw or heard from his mother again. He was eight at the time.

So Dad was raised by his father without any contact with his three older siblings – who went with their mother after the divorce. This was less than ideal. With his father doing his best to throw his money away on trips to Wimbledon and a series of ill-advised investment schemes, including something to do with string beans, while insisting on regular correctional coaching for Dad to sort out his stutter *and* left-handedness, all to no avail, things after the divorce went from bad to worse. With the last of his money, his father bought a farm in the lower Blue Mountains and before long ran out of the funds to employ people to work it. His answer was to take Dad, then fifteen and top of History and English at Sydney Grammar, out of school to milk cows on the farm.

Four years later, on his nineteenth birthday, the minimum age for enlistment, Dad was finally relieved of the job of milking cows by the outbreak of World War II. The only trouble with this otherwise convenient development was that Dad was practically blind without his glasses and they didn't let soldiers wear glasses. But keen to get away from those cows – and his father by now – and in possession of a photographic memory that hadn't been put to good use for a while, Dad memorised the eye chart during the early part of the medical examination and sailed into the war with flying colours – if half blind. Somehow he survived, but his family name didn't. He returned from the war just Jones.

* * *

Whoever said 'what's in a name?' clearly hadn't met my family, because Mum's family were name-changers too. Born in London in 1923, Mum was officially christened Margaret Ethel Burke but unofficially called Peggy, the name her parents preferred but one that at the time was not on the register of acceptable names. Her last name, Burke, was not strictly her real name either, as her father's family were Germans by the name of Boecker. But after the Germans killed her father's younger brother in the First World War he was so offended he officially anglicised his last name from Boecker to Burke and his first name from Rudolph to Rupert. Mum's older brother and only sibling, Walter, born during that war, was then named after this unfortunate uncle. Otherwise he was to be called Sydney after his mother's place of birth, his mother being the original Charlotte. Some would say a lucky escape for him.

Mum also had a lucky escape in war. During the Battle of Britain, she was a teenager living with her mother in Croydon, a target for the German campaign, when a Luftwaffe bomb landed in the next-door neighbour's garden blowing out all the glass in their tall windows, upstairs and down, and collapsing the roof, while she took shelter with Nana in the cupboard under the stairs. The neighbour's house was obliterated entirely, so it was just as well that *they* had taken the precaution of moving out during the battle. Nana evidently had taken a more Australian approach to evacuation: she'll be right, mate. And she was, but only just.

Nana, although Australian, must have been terrified for her teenage daughter and wished she herself had never left Bondi. Why she did leave Bondi for Croydon was down to Rudolph (Rupert, Ru), who had travelled to Sydney from London on the brink of World War I in his capacity as a hide-classer. When Ru turned up in Bondi in early 1914, Nana was 27 and the only daughter (of five) yet unwed, quite happy riding her horse through the waves of Bondi, her mother calling out from the shore when the sea was particularly rough: 'Hold on, Ethel!', because Nana mostly went by her middle name. Why she went by Ethel instead of Charlotte I used to wonder about as a child; surely Charlotte is a better name than Ethel. But I guess *some* people can be fairly strange about names.

Ru, however, had other ideas, and after a short time proposed to Nana over the washing up one day, seizing a tea towel as he valiantly stated his case, concluding by asking Nana: 'Is there any hope?' Nana, encouraged by the tea towel, said that there was, not knowing that it would be the last tea towel Ru ever held.

Nor did she know she would be more than 50 years in England before returning to Australia after Ru died and Mum had travelled to Australia herself, charmed by the bareback-in-Bondi story as well as the Australian accent that she used to hear on the radio in London. She was also hoping to find a partner, which she finally did, just in the nick of time. How *this* came about is another quite unlikely story ...

* * *

My parents met late in life in a sharebroking firm in Sydney, where Dad was working as an accounts broker and Mum as a secretary. Mum was going on 40 and Dad was 43. What had taken them longer than most to find a partner is not altogether clear. In Mum's case, she had two broken engagements to her name due in part, it seems, to her preference for finding someone who looked like the film star Clark Gable. For Dad, the war had interrupted his stride somewhat, as he spent most of it in Papua New Guinea without his glasses. It's possible, too, that his own parents' marriage put him off the idea a little. But by this late stage in the game they were similarly ready to take the plunge and perhaps a little less picky than they might have been otherwise. Dad, indeed, did not look *anything* like Clark Gable, nor did he have much of an Australian accent thanks to his posh, if unfinished, schooling.

Still, their place of work was a large firm and Mum and Dad had been working there for more than a year without having met. And it seems they may never have met if not for some visiting Germans, a trio of wise men who came unannounced to the office one day and asked – in German – to speak to someone in charge: *'Bitte können wir sprechen Sie mit Ihrem Chef?'* or words to that effect. Possibly confusing the outcome of the war, these perhaps not-so-wise men seemed to assume everyone in Sydney spoke German. And when they received blank stares to their question, even after it was repeated slowly, a crowd formed around them until someone figured out they were Germans. Once this vital detail was ascertained someone else piped up: 'Peggy Burke speaks German!'

Now, if you've been following this brief if somewhat entangled family history you will perhaps recall that Peggy Burke is the name, albeit the unofficial one, of the woman who would become my mother. You won't know she spoke German, however. And as it happened she *didn't* speak German nearly as well as she had done while working in Austria as a code breaker's assistant after the war. At *that* time she was fluent. But since then she had been somewhat distracted, looking high and low for Clark Gable and travelling to Australia, among other things that had not improved her German any. So when she was eventually accosted by the trio of Germans and tasked with explaining what they wanted, she found that their speech, heavy in stockbroking jargon, was barely comprehensible.

Happily, this small detail proved an incidental footnote to my parents getting together, because standing in the crowd gathered round these three not-so-wise men, overhearing this statement about the German-speaking Peggy Burke, was none other than the man who would become my father. And for some reason that he was never quite able to explain, the idea caught his curiosity and he resolved to make the acquaintance of this bilingual Peggy Burke at the nearest possible opportunity, which he duly did. Mum kept *schtum* about the three wise men, Dad never asked, and the rest, as they say, is history.

They were married in a civilised sort of haste the day after Dad's final exam for his also much delayed Bachelor of Economics degree at Sydney University and with Mum insisting on keeping the word 'fruitful' in her vows, against the minister's discreet suggestion that the word be left out because it was not appropriate at her age. But Mum, like Dad, was not one to be constrained by practicalities if she could help it. And, as it turned out, she could. Eleven months later, my brother Timothy Lloyd Jones was born; roughly two-and-a-half years after that, my sister Barbara Lynette Jones arrived, and almost exactly halfway in between, in the hottest month of 1966, a hellishly hot year, Sally Charlotte Jones, aka Sacha, the future brave defender of mankind, turned up in the land of fake forests and improbable fruits. With three children under three, the doctors hurried to tie Mum's tubes or she'd likely still be making improbable fruit in the fake forest, where she continues to live at the ripe old age of – well, I'll let you do the math.

Chapter 2

The Girl with the Long Second Toe

'It's a girl!'

Mum was asleep when I was born, as she was for all three of us, due to Tim's *massive* head and her small pelvis (and large age); factors that combined in those days to mean we all had to be born by Caesarean section under a general anaesthetic. Mum says she was bitterly disappointed by all of this, but it couldn't be helped. It certainly wasn't *my* fault. When you make improbable fruit in the fake forest at a ripe old age you can't expect it to be straightforward.

Mum claims she came to during the operation just in time to hear the nurse cry: 'It's a girl!' before falling back into a satisfied state of unconsciousness. But she was probably dreaming. She had wanted a girl second and a boy first, all in the right order, as she saw it, and so she probably imagined hearing what she wanted to hear. We can all be guilty of *that*. Whatever the case, it was a girl and Mum would wake up to meet her eventually, when she was delivered to her bedside, already washed and swathed, by one of an efficient team of nurses at Sydney's Royal North Shore Hospital. Dad was on his way.

As new mums are wont to do, while waiting for Dad (who was at the florist), Mum peeled back the hospital swathe to check fingers and toes, and was pleased to see that not only did her daughter have ten of each, but the second toe on each foot was extra-long. She had read somewhere that a long second toe was a sign of intelligence and felt – at that point at least – that intelligence was generally a good thing. Later, it seems, she would not be so sure.

But there was little time to ponder the wider ramifications of this long toe, or to check the rest of me for signs of other useful attributes, before Dad came bounding in bearing a dozen red roses and his own big news. 'I am going to write a book, hon!' said he. 'I've got it all figured out!' was Dad's big news, announced with such enthusiasm that Mum's news – about my birth *and* extra-long toe – had to wait. Mum didn't mind, she was always pleased to receive good news, not least when she was high on painkillers. She was also happily distracted by those sweet-smelling roses that a nurse obligingly whisked away and returned in a vase for her bedside table. 'That's wonderful, love! I'm so pleased', Mum will surely have said, gazing at those blushing roses, not altogether meaning to encourage Dad to expand further on his plan to write a book about the Third World but inadvertently doing so.

And so as Dad began to expound on his plan to write a book on development economic theory that he hoped would one day save the Third World and Mum listened as keenly as she could, understanding about as much as she would have done had he been speaking in German, I lay in her arms, less than an hour old, my long second toes wriggling with a sense of disquiet that all was not quite right in my world, wanting to tell my parents, but not being able to get a word in edgewise, that for starters: 'You've got the wrong name!'

So my timing as well as my destination was a little off when I arrived in this world, the very day Dad decided, in a somewhat unlikely mid-life crisis, that he wanted to save the Third World. For looking after *one* baby in the fake forest with Dad holding down a full-time job during the week and trying to save the Third World on the weekends would have been quite challenging enough for people in their forties of less than practical dispositions. But looking after two babies in these circumstances was simply asking for trouble. It would be touch and go if we would be saved, let alone the Third World.

At least Dad had given up the gambling by this stage. In his bachelor years he had been quite a heavy gambler on the horses, winning and losing a fair amount of money along the way, having something of an easy-come-easy-go attitude to money. But money was not quite as easy come now that he had a wife and two babies under the age of two to support, as well as a pressing desire to save the Third World, so it was just as well that he gave up gambling when he got married. But he continued to have an extravagant streak, even after he made his commitment to saving the Third World, which did not exactly help the situation in anyone's world, except for maybe the world of Prouds jewellers, Sydney's most expensive jewellery shop, where Dad liked nothing more than to buy extravagant pieces of jewellery for Mum, as well as our local Chinese takeaway where Dad tipped excessively. The staff there must have thought Mr Jones was the richest man in Australia. He wasn't.

His father might have been once, but those riches were long gone. The deposit for our modest three-bedroom house in the fake forest had been paid for in large part by the sale of Mum's father's stamp collection; nothing to do with David Jones. The car Dad drove to the hospital to deliver his dozen red roses and big news to Mum was an ancient Austin A30 with a gaping hole in her floor, held together by her good name alone. For naturally Mum and Dad named all their cars as a matter of priority. This one was called Patsy. But Dad was not a car man by any stretch of the imagination, and so was disinclined to spend money on anything as practical as fixing Patsy's flooring. He much preferred to spend the money on extravagances such as the dozen red roses he delivered to Mum's bedside *every* day of her two-week stay in a private maternity ward, to the point that she became so embarrassed by the profusion of red around her bed that she asked the nurses to distribute the roses around the ward. The money spent on those red roses alone, not to mention the jewellery, would probably have been enough to save the Third World right there.

Indeed we were none of us practical people. Nana, who had just arrived back from England after 53 years away to look after Tim while Mum was in hospital having me, was the most practical, or least impractical, member of the family. But she was a couple of months off 80 when I was born, and having looked after Tim for the entire two weeks of Mum's confinement, taking him in on the weekends to wave at his mother through the ground floor window of the ward so as not to disturb the mothers and their roses, she was quite ready to leave Mum to it when the time came and return to the peace and tranquillity of her two-bedroom unit in Queenscliff, a safe distance away. Dad, of course, had to carry on working at his First World job during the week, there being no such thing as paternity leave in those days and him needing to work overtime to pay for all those roses anyway, as well as devoting his time to the Third World on the weekends. So that meant it was largely left to Mum to make the adjustment from the sweet-smelling efficiency of the private maternity ward of the Royal North Shore Hospital to our not quite so sweet-smelling situation, deep in the fake forest.

Tim was also going to have to make a tiny adjustment too. Fifteen months young and traumatised by the unexplained disappearance of his mother for two long weeks, his adjustment was not going to be easy. Indeed it was more a question of how long it would take him to adjust and what lengths he would go to in the meantime to return the situation to the way it had been before his mother had disappeared and I had appeared.

A few weeks went by without incident, a period that might be described as the honeymoon period, with all the delusions of easy happiness that that implies, as Tim bided his time and Mum thought: 'This is easy. I could do this two-babies-under-the-age-of-one-and-a-half-at-the-age-of-forty-two thing with my eyes closed' and promptly closed her eyes, because in fact she was more tired than she'd ever been in her life. That was Tim's opportunity to strike. One fine morning when I was about four weeks old and Mum was occupied in the kitchen humming, because it helped her keep her eyes open, I was lying in my open-topped bassinette in the living room – with Tim. Within short reach stood an empty glass milk bottle; it was a one-litre capacity bottle with extra thick glass to withstand the knocks, and, held upturned by the neck, was practically a purpose-built weapon for a sixteen-month-old baby boy, with attitude, to wield. To his credit, in a law-of-the-jungle sense, Tim saw its potential as a weapon immediately, much sooner than Mum did. And with Mum's back turned Tim, quick as he could, tottered over to the table, seized the weapon by the neck in his fat little fist, and tottered back to my bassinette. There, he raised the glass club up over his head and prepared to bring it down onto mine.

'No!' Mum assures me she screamed out as she emerged from the kitchen to see Tim poised to strike with the upturned milk bottle in his hand, an expression of intent on his face. She seized the weapon from him, just in the nick of time.

No doubt deeply displeased by a good plan foiled, Tim would not wait too much longer before his next attempt, which would be a little more successful than the first. With the glass clubs put out of reach, he would have to find some other weapon to use. But gaining in strength all the time, it was not long before he found that his own bare hands were pretty effective weapons in themselves. I was just sitting up, surely an added affront, and with Mum's head turned again, Tim, sitting next to me, took hold of a chunk of skin on my arm and gave it such a pinch that Mum, who turned back just at that moment, saw my face go rose red with what she took to be fury, before I toppled over onto the bare floorboards and promptly passed out. Tim could not have been more pleased.

Not being able to rouse me and finding my body quite limp, Mum thought she had better take me to the doctor, who was concerned enough to send me back to hospital for my head to be plugged with monitors to see if any damage had been done to my brain. The results of those tests remain inconclusive. Apparently, as one of the nurses told Mum at the time: 'These tests can be very difficult to read.'

Fortunately Mum was not one to worry too much, and being already pregnant with her next child by this stage, she could not afford to waste too much time thinking about whether or not I was brain damaged. As to Mum worrying about *Tim's* brain, in terms of his behaviour suggesting anything untoward, she didn't even consider it. 'It's perfectly natural for a little boy to be threatened by his younger sister. You shouldn't take it personally,' she told me, much later on, when I ventured to inquire about her thoughts on the matter. I don't know what she expected those long second toes to be good for, but it clearly didn't include taking offence to my brother trying to do me grievous bodily harm.

Not long after this fury faint I poked Mum so hard in the eye that she thought I had blinded her – I had not. But thinking I had (albeit only in *one* eye) she abandoned me to the floor, and to Tim, to run tearing round the neighbourhood, clutching the wounded eye, frantically knocking on doors to find someone to drive her to the doctor. Though there was no lasting physical damage from that eye poke, Mum did have to wear an eye patch for a while afterwards and continues to maintain that she has 'never felt such agony' in all her life. It's difficult to say exactly what my motives were for this attack. At eight or nine months old I'd like to think I was innocently drawn by the twinkle in Mum's eye as she held me up over her head lying back on the floor, as mothers without a care in the world are wont to do. But these things can be difficult to read. The important thing is not to take it personally.

* * *

It was around about this time that Dad decided, in a rare flash of practicality, that Mum wasn't quite coping and needed help. Although Dad was by all accounts a great help to Mum when at home, even changing nappies, something most fathers of the day apparently avoided on pain of death, he was not home much during our waking hours. Monday to Friday he was away from seven in the morning till six in the evening, and every Saturday from the week of my birth, come rain, hail or shine, he was in the State Library of NSW, researching the economic problems of the Third World. So just as soon as Tim reached the minimum age of admission (two) he was enrolled at the local private kindergarten for two full days a week at the considerable expense at the time of $1.80 per day; the most practical money Mum and Dad ever spent. And for a while all was rather quieter on the home front, until the fun began all over again with the arrival of number three.

My sister Babs, as she would affectionately be known by one and all, was born a few months later; the cutest baby you ever saw, with huge round, deep brown eyes, the same colour as Mum's. I was not threatened immediately by the arrival of the cutest baby ever born, and did not reach for the nearest weapon;

nothing to do with the fact that the glass clubs had been put out of reach. Nor did I use my bare hands to pinch Babs into a fury faint. She was not quite as prone to fury as some, so this probably wouldn't have worked. Still, credit where credit's due. In the first year of Babs' life I am on record for being 'very attentive' to my little sister, as Mum wrote in one of the many letters she somehow found time to write back to her friends and relations in England. Whether I wanted to be attentive, or it was more a case of *someone* having to look after Babs while Mum was busy typing, remains unclear.

But in Babs' second year, as she became less of a baby and more of a rival toddler and I was packed off to kindy with Tim, leaving Babs at home on her own to receive Mum's undivided attention, I began to be rather less attentive and rather more antagonistic towards my little sister. According to another one of Mum's letters to England, I enjoyed 'teasing' Babs by stealing her favourite 'pubbah' (pillow), and refused to dress myself when Mum dressed Babs on mornings when we were rushing off to kindy. 'Sally becomes annoyed and irritable very easily at the moment,' Mum wrote in that letter, without offering an explanation. But later in the same letter she writes: 'Tim never stops talking, issuing instructions to the girls,' which would seem to me to be an explanation, at least a partial one. And given that Mum's solution to my refusal to dress myself was to get Tim to dress Babs, which promptly got me dressing myself again to be sure, it would seem that Mum wasn't entirely on top of the situation. If I were a *totally* impartial observer looking in on this scene, say a child psychologist specialising in Middle Child Syndrome, I might be inclined to observe a middle child squeezed uncomfortably between a big bossy rock, on the one side, and an annoyingly cute, deceptively hard pubbah on the other. But as I am not that impartial observer, I could not possibly comment.

Then there was kindy. It's fair to say I did not take kindly to kindy. Not only was I there with the big bossy rock, stressing over Mum re-dressing Babs at home to their mutual hearts' content, but for almost half the day at kindy we were shut up in a room and told to sleep. I believe there is such a thing as sleep torture where a person is prevented from going to sleep for many days and nights; a terrible thing indeed. Well, at kindy they practised this torture in reverse, and it was no less terrible. Tim could sleep anywhere, for any length of time, to the point that when he was a baby the doctor had actually reprimanded Mum for letting him sleep *too* much. She'd thought you should never wake a sleeping baby. Evidently there's a limit. Tim was that limit. But I had quite a different approach to sleep. I had to be driven around, first in Primrose, Patsy's replacement, who didn't last long, then in Deirdre, our faded brown Holden station wagon who came next, in order to get me to sleep at night. To get me to sleep during the day, let's just say they would have had a tough time torturing *me* with sleep deprivation.

It didn't help that the sleep room at kindy had a loud ticking clock on the wall and pale curtains that failed almost entirely to dim the daylight. Nor did it help that we slept, or didn't sleep, on the floor in a sea of children, at least one of whom – Tim – snored, as if to emphasise the fact that *he* was asleep and I wasn't. I looked across the room in his direction, willing him to open his eyes so I didn't feel quite so alone in that sea of sleeping children, but he never did.

From the age of two I was at kindy for fourteen hours a week, and for some of that time we were allowed to be awake. This time was a little less trying and I did my best to make the most of it. We had regular group singalongs with our teacher, Mrs Hooper, conducting and energetically mouthing the words to the songs. As one of the youngest and shortest girls I was always in the front row. This became the frontline when Mrs Hooper, standing at close range, got particularly carried away with mouthing the words. She seemed to have a huge mouth and when she mouthed the words to the chorus of 'Waltzing Matilda' I had to look away for fear of being swallowed up by that mouth. We were supposed to look to the front at all times, so Mrs Hooper would respond when I looked away with 'Waltzing Matilda, eyes to the front Sally, you'll come a waltzing Matilda with me,' which was sure to produce giggles from the group and get my eyes to the front promptly. I don't know if this was why I confused the lyrics of 'Waltzing Matilda' for 'Wall *sing* Matilda,' while spending the best part of these song sessions staring at the wall, or if it was the confusion that drew my eyes to the wall in the first place, but for some time I did suffer this confusion, wondering why the walls were singing and why we would be singing about the walls singing. Sleep deprivation might also have been part of the problem.

Still, it wasn't all wall-to-wall confusion and conflict at this age. When the sibling stars all lined up, we three young Joneses could almost work well enough together to give the impression that we were getting along, at least for a very brief part of each day. It helped when Dad was at home to relieve Tim's sense of obligation to boss us girls around when he was the only male present, and before Dad went off to work of a morning we would give him a proper send-off, each performing assigned tasks, even Babs who was barely two. Babs (with Mum's help) brushed Dad's suit with a special brush once Tim had selected which of three suits he was to wear that day, and I had selected which tie – a much more demanding task than suit selection, as Dad had about twenty ties. I had a favourite tie, a pale blue one with cute little crimson cubes tumbling all over it, which seemed to know it was the best tie and always wanted me to choose it. This didn't help. If I took too long Mum would appear at my elbow to hurry me along and find me talking to the ties, trying to explain to my favourite tie that it had to give another tie a turn. But otherwise it all ran smoothly.

I was on prune duty as well, 'assisted' by Babs. Dad had exactly three prunes in his lunch bag – as well as some other things which Mum had prepared earlier; we weren't that hard up that Dad only got three prunes in total for lunch – and at least two of those prunes were my responsibility to get from the fridge into a little piece of greaseproof paper, and safely delivered to Dad's briefcase. After selecting Dad's suit, while Dad got dressed and Babs and I did the prunes, Tim waited like a sentinel by the front door, clutching Dad's briefcase as if his life depended on it, ready to close it upon the important prunes, before handing it to Dad in the grand finale of the send-off ritual. As Tim handed Dad his briefcase he had to say, in the most reverential of tones, being, at that age, totally in awe of his father: 'Have a good day at work, Dad.'

Babs could not always be relied upon to place her prune neatly on the piece of paper next to mine, which could sometimes cause a delay in the prune procedure, as I repositioned her prune and she said 'Mine!' or some sound I understood to mean mine, and took up her prune again to put it where she thought it ought to go. As she could barely see up to the top of the card table that had been set up in the kitchen for the purpose of Dad's prunes, the final positioning of the prunes could take some time. 'Huwwy up with Dad's poones!' would then be heard coming through from the front door where Dad, Mum and Tim were now assembled, ready to go, but for the delivery of those poones.

Somehow we got there before Christmas and Tim got to say his important final send-off to Dad. Although sometimes he would be so overcome with the grave importance of the task he'd be unable to get the words out. *Once* I leapt into the breach that seemed to be much too long for Dad, who was in a terrific hurry to get to work, and said Tim's farewell wish for him. 'Have a good day at work, Daddy,' said I on that one brave occasion – never again.

Dad's homecoming I left entirely to Tim. On Fridays these would consist of him standing hand-in-hand with Mum on our front veranda, which was elevated above the street level, not unlike a stage, and when Dad pulled up in Deirdre to park on the verge down by the road, Tim would yell out in his best stage voice: 'Have you got the grog, Dad?' for Fridays were grog-buying night and thanks to Tim the entire neighbourhood knew it. There was nothing Mum could do to curb his enthusiasm, try as she might, and despite the needlessness of his inquiry. Dad always had the grog.

* * *

When Mum and Dad bought into the fake forest, our street was a quiet cul-de-sac with a deep gully of dense bush at one end. But not long after they moved in, the gully was sold off to developers and the earth-movers and rock-exploders moved in to blast the rock face and dig up the bush to make a through road for houses either side. The birds no doubt saw it coming and laughed loud at the poor fools who didn't: 'Mwa-ha-ha-haaaa.' It was all the same to them whether they perched on a clothes line or a branch. But it was not all the same to us, although Mum and Dad, who were the last to buy into our street before it was sold off, probably couldn't have afforded to buy our house otherwise.

By the time we were old enough to be playing with the neighbourhood kids our street had become a busy through road and an accident waiting to happen, especially in the vicinity of our house, which was only one house back from the top of the steep rise at the opposite end of the street from the development. In fact, our house was at the top of two steep rises; *three* if you include our driveway. Today there is a speed bump installed directly opposite our house. But that took about 30 years to arrive. In the meantime, many cats were hit and killed or nearly killed by a speeding car right outside our house; as was at least one child.

The Faheys lived directly across the road from us and had three children, Phillip, Beth and Jan, the same gender order and roughly the same ages as us. When I was not at kindy, Babs and I often played across the road with the Fahey girls or they played at our house. Mostly we played at theirs, either because Jan was the youngest or because Mrs Fahey was a bit more of a worrier than Mum. The routine was for Mrs Fahey to phone

Mum when it was time for us to go home and Mum would come and stand on our veranda, which had a good view of the place where we crossed the road, to supervise our crossing from a distance. Why she didn't come and get us I don't know, but it was probably a combination of her not wanting to go down and up our steep driveway more than she had to, and her knowing that I liked the responsibility of getting us across the road safely, which I did, for the most part.

Babs was two-and-a-half and I was not quite four when we embarked on one such crossing. Being the eldest I was in charge of the crossing and had successfully crossed us over several times before. I played it safe. Because of the steepness of the rise at the near end of our street where we stood waiting to cross, and my lack of height, I could not rely on my eyes to see if there was a car coming in time and had to trust in my ears instead. Careebong Road turned off our road just before the top of the rise and sometimes I'd be waiting for a car I could hear approaching that never came, which was frustrating. It may have been even more frustrating for Babs, for her only job was to hold onto my hand and wait for me to say 'Go!' before we both ran across the road, holding hands for a bit then breaking apart to run up the driveway to Mum.

I remember on this day we had been waiting a while, with cars coming at regular intervals from both directions, and more than one turning off into Careebong at the last minute. I don't remember loosening my grip on Babs' hand, but I do remember being a bit more frustrated with the wait that day than usual, and perhaps being a little tired of the responsibility, too. Mum waved down from the veranda and I turned to see Babs' face light up with a beaming smile in response, right before she suddenly broke free and took off across the road. I screamed out 'No!' and stepped out onto the road to pull her back, because the sound of the approaching car was so loud I knew it was almost upon us. I managed to get hold of Babs' hand and pull her back a ways but it was not enough. The speeding car that came flying up over the top of the rise at that moment caught her other arm and wrenched her hand from mine, flinging her up high in the air, her white dress billowing out like a mini parachute before coming to land with a terrible thud. The car screeched to a halt with Babs lying on the bonnet, unmoving.

Mum was running down our steep driveway, screaming, 'My baby! My baby! They've killed my baby!' I remember her saying 'they' because I thought she meant me as well as the driver.

The next thing I remember is driving in the woman's car, the car that hit Babs, sitting next to Mum in the back seat, with Babs lying unconscious on her lap and Mum rocking her back and forth, crying 'My baby is dead; My baby is dead', over and over. I had never even seen Mum cry before, and I couldn't speak for fear that it was all my fault.

The woman drove us to the Warringah Road medical centre on the corner and Mum ran straight in with Babs in her arms. I sat outside in the waiting room with the woman. She was saying she was so sorry and crying too. I wanted to tell her it wasn't her fault, but I still couldn't speak. I couldn't even cry.

Then Mum and the woman were in the waiting room crying and hugging each other, but now they were happy and everybody everywhere seemed to be smiling. It was some kind of miracle. Babs was not dead. Not dead at all. She only had a mild concussion and was going to be completely fine. The doctor told Mum it was because her bones were so young and still floppy, and because she had landed on the bonnet, not on the road. Babs didn't even know what had happened and we never talked about it afterwards. She has no memory of it today.

Many years later Mum told me I had saved Babs' life that day by pulling her back from the full force of the car. After that I didn't feel quite so bad for letting go of her hand.

Chapter 3

Keeping the Joneses up

I have mentioned already that our house was in an elevated position with a veranda. This could give the impression that our situation in the fake forest was a little grand. This would be the *wrong* impression to give. For a while we did have a fairly nice view over the houses opposite, on the lower side of the street, across a bush-clad valley beyond, all the way to the Sydney Harbour Bridge, twenty-odd miles as the crow and kookaburra fly. But then the gums of Careebong, many metres below the level of our street, grew so tall they obliterated the Harbour Bridge itself. After that you could just see enough of the night lights on the bridge arch and city skyscrapers peeping through the gum leaves to know what you were missing. Still, even before that, our situation was never grand.

Directly behind the houses on our side of the street ran a thick, above-ground water pipeline, in steely silver, like a varicose vein upon the leg of the land. 'The pipe', as we called this unsightly vein, provided water to the whole Manly

Warringah Shire in which 'the Forest' is but a part. It was thick enough to carry passengers along its spine and at any hour of the day or night people would appear, as if walking on air, or along the top of our back fence, peering in at our lawn and kitchen window as I hid in the lawn locker, pretending to be looking for a ladder, and not in fact practising my cartwheels on the lawn.

Eventually Mum found the sun's glare off the silver pipe from the vantage point of her kitchen sink at the back of the house so blinding that she rang the Council to ask if they would paint it. Incredibly, they did. So in another year or two the whole pipe running the length of the Warringah Shire was painted a deep forest green. Why it took someone from England to point out the need for green in a shire and forest I can't imagine. She was less successful, however, in persuading the Council to clean up the wasteland of rock and weed that ran either side of the pipe, and spent a great deal of time and energy lamenting that wasteland, and now and then getting out there herself to do what she could to try and tame it.

To add to the industrial aesthetic, three doors down, directly behind the Henderson's house where Sally the dog lived, loomed a towering power pylon and bulky red brick power station branded with High Voltage warning signs. Shaped like a spire but with a flat top that made no pretence of reaching up to the heavens, this giant pylon sent out thick black tentacle wires across the backs of our houses that moaned in the hot wind and sizzled with a sinister sound when it rained, burdened under the weight of all that power, presumably. Whether or not the leukaemia that struck the Henderson family when we were growing up had anything to do with that sinister sizzling is difficult to say; many parents worried as much. But not ours, who tended to have their minds on matters less practical. This was probably just as well, for there was nothing to be done about it.

The young Henderson girl, who was about six at the time, the same age as Babs, survived her cancer. But a few years later the family moved to a newer, fancier suburb on the outskirts of the fake forest that sensibly kept its power tucked underground, safe and sound. They took Sally the dog with them, so that was at least one problem solved – or relocated.

* * *

French's Forest was an up and coming region of the wider Warringah Shire, but where we lived, in the older part that was settled in the 1940s after the fires of '39 destroyed the first attempts at European settlement along with much of the surrounding bush, was fairly modest. The people who built the houses in the older part of 'the Forest' were not, of course, the first people to visit the area. The indigenous Aborigines of the Kuringai tribe had been visiting the general area for approximately 30,000 years prior, leaving carvings on the rock faces, which, had we been able to understand them, I would imagine would say something like: 'Nice place to visit, but whatever you do don't try to set up home here.' But not understanding, that's exactly what those settlers did; some of them, like the people who built our house, not even taking the precaution of building in brick to provide a degree of insulation against the high fire risk of the Eucalyptus forest (bush) that surrounded us. For our house, unlike the majority of houses in the older part of 'the Forest' and all in the new, was built in weatherboard wood. This, according to our Uncle Walter, who some years earlier had also moved to Australia and built himself a solid brick house in Perth, clearly more versed in the tale of *The Three Little Pigs* than his sister was, was foolhardiness in the extreme, and he expended a considerable amount of energy trying to persuade Mum and Dad out of their weatherboard house and into a brick one. Alas, we were not to be moved, as Mum *liked* our weatherboard house, whose white and grey colour scheme matched the colour scheme of her dream home exactly. Also, we couldn't afford brick.

And she may well have been right to focus on the colour scheme of the house rather than doing what she could to reduce the risk of it all going up in flames in the next heatwave. Because as it turned out, we only had one close call with fire when we were growing up. On that occasion the flames reached the bush of Bantry Bay less than half a mile away and Tim, ten at the time, was dispatched to the roof of our house to put wet tea towels in the gutters. Dad passed him the sodden towels from the ground, being no good on rooftops on account of his bad back – a legacy of the war. But had the fire come that extra quarter-mile we would have been ready for it with our wet tea towels.

The houses built at the new end of our street, in the development we called 'the Subbo' (Australian for sub-division), were brick clad *and* framed for added fire protection. Mum sometimes referred to these houses, almost all of them two-storeyed and double-garaged *with* pool, as 'monstrosities', to make herself feel better about our house, no doubt. But as we grew up, and our three-bedroom, one-storeyed, no pool, no-garage-or-even-carport weatherboard house began to shrink and ache under the strain, she decided a second storey might not be so monstrous after all. She had plans drawn up for a top storey and I spent a good amount of time gazing at these plans, imagining having my own room upstairs looking out across a back lawn that was as green as any lawn ever was. But when it came to it, we didn't have the funds for a top storey and Mum's revised plan for a more modest extension to the back of the house was turned down by the Council, who wouldn't let us extend our house further back as this would increase our proximity to the high voltage power pylon and station.

So in the end, Mum's extension plans were reduced to the installation of a second toilet in the outside laundry, which at least took care of the queues for the bathroom and stopped people pounding on the door to be let in to use the toilet when you were in the shower or bath – and having to let them in and wait outside dripping on the carpet until they were done. Then going back in ...

It was good of our laundry to squeeze in a second toilet, because it had recently been called upon to accommodate a second fridge – chiefly for the purpose of storing Dad's back-up grog. Toilets and fridges are not entirely natural roommates, and indeed the arrangement may well have been illegal. And because of the lack of space in the laundry, when you sat on the toilet, one knee bumped the washing machine and the other the second fridge. This leant a certain rustic quality to the experience, but the advantage of the arrangement was that if you ever overheated while sat on the toilet, a not uncommon experience living in Australia, you could reach a short arm out and relieve yourself by the cool of the open fridge door. And while there, you were free to peruse the contents of the fridge, beyond the grog, to consider your next meal while eliminating your last. Some might call that efficient.

Efficient or not, I avoided the laundry toilet for all but the gravest of toilet emergencies, especially at night when the slugs came out. I did not like slugs. Indeed sitting with the slugs I felt was only fractionally better than literally exploding with poo, which is why I put it off until that was nearly the case. The laundry door naturally did not reach all the way down to the concrete floor so it was a free-for-all for the slugs to come and go as they pleased, congregating around the base of the toilet, possibly because it was inclined to leak. And being Australian slugs they were naturally well fed, and closer to the dimensions of your average-sized seal.

If the seal-sized slugs were not enough to put a young, *sensitive* green-eyed girl off venturing outside to the laundry toilet at night, the black hole the size of a basketball in the low-lying ceiling was. All sorts of things can live in Australian black holes. As far as I knew, no-one had ever been up into our black hole to find out what was up there, and we knew people who had a python living in their attic (not by choice). I was told pythons were not poisonous and quite harmless unless provoked. But sitting on the toilet, directly beneath the black hole at night, I was not entirely sure that what I was doing would not be provoking to a python and undertook these emergency ablutions with one eye watching out for a python from above, and the other for the seal-sized slugs from below, altogether feeling that my situation, sitting with the slugs and suspected snake, was rather a long way from where Dad had once sat next to a queen, if only the Queen of Sweden, when a child of six, watching his father compete at Wimbledon.

Actually, as a young child captivated by this sitting-next-to-a-queen story, I got a bit carried away and confused, telling people that 'my daddy once sat next to the Queen of Sheba', possibly due to the Sunday school sessions we attended for a few years. When one of the parents at kindy heard this she told me, with feeling, to 'Stop telling stories, little girl!' which was a bit upsetting, because I *wasn't* telling stories, as far as I knew. My daddy really had sat next to a queen, as difficult as that might have been to believe now.

This lack of grandeur would have been less of a problem had it not been for the fact that we were the Joneses, supposed to set an example for everyone else to keep up with. Never mind the *Lloyd* Joneses; never mind them indeed. We had our work cut out for us keeping the ordinary Joneses up.

In pursuit of this demanding goal, it was decided that before Tim started school a family trip to the zoo was in order. Animals are important in Australia – especially Australian animals – and our animal awareness and education as a family was somewhat limited, unless of course you count slugs, which one generally doesn't. Dad's dysfunctional childhood had bypassed the zoo entirely, and Mum was from England, where they don't really have animals as such. That left Nana as our resident authority on the subject. Nana had once known a thing or two about horses, 60 years ago, but when it comes to animal awareness horses are a bit like slugs in that regard; they don't really count. And as Nana was not even a Jones, it wasn't her job to keep us up to the minute on animals that *do* count, and so, one way or another, it was decided that our animal awareness left rather a lot to be desired and it was time to do something about it.

So it was in the spring of 1969, with me recently turned three, Tim 'four and two-corters', as he proudly told anyone who asked and many who didn't; Babs not quite two and Nana 82, that we Joneses and one honorary Jones set off for Taronga Park Zoo in Mosman, dressed in our Sunday best, as unlikely a party for a zoo safari as ever there was. Dad rarely ventured outside without his large straw hat on, shorts and long socks to the knee; Tim never ventured even as far as the Faheys without his red clip-on tie, and Nana only had one pair of smart shoes; heeled black court shoes that looked like, and probably were, relics of the Victorian era, not expressly designed for zoo safaris. Babs and I wore matching hand-embroidered party frocks and black patent leather shoes. I'm not sure what Mum wore, but it wasn't a safari suit.

We began with the classic Australians, which were first in line as you entered the zoo. These days zoos are rather more intentionally interactive than they were in my young day, and so our first animal encounter was not with a koala that we could hold, as we could today, but with a *suspected* koala at the top of a tall gum that we could barely see. 'Where is it, Dad?' Tim was quick off the mark to ask his hero in all matters, as we crowded round the base of the tall tree, peering straight up, trying to distinguish grey koala from grey tree trunk and cloud. It didn't help that we were all vertically challenged, even Nana in her two-inch heels, excepting Dad, who was of average height, but struggled with weak eyesight and a profound disinterest in ever seeing a koala or any other animal as long as he lived. 'Where is it, Dad?'

When we did finally manage to locate what we were fairly sure was a koala, it was only to discover that it was fast asleep with its face, the most interesting part, turned towards the tree trunk, and would not wake up no matter how often, or how loudly, Tim ordered it to 'Wake up, Kwala!' After this turned to 'Why won't it wake up, Dad?' issued at seven-second intervals, despite encouragements from one and all, including several strangers, to perhaps make a *little* less noise and then it might wake up, Dad felt obliged to consult the *Habitat and Behaviour Guide* directly. 'What does it say, Dad?' Before much longer it was suggested, again by strangers, that we proceed to the kangaroos.

I believe we had a little more success with those slightly more lively Australians, including a fleeting sighting of a joey in its mother's pouch, before the mother sensibly bounded off out of sight. 'Bunny?' said Babs, pointing from her stroller at the bouncy kangaroos, which provided a welcome bit of light relief for everyone – especially Dad, who was already beginning to wonder if they had a pub at the zoo (they didn't). Babs' kangaroo bunny was not quite as silly as it sounded, because kangaroos with their long flat feet do look a bit like Bugs Bunny, a rabbit she had recently been introduced to on the television that had arrived in our house a few months prior. In fact 'bunny' was her first proper word, an early indication of the animal lover *she* would become.

From my point of view I was ready to go home after the 'bunny' and wanted to deploy *my* first word – 'no' – to suggest we'd seen quite enough animals for one day and *no* more, please. But no-one listened to me. By the time we got through all the Australians, including some fantastically fat snakes squashed behind glass without start or end that left even Tim speechless, and made our way to the Africans, with Nana in her Victorian heels slowing us down to the point that others appeared to be running past us, and probably were, I was ready to run for the hills; next stop Russia. When we made it to the zebras and Tim launched into: 'Why do zebwas have stwipes, Dad?' I realised it was now or never. Nana, Mum and Babs were still somewhere between continents, and camouflage, the usual explanation for why animals have anything, was not going to cut it with the zebwas' stwipes. I didn't know this exactly, but I *sensed* it, possibly with the help of those long antennae toes.

Then I saw the crocodiles ... Unlike all the other animals I had seen at the zoo, the crocodiles struck me as my kind of animal. They weren't slimy or squashed or sleeping or jumping, nor were they striped for no apparent reason. They had character, it seemed to me, and were the best looking animal by far. They must have been African crocodiles, being in the African section, but they were behaving very much like good-looking Australians often do, lying there sunning themselves by the water's edge, wearing self-satisfied grins and not much else. But whether African or Australian crocs, I wanted a closer look. I snuck off quietly so that no-one, not Dad, or Tim, or even the zebwas noticed ...

The crocodile enclosure in those days was bordered by a low wire mesh fence that appeared to be designed more to keep the crocodiles in than the visitors out. This was ideal. Although I was not entirely dressed for climbing, in my shiny shoes and elaborately smocked dress, I found that the toe of one shiny shoe fit neatly into the wire mesh holes, with only a few scratches incurred, and in no time at all I was up and over that low fence and standing on the inside with the crocodiles. I smiled, a little shyly, at the croc closest to me, and was pleased to see that he (or she) smiled back. I was a bit nervous at that point as to what would happen next, but I was nonetheless extremely pleased with myself to find myself on the *right* side of that fence.

I am told that Dad – not a running man by any means, on account of his bad back – ran that day, possibly *away* from Tim and the zebwas as much as towards me and the crocs. Mum had rounded the corner just in time to see me in my Sunday best clear the top of the wire fence and screamed out to Dad to get his attention. Dad, who was somewhat closer and had longer legs that could be used to good effect in an emergency, apparently made an impressive dash to the neighbouring enclosure to retrieve me from inside the crocodile enclosure in the nick of time, just as one of the crocs was beginning its approach. Tim, meanwhile, left alone with the zebwas, wondering where his hero had taken off to in such a hurry, possibly decided to fill the time by letting the zebwas know that he was 'four and two *whole* corters' and would soon be starting school. Frankly, it couldn't come soon enough.

* * *

When we weren't at the zoo showing everyone else how it's done, we were keeping the Joneses up by appearing on television. Mum appeared on the general knowledge game show *Temptation* and won a lawn locker – she was going for the car, because Deirdre was now on her last legs – and I went on *Romper Room* and recited the alphabet backwards. Unfortunately, my backwards alphabet was not deemed essential viewing for the children's show that was aimed at preschoolers, and did not make the final cut. But Mum and Nana, who were sitting in the studio audience during filming, said it sounded impressive, at least what they could hear of it did; evidently there was something wrong with the studio sound system and my backwards alphabet was not altogether audible.

But at four, I knew my backwards alphabet backwards. Nana had drilled it into Tim and me during the long Saturdays we spent together down at her Queenscliff unit, giving Mum a break while Dad was in the library looking into the Third World. Why I appeared on *Romper Room* nobody can tell me exactly, so I can only assume it had something to do with my special skills, and the fact that most of Sydney's four-year-olds appeared on the show at one time or another. It was a bit disappointing that my backwards alphabet didn't make the final cut and wider Australia was deprived the chance of seeing what one young Jones could do backwards. But never mind; there were bound to be countless other opportunities to use my backwards alphabet in later life.

I can't say that I remember reciting my backwards alphabet on *Romper Room*, nor do I remember much romping (apparently there was quite a bit). What I do remember is the drawing. By the time I appeared on *Romper Room* I had roughly two-and-a-half years of kindy under my belt. And apart from the principal activity of watching other children sleep, and repeated renditions of the singing-wall song, I spent my time at kindy drawing with crayons. And as with my backwards alphabet, at this age I liked to practise a thing until it was perfect, rather than take a stab at lots of different things. And the one thing I drew to perfection at this age was my dream home, complete with two, properly green and shady, dream trees.

The main feature of my crayon dream home was that it looked nothing like our house, and the same for the dream trees. My dream house had two storeys, four picture-book windows, and a brick chimney. I was particularly proud to have mastered the art of drawing bricks; it was not easy drawing bricks with blunt crayons. Crayons were always blunt in those days. There was a meandering front path up the centre of my dream home to the front door, and one bright green broccoli-shaped tree on either side of the path. To cap off my dream home, the chimney had a soft squiggle of smoke rising up to show that a cosy, *gentle* fire was burning inside, and a few blades of bright green grass here and there, to show that the grass around *my* dream home was the proper colour.

All this was good clean fun for a four-year-old plotting her escape from the fake forest for a better life until I went on *Romper Room* and was asked to draw a series of *different* pictures for the three shows we were filming in the one day. I could have shown them different singing or sleeping, perhaps, but different drawings I could not do. The whole idea was to get my dream home and dream trees *right*, not to draw for the sake of it.

Apparently this was not the *Romper Room* spirit. 'Are you *sure* you don't want to draw something else today, Sally?' I can distinctly remember the young woman host of the show asking with an irritated hiss over my shoulder as she came round with the cameraman to where I was launching my third dream home, not *identical* to the first two, to the trained eye (think Monet and haystacks), but somewhat similar if you weren't prepared to take the time to study the differences, which she wasn't. Grammatically, my answer should have been: '*Yes*. I am sure.' But on account of my continued fondness for my first word, I remember replying, with feeling: '*No*'; meaning no I didn't want to draw anything different. To which reply the host hurried off in a huff, taking the cameraman with her, never to return, to focus instead on young Johnny's drawing, further along the table. This, from where I was sitting, looked like yet another messy ball of coloured wool. But according to young Johnny, when he was asked by the smiling host, was an 'eshploding cavavan' and not in fact an 'eshploding car' or 'eshploding twuck' of the previous two attempts. The host seemed satisfied.

Never mind, I was pleased enough with my first television appearance, feeling I had done myself and all the Joneses of Australia proud by setting things right across the entire country on an architectural and landscaping front.

Mum claims I was Dad's favourite at this age; indeed it is not difficult to see why. I don't remember much about being Dad's favourite, if in fact I was. But I do remember him calling me 'Sally-Wally-Wally with a fringe on top', and that being about the only time I didn't mind being called Sally, though I could have done without the fringe. Later on, when I was *not called Charlotte for nothing* and Sally-Wally-Wally was long gone, Dad would call me Sally when he was cross with me and I seemed to be anything but his favourite, and Sal when he wasn't so cross; increasingly rare occasions. I don't know precisely when Sally-Wally-Wally was replaced by naughty Sally who was too clever for her own good, but what happened at the Nestlé Christmas picnic that year probably didn't help.

Since graduating with his Bachelor of Economics, Dad had left accountancy work to join Nestlé's market research department. This work was precisely the sort of 'economics' he did not want to do, but if he was going to save the Third World he needed to pay the First World bills first. At the end of every year, Nestlé put on a Christmas picnic for all its employees and their families, hiring out a football field for the purpose. Along with the barbecued sausages, Nestlé provided a substantial present, boxed and wrapped, for each child under a certain age, to be delivered in person by Santa, who arrived on the football field towards the end of the picnic, sweating in his thick white beard and red Santa suit, standing on the back of a truck, ho-ho-ho-ing with admirable enthusiasm, about as far from the North Pole as Santa gets.

I appreciated Santa coming so far. Indeed I was a fan of Santa and all things Christmas at this age, even more so than most children, it seemed. The magical world of Christmas was a world well beyond the fake forest and I was more than ready to be transported to that world and rewarded with presents when I got there. When I was a bit older, seven or eight, I started anticipating Christmas on the first day of September by making a cardboard calendar, on which I eagerly crossed off the days until Christmas – all 116 of them. When I was a bit older still, I started making my own multi-paged Christmas cards for each member of my family, including Nana, with much green, red and silver (for snow) glitter, to extend the magical world of Christmas for as long as I could.

But at four I was not quite making my own calendars or

cards, so the extension of Christmas was left up to the grown-ups, who could be unreliable. We had Christmas concerts at kindy that were quite fun, though largely because they spelled the end of the kindy year. So the pre-Christmas highlight for me at that age was, by far and away, the Nestlé picnic, and I pressed Dad well ahead of time to tell me when precisely it was going to be, especially that year, as it was the first year I could clearly recall the fun of the previous picnic – and the last, as it would turn out.

The highlight of the picnic was of course Santa's arrival with the presents. By the time the presents were piled onto two long trestle tables, one for the boys and one for the girls, and all the children, possibly 50 in total, were told to line up in front of the appropriate table, I was fairly bursting at the seams with excitement and anticipation. I made sure Babs, whose hand I had to hold while we lined up in the girls' queue, did not peek at the presents while we waited. I covered my eyes with my spare hand, and tried to block my ears too. For the only *slight* problem with the Nestlé Christmas presents was that all the girls got the same present, as did all the boys. Nestlé could not be expected to get a different present for each child, Dad said. This meant that the girls in front of us in the queue, of which there seemed to be about a million, girls who didn't have sisters to slow them down getting to the front, could spoil our surprise if they unwrapped their present on the spot. They were encouraged to 'run along now' rather than do this, but they didn't always follow that instruction.

'Put your hand up!' I scolded Babs, whose enthusiasm for covering her eyes never came close to mine, to the point that I was tempted to let go of her hand and cover her eyes for her. But she wasn't too keen on that idea, and it was hard to block my ears at the same time. Santa's helpers, who were standing behind the tables handing out the presents, were ordinary ladies dressed in regular summer clothes. This was a considerable disappointment to me, as they were clearly *not* Santa's actual helpers and only pretending to be. How Santa tolerated this I did not know, but I decided that his real helpers must be back in the North Pole busy with preparations for Christmas, and did not let the disappointment ruin my excitement too much.

Then I peeked out from behind my hand across at the boys' queue in which Tim was standing almost at the front, and saw with perfect astonishment, that the wrapped boxes on their table were not all the same shape. There were two distinct shapes: one square, the other tall and narrow. I could scarcely believe it. 'The presents are not all the same! We get to choose! Babs won't get the same as me!' It was all too good to be true. I didn't shout these things out, but I almost did. The previous year Babs and I had both got a brown-haired doll called Clarabelle, who I was already bored to tears with. If there were *two* presents this year that meant that at least one of them wouldn't be a doll. I was extremely pleased about this; Babs could have the doll. But it was the thought of getting to *choose* a present that was the most exciting thing of all, and I was tempted now to peek around the girls in front of us at the boxes on our table to get an idea of which one I would choose. But I'd come too far now and the surprise was too good to spoil, so I kept my hand over my eyes and made Babs' more or less keep her hand over hers.

The wait was almost over; just two girls in front of us. Tim had run off with his present, back to Mum and Dad, so I didn't know yet what he had got from Santa, though I did see him choose the square box over the tall one. This not knowing added to my excitement. The more surprise the better.

'It's just a doll,' I heard the girl in front of us say then and my heart practically stopped. 'A *doll*? What does she mean, just a doll? It can't be *just* a doll. What about the other present?' I couldn't, I *wouldn't* believe it. 'She must be wrong,' I told myself, and clung in desperation to that thought for a few frantic seconds before we were standing in front of the table and what was left of the presents, and I saw, with jaw-dropping disappointment, that the boxes on the table were all the same shape and that that shape was almost certainly a doll.

'Isn't there anything else?' I asked the woman behind the table, when I'd recovered my voice, as I stretched up and over to peer behind the table, looking for a different shaped box. 'Anything *else*?' the plainly dressed woman said, with pure disgust in her voice, frowning and saying she'd 'never heard of such an ungrateful little girl', before shoving one doll-shaped box at me and another at Babs and telling us to run along.

The drive home from that picnic in rattling old Deirdre I remember even more clearly. As usual Dad was driving, though he hated driving and Mum loved it, and Mum was in the passenger seat, with the three of us in the back, a regular family of five, as far as outward appearances went. There was not much being said, as Dad hated 'distracting noises', especially when he was driving, and the mood was subdued. We hadn't exactly left the picnic on a high note. When the girls' present turned out to be indeed just a doll, this one with blonde hair called Kandy Kisses, but otherwise identical to last year's doll, I had cried quite a bit and stomped my foot, sobbing: 'It's not fair!

Tim got to choose a present but we didn't!' A shiny red truck, it turned out to be. Other boys got a cricket bat. 'We *always* get a doll!' I cried at Dad until he called me 'an ungrateful little girl' too, and with more anger in his voice than he'd ever used to talk to me before. 'Other little girls don't get to have any presents for Christmas at all,' he added, stuttering as he spoke, which made him sound even angrier, as if it was my fault about the stuttering as well as the other little girls.

Staring at the side of his face from where I was sitting behind Mum, I decided I didn't like him anymore. Babs, sitting next to me, had her Kandy Kisses doll propped up on her lap and was talking quietly to it, telling it to 'be a good girl for Mummy'. Tim, over by the other window, was arranging his favourite matchbox cars that he took everywhere with him in his pocket, in the back of his new pick-up truck. My doll, still in its box, was lying on her back on the dirty metal car floor beneath my feet, staring up at me through the plastic, with such a stupid look on her face, as if she didn't know what she'd done wrong. If I moved my foot to the side a bit it looked like I was standing on her face.

Chapter 4

Pink milk blues

Children don't really know what's going on in their parents' lives any more than parents really know what's going on in their lives, least of all when there's a double generation gap between them, as there was with us.

Mum told me many years later that Dad hated going to these Nestlé picnics, not least of all because his much younger co-workers, with children our ages, used to make a point of taunting him about being such an old father. 'I see you brought your grandkids with you again, Mark,' they would say to him, the same every year, and in front of Mum, which Dad found distinctly unfunny. He only went to these picnics for our sakes, according to Mum. I never knew this. Unfortunately, Dad didn't exactly wear his age well. With his grey hair, and not much of that, his thick-lensed glasses, slight stoop from his bad back, and badly sun-damaged skin, he looked even older than he was, and as I got older I was embarrassed about this too. When friends asked me, 'Why is your Dad so old?', or, 'Is that your grandfather?' sometimes I just said it was to avoid further embarrassment. But it never occurred to me that he was sometimes embarrassed about it too.

In 1971 Dad was promoted to Market Research Manager for Nestlé Australia. With a bit of luck that put an end to these taunts from his co-workers, because it didn't seem to do him a lot of good otherwise, moving him onto the frontline of the First World, with annual trips to Nestlé headquarters in Switzerland that took him away from his precious Third World research – as well as his family. Mum said he hated these trips away. The promotion did mean a new company car, which parked, all shiny and new, on our front verge, as if it owned the place. Poor old Deidre seemed quite upstaged in its shadow, faded and squashed as she was now at the top of the driveway, between house and fence, so that her doors couldn't open without a collision with one or other surface. But not being a car person, Dad cared very little for this shiny upgrade that meant he had to contend with peak-hour traffic into the city every day, rather than just on Fridays when he picked up the grog, which made the battle worthwhile. And his company cars that were upgraded every year were never named. They were never really *ours*; never members of the family like Patsy, Primrose and Deirdre, and later on, Dilly. Don't ask me how Mum and Dad chose the names of their cars. I think there was some method in their madness involving the car's registration, but I wouldn't be sure of that.

I would have felt more for Dad *and* for Deirdre having to cope with all these changes and upheavals, if that year had not been the year I started school and was thrust into a hell of epic proportions – and I don't mean in the classroom. I hardly spent any time in the classroom that year, being either in the school sick bay, at home in bed or in hospital, with one disease or disability or other. I started school at the height of the summer and every morning, with temperatures reaching 30 degrees by nine o'clock, we were made to stand outside for a 20-minute assembly, squashed into a tight group, listening while the headmaster told us, more than once, about the importance of paying attention at school and various other vital matters I found very hard to pay attention to; until I fainted. I can only think I managed to avoid braining my head on the concrete because of how tightly packed we were. As a consequence I became very familiar with the sick bay that year, waking up there and wondering how I got there. 'You fainted – *again!*' would be the somewhat unsympathetic reply of the school nurse.

After a while I didn't need to ask. These days, most schools have sun shades and sensible sun hats. The girls had hats back then, but they weren't sensible. They were short brimmed straw hats with a cutting elastic chin strap that nobody wore past the first week, because they were hot and scratchy and blew off in the wind when you ran, despite the elastic, unless you tightened it to the point of strangulation.

Possibly as a result of all this fainting and heat stroke, I became a sickly child soon after starting school. First was the hepatitis, then the impetigo, followed by the chickenpox and asthma. Naturally, Mum wrote to tell her friends and relations in England all about it:

Poor kid, she's had a rough time this year what with the hepatitis, chickenpox, impetigo and then the asthma. She was close to having to go back to hospital, her breathing was so laboured, but the suppositories eased it – though they then made her vomit!

Poor kid indeed. I would have had to go *back* to hospital, because I had already spent three weeks there for the hepatitis. Mum always used to say England was dreary compared with Australia. I think her purpose here must have been to prove it – also to relieve the dreariness. I was happy to help relieve the dreariness where I could, but only up to a point. I think having everyone in England know I had something shoved up my bottom that made me vomit is going a bit far to relieve the dreariness. Sometimes dreariness can be a comfort. As to what was going on in this not-so-dreary country on a medical front, treating asthma with suppositories, I can only suppose it had something to do with Australia being the land Down Under, where things tend to be done upside-down and round the wrong way.

The doctors, mind, did have more regular methods for treating diseases as well, such as needles. In fact needles came so regularly and so relentlessly that year for me, that one day, hearing the doctor tell Mum another was on its way, I said enough was enough and took off out of the surgery running for my life, next stop Russia. I would have made it too, if not for Mum and the doctor, needle poised, giving chase, calling out for me to stop, as if I were a thief, alerting the nurse who cut me off at the main door and held me down until the doctor could catch up and give me the jab there and then, Mum tut-tutting all the while. If I'd been able to breathe properly, they would still be looking for me in Russia.

Babs got chickenpox – the easy disease – at the same time I did. This wasn't quite so bad as we spent two weeks sitting up in bed playing Lego lent to us by our next-door neighbours, the Martins (or Martians, as we called them, because they were skinny boys who were into science). The Martians kept chickens in their backyard so I decided they had lent us their Lego because they were feeling guilty about those chickens having given us chickenpox. Missing as much school as I was I was happy that at least something made sense.

In hindsight it seems clear that part of my problem was the amount of dairy I was consuming all of a sudden, which was causing me to put on weight and have difficulty breathing. I was probably allergic to it. But the dangers of dairy were evidently not known by the medical establishment in my day as it was in hospital for the hepatitis where I developed a taste for milk, which was served with a sweet pink additive (Nestlé's strawberry Quik). Indeed for the entire three weeks of my hepatitis hospital stay I refused to consume anything but pink milk, by way, I like to think, of a gender and age-appropriate hunger strike. Then out of hospital, and off my hunger strike, I was free to continue consuming as much pink milk as a I could get my hands on, which was practically unlimited, on account of Dad working for the manufacturers of the pink stuff, in addition to my regular food intake, which I resumed with a vengeance. On top of this, at school, when I was actually there, I was being made to drink half a litre of white milk every morning, which probably amounted to more milk in total than any child of five had ever consumed, and certainly more than I needed.

My regular food intake also left something to be desired in the way of health; I cannot blame it all on the hepatitis. Starting from the day of my first birthday when I seized the feeding spoon from Mum's hand, uttered my first word 'No!' and refused henceforth to be fed by anyone, it seems I was pretty sure about what I did and did not want to eat, and in what quantities. And what I most wanted to eat, and in large quantities, was meat, so much so that Mum described me to her friends back in England as a 'meat addict': 'Honestly, you should have seen Sal tucking into the chops ... she's much more of a meat addict than Tim,' she wrote, no doubt exaggerating to relieve the dreariness. The fact that this chop-chomping incident was on the occasion of our very first home barbecue and as an Australian it is practically a patriotic duty to embrace the barbecue – I don't know what Tim was doing – Mum does not explain, which seems a little unfair. That said, I am also on record for having replied, at the age of two, when asked if I had a special boyfriend at kindy: 'I don't like boys, I only like food!' which does suggest that my interest in barbecued meat might have gone a *little* further at this age than patriotism required. But still.

Whatever the case, that year wasn't working out too well for me on the weight, breathing and general health front, and it must have had something to do with my particular predicament and predilections, as the same could not be said for Tim and Babs, who both survived that year, and most others, without giving Mum much to write home about. And because asthma is stress related I can't help thinking that part of the problem was my increasing jealousy of Babs, who that year got to be home alone with Mum all week. Indeed Mum more or less admitted as much to her friends (in typed letters, copies of which I have acquired with the assistance of a private detective), when she wrote: 'After Sal's second attack [of life-threatening asthma] I decided it was probably my fault, as I'd been inclined to make too much fuss of Babs, being the baby and my last.' *Probably?* I'll let you be the judge.

The other problem with Babs, which might also explain the first problem, was that she was getting cuter by the minute, whereas I seemed to be prematurely aging – and not in a good way. Babs' hair, for instance, was thick, wavy and a rich dark blonde, whereas mine by this age was bright white, straw-like, and so thin you could see my scalp through it. Although I'd started out with a good amount of thick, normal-coloured hair, something appeared to have gone radically wrong since then, with my hair at five resembling almost exactly the hair you see on the oldest of people. Also, just to keep everyone guessing, my skin was not white but tanned, and rather more so than either of my siblings' skin. Mum explained this as an 'olive complexion'. This didn't help me much. We were an olive-eating family and the olives we ate were green. I had green eyes; perhaps my skin was green too. I *liked* green, certainly, that much has been established, but not so much in skin. And why was I the only one in the family with green eyes and skin? Where had I come from and why was I here? These were all good questions that were difficult to answer when I was getting so little schooling.

Over and above the hepatitis, sunstroke, impetigo, chickenpox, asthma, vomit-inducing suppositories, needle phobia, excess weight, dairy allergy, premature aging, green skin and excessively cute sister, when I was at school I was *also* being terrorised by giant furry black caterpillars that lived in seething swarms in the only shade trees in the junior playground. I was no more fond of caterpillars than I was of slugs, it's fair to say, and when one landed with a weighty thump in my lunch box one day, I leapt up and ran for the hills, abandoning my lunch to the caterpillar in a most uncharacteristic sacrifice. After that I gave those shade trees such a wide berth that I had to circle the whole junior school to get back to my classroom every lunchtime, which might also explain why my hair and skin were a different colour to everybody else's. So in one way or another I had more sun, stress and sickness than most in my first year at school. And I think it is in this sympathetic light that my actions that Christmas are best explained. It had been a tough year.

* * *

Having no blood relations nearby with whom to share Christmas Day, we spent every Christmas with the daughter of Dad's father's fourth wife and her family, the Gileses. Auntie Robin, Dad's stepsister, was married to Owen and they had three sons of similar ages to us, only better spaced and with enviably interesting names: Evan, Ross and Marcus.

With our Nana and their Nana Marion – Eric's fourth wife – and Uncle Frank, Uncle Owen's father, we made a good-sized party of thirteen that squeezed into our small living-cum-dining room with great difficulty. Then we turned on the oven. For Christmas at our house involved a traditional sit-down, midday winter feast of roast turkey, chestnut and sausage stuffing, gravy and roast veg and whole leg of ham, followed by a homemade Christmas pudding and brandy custard that naturally had to be set alight, despite the fire ban that was invariably in place on Christmas Day. And we did have a fire one year after Uncle Frank got a bit too close to the flaming brandy pudding and his paper crown caught alight. Fortunately, Dad was nearby with a recently refilled glass of wine and only hesitated briefly before emptying his glass over Uncle Frank's flaming head. After that we all had to remove our paper crowns before the flaming pudding was delivered to the table, as a precaution. It would probably have been easier to forgo the flame, but that wasn't our way.

This was all good clean fun, up to a point. With so little room, we six children were crowded round the card table down one end, in front of the turned off TV, as far from the business end of the feast as possible. We were served our food on small plastic plates that tended to get smaller by age and gender. Babs' plate was barely bigger than her hand. Uncle Frank's was *almost* as big as his head. More often than not the adult responsible for serving us our food was Auntie Robin. This was a problem. Don't get me wrong; I was very fond of Auntie Robin. She was beautiful, young, and a former ballet dancer. But as she was also built like a gazelle – or a ballet dancer – with an appetite to match, and didn't have any daughters, she seemed to have trouble appreciating that *some* girls have the appetites of much heftier animals altogether; pigs, for instance.

And so it was that Christmas, at the end of my annus horribilis, that Auntie Robin did indeed serve the children's meals and not only failed to serve me a tenth of the turkey meat and stuffing I required, but served Tim, who wasn't even a meat addict, more! I swallowed that good-little-girl serving in one gulp, to make a point and in the hope that Auntie Robin might be fooled into thinking she hadn't yet served me. Then, in my sweetest well-mannered voice, asked: 'May I have some turkey and stuffing please, Auntie Robin?' cunningly leaving out the 'more'. But Auntie Robin wasn't as easily fooled as she was slim, and told me I had to wait for my seconds until after everyone else had been served their first helpings. This was hopeless. It took half the day just to serve Uncle Frank, who largely came to Christmas for the food and was *not* built like a gazelle, and who wore his belt under his armpits so his stomach had free rein to expand without anything tightening to tell him when to say when. So he never said when. I practically wept with the unfairness of it all.

The one saving grace in this cruel Christmas conspiracy to starve me to death was that Mum always made sure to buy the biggest turkey in the shop. So when the adults *finally* finished their seconds and Uncle Frank his third serving, and everyone had left the table, the boys and men to play a round of Christmas cricket on the back lawn, the women to clear the table, stir the custard and ready the pudding in the kitchen, and Uncle Frank to quietly pass out in a chair, I was free to eye what was left of the turkey squatting stoutly on the kitchen bench, exactly at my eye level. There must have been a breeze coming in through the open back door next to which the turkey had been placed, in all its greasy glory, presumably to cool. I was extremely pleased to see there was still a good amount of flesh on the bones and rich meaty stuffing spilling out of the stomach, and with everyone's backs turned, occupied with either custard or cricket (or clinging to Mum's skirt, as Babs was), I saw my chance to grab said turkey and make a run for it, perhaps not quite as far as Russia.

There was a flyscreen door between me and my great escape, but it was a flimsy thing that didn't close properly, so I calculated I would not have too much difficulty kicking it open with my left foot while balancing the turkey and tray in both hands, to charge across the lawn unnoticed by the Christmas cricketers, who could usually be counted upon to get so involved in their game they wouldn't notice a meteor strike, or even a five-year-old girl running across the lawn hauling a large turkey carcass. Still, I thought it was best I asked permission. Manners were important in our house.

'*May* I have this bone please, Mummy?' I asked, using my best grammar, as it was no time for a debate about *can* versus *may*. Grammar was also important in our house, more important than basic hygiene, for instance. Clearly my good grammar did the trick, because Mum, standing by the stove a couple of metres away with her back turned, chatting with Auntie Robin and the two nanas, taking turns to stir the custard, did not even turn around to see to which bone I was referring, before agreeing to my request.

I had to move fast. Lifting my arms up to the level of the tray, I remember being a little surprised by the weight of the stuffed turkey when I finally held it in my hot little hands. But I bore up well and lowering it carefully to the level of my chest, I stood on one leg to kick the flyscreen door open with the other, as planned. As the screen door flung wide I charged out across the crazy paving stones then behind the wicket on the near side of the lawn, unseen by the Christmas cricketers, who indeed must have been absorbed, to make my way to the far back corner of the lawn, where I found a modicum of shade almost big enough for me and my turkey, and sat down cross-legged on the grass, bindis in the bottom be damned, and balancing the turkey and its tray on my folded knees, happily set my ravenous fingers to work.

It was the happiest moment of my life and a fitting end to a difficult year, I thought, for a few blissful seconds.

Unfortunately, all good things must come to an end, and, it seems, the more good the thing the more abrupt the ending must be. Because I never got to finish that stuffed turkey before I was discovered, with my face and fingers covered in grease and a large chunk of stuffing sausage stuck to my nose, by none other than the gazelle! 'Sally!' was all the gazelle said, in her horror, and all she needed to say to ruin the moment entirely.

But never mind. I got to have my turkey and eat it too, if only for a few glorious moments. Better still, not long after I ran off with the Christmas turkey at the end of that difficult year, overweight and struggling to breathe, Mum took me back to the doctor. And this time, instead of suppositories, which clearly *weren't* working, he prescribed ballet, which he thought might teach me to breathe a little easier. And it was ballet that eventually got me out of the fake forest.

* * *

So, you see; it was all just as well in the end. Because no-one else in my family, least of all Auntie Robin, would have been likely to recommend I do ballet. And indeed when Mum took me along to meet the Russian – yes, Russian! – ballet teacher at our local dance school to have my potential for dance assessed, *she* was highly sceptical too, and quickly took Mum aside to tell her: 'I am sorry, Mrs Jons, but she is not billt for barllet', looking my way with a pitying smile, and speaking with a slightly terrifying accent. Fortunately Mum was able to impress upon this straight-talking Russian, who was none other than 'Mrs P', aka Tanya Pearson, formerly Tatiana Jakubenka of Moscow and future recipient of the Order of Australia Medal for services to dance, that it was a matter of life and death that I do ballet. But, Mum insisted, she need not teach *me* how to dance, merely how to breathe a little easier.

And so it was, on this rather more modest basis, without expectation on either side that I should ever learn to dance, that I was accepted into Tanya Pearson's Northside Ballet Academy early the following year.

But Mrs P nearly need not have gone to even that much trouble on my account. Because two weeks before that inauspicious start to my ballet career, I nearly drew my last laboured breath and saved her and everyone else the bother of trying to teach me how to breathe, much less dance.

We were on a family holiday up at Avoca Beach, a big wave beach some 100 kilometres north of Sydney, where we had spent our summer holiday for the previous two years. This time we drove in Dad's new company car, which was a special treat that made me feel important, until it transpired that new car upholstery made me sick. I was not used to new things. The raw, overripe smell was enough to turn my stomach before we'd even cleared the fake forest; most of the time Dad used his car and we drove in dear old Deirdre whose much older upholstery I could stomach. But at least in the new car when I cried out: 'I'm going to be sick; stop the car!' and was sick, in the curb, I got a window seat. Before that, Babs had been allowed to have the second window seat in case she wanted to go to sleep on the three-hour drive (Dad drove slowly). Tim had the other window seat as a birthright. Even so, carsickness was not what nearly killed me on that holiday.

Our motel unit was a short walk over a low sand dune to Avoca Beach. This suited Dad perfectly, because he was the only one who could drive his car, either for insurance reasons or because he was the man of the family, and being that close to the beach meant he didn't feel obliged to drive us anywhere. While Mum walked us to the beach, he spent his day in the motel immersed in the Third World. Dad did not come to Avoca for the big waves, indeed. His sun-damaged skin and bad back combined to make the beach a bad bet for him; even worse than the zoo. But even if he had been in perfect physical health Dad would have preferred the Third World over the beach any day. He was waiting to hear back that year from a professor in Massachusetts he had sent his work-in-progress to, after Sydney University had turned it down on the grounds that it was 'too big and ambitious' for a Master's thesis. And sure enough he did hear from this professor during that holiday (as I later learnt), expressing the opinion that the folks at Sydney University need their heads read if they rejected what Dad had sent him, and encouraged him to go it alone with his book, which he then did.

Meanwhile we went to the beach all day every day for two whole weeks, coming back for lunch at half-time. All went well for the first week, as the weather held and we loved the water. And a bonus of all that salt water was that the impetigo sores I'd had all year finally cleared up, including a giant blister almost the entire length of my thumb. I was standing outside the motel when it burst, and the relief I felt to have my thumb back would not be dampened by Mum, who was with me at the time, joking that Nana probably heard it burst back in Sydney. Still, it was not bursting blisters or cruel jokes that nearly killed me up at Avoca that year either.

We were nearing the end of our holiday when the weather turned. A high wind whipped the surf up and only the staunchest swimmers and surfers were braving the open waves on the beach without flags. Everyone else was crowded into the rock pool down one end of the beach. Because it was quite a hike from the motel to the rock pool, Mum took a packed lunch, rather than come home for lunch, and so we stayed all day at the beach. Dad must have been happy. I was happy too as this meant more time to practise my dolphin dive, which needed as much practice as possible. It also needed a fair amount of space, but in the crowded rock pool that day it was difficult to find the space to hold my breath, crouch down, then leap up in the air and throw myself over to one side, with my arms forming a perfect point above my head, to land with a satisfying slap back onto the water, just exactly like a dolphin. There were so many children and adults in the shallows that I kept being pushed deeper into the pool to find enough space for my dolphin dive, until I reached a long second toe down to find no sand.

Instantly I knew I was in trouble. Because even though I made a pretty convincing dolphin, if I do say so myself, I could not, in fact, swim and needed the sand for safety. Mum was on the shore with Babs, chatting to another Mum. Tim was in the pool somewhere but there were far too many people to see where. He did not favour the dolphin dive and we didn't usually play together in the water.

After realising I was out of my depth I tried to madly kick and paddle my way back towards the shallows, but the water was pulling me in the opposite direction out to even deeper waters. I don't remember if I screamed for help, but it was so noisy with people playing and the crashing sea just beyond the pool that even if I had screamed it's unlikely anyone would have heard.

The pool was so swollen that day that as I approached the back of it, being held up by the tide rushing to meet the sea, I couldn't even see the jagged tops of the rocks where the pool ended and the dark churning sea began. I had never been out to the back of the pool before, not even on calm days, as the water was over my head even then. So to be approaching it now and at such an alarming rate, with no rocks to grab onto when I got there, was truly terrifying. I was sure I was going over.

I can still see those dark churning waves beyond the pool as I was being sucked out towards them, close enough now to just make out the jagged tops of the rocks about a foot below the surface of the water as I came on top of them, about to go over. But then, out of nowhere, as my hand scraped one of those jagged rocks, desperately trying to grab on, and the surging sea prepared to claim me, came a strong arm around my waist, dragging me back from the edge of the pool against the ferocious force of the tide. I couldn't believe it or even understand it. I half thought I was dreaming. But the man with the strong arm was real enough and he dragged me back against the strong current all the way to the shallows then lifted me up out of the water, over the heads of all the people, to sit me down on the safe sand and ask: 'Where's your mother?' the only words he spoke to me. I pointed in stunned silence to where I could see Mum still sitting on the sand, chatting, with her head turned the other way, with Babs sitting nearby, exactly as I'd last seen them what now seemed like an eternity ago, as if nothing at all had happened. The man then left without saying another word and I sat there, feeling the warm, safe sand beneath me, listening to the happy sounds of people playing in the water, not quite believing I was lucky enough to be alive.

Chapter 5

Green eyes, brown socks

Altogether, being five was a bit of a touch-and-go age for me. But never mind. They say what doesn't kill you makes you stronger.

I came home from Avoca that year more stressed than I'd ever been, with car sickness and a fear of drowning at sea to add to my long list of issues. But if I hadn't been at a stress maximum, wheezing and spluttering and generally carrying on as if I was still drowning when I got home from Avoca, Mum probably would not have taken me back to the doctors the following week. And if she hadn't done that I probably would never have done ballet. And that really did make me stronger, even if it, too, nearly killed me.

I never told Mum about what happened in the rock pool up at Avoca that wild weather day, at least not until many years later when she frowned and said, 'I never knew anything about that', in a way that made it clear she didn't quite believe me. And I think part of the reason I didn't tell her, much less Dad, was because I didn't want to believe it had happened either, and thought it was my fault, which it was, really. I was not quite the dolphin I thought I was. Also, I think I was in shock for approximately 25 years afterwards.

I started ballet and my second, slightly less disastrous year of school, two weeks later; a few days before my sixth birthday. Ballet was immediately a haven from the world of fake forests and wild seas, raining caterpillars and suppositories. In the dance studio, trees and seas were taken out of the equation entirely, as were caterpillars, compulsory milk and sun so hot it melted my hair off, as the first thing about ballet is that it is usually undertaken on land and indoors. Indeed hair was taken out of the equation too, tucked into a bun, and forgotten about. This all suited me. I did not need to think about hair or sun or sea or caterpillars any more than was absolutely necessary.

The second thing about ballet, if you're lucky, and for some reason I was in this case, is that it is undertaken within doors that are not any old ordinary doors but fancy, stylish doors, as the Northside studio was. Indeed Mrs P's studio at the Crown of the Hill on the edge of the fake forest looked like a cake; a fancy two-tiered gateau cake with circular, whipped cream walls and sweet mint leaf ivy climbing all over it. Hansel and Gretel's witch could have done worse to entice children in. The mistress (some might say witch) of this particular cake building had other things in mind for the children she enticed than fattening them up, indeed; but I wasn't to know that then.

I was enchanted from the moment I saw the *outside* of the cake studio that stood out among the blocky red brick and white weatherboard houses of the fake forest, like an oasis of sense and style. Even at six I could appreciate this and adjusted my dream home immediately. Inside it was even more magical, though I was slightly disappointed to find it wasn't actually cake. The polished wooden floor boards sparkled from delicate shafts of sunlight that shone in through three tall, elegant windows, as the tinkling piano music bounced off those shiny boards and whipped cream walls, like *it* was merrily dancing too, drowning out the roar of the six-lane Warringah Road highway beyond. The final charm was a black spiral staircase leading mysteriously upstairs to what further delights I could only imagine. I added this feature to my dream home and envied Mrs P's children, who lived up there, especially her two girls who were not that much younger than I was. If I could ever get past Mrs P, I was going to sneak up that staircase to find out how lucky little girls on the edge of the fake forest, inside a cake, live, and see if there was any room for one more.

That never happened, alas, but it didn't matter much. Because dancing to that tinkling piano in the ground floor studio was so much fun I almost forgot about the spiral staircase. And against all the odds of a bad build and laboured breathing I took to ballet immediately. Even Auntie Robin, who came to watch a few classes at the start, had to admit I had 'a real feel for it', as she told Mum, and Mum hastened to write to tell her friends and relations back in England about, lest they think life in Australia was all about suppositories, vomit and pus. And when the piano played and Mrs P said 'and …', clapping her hands for us to keep time, encouraging us to 'pull up' and 'turn out', there was nothing I wanted to do more than pull up and turn out, as I danced to the pretty music, feeling like I could breathe properly for the first time. If only *all* of life could be about pulling up and turning out to pretty music, inside a cake.

Alas, it could not. And finding this oasis in the fake forest had a downside too, in that when I had to leave it behind, which I did most of the time in the early years, what I returned to seemed all the more like a dry and dreary - if dangerous - desert. Although I was under doctor's orders to dance, apparently there was no need for me to dance a lot. Rather, I should dance just enough to know how much easier it was to breathe when I did. The rest of the time I still had to dodge the sun, slugs, surf and various other stresses of life that kept me on the brink of the sick bay, all the while drinking enough pink and white milk to drown in, and let's not mention the meat. It wasn't easy. And the worst of it were the socks – the *brown* socks, of course – that were part of the girls' all-year uniform at French's Forest Primary.

Dad's promotion did not seem to have brought any major improvement in our situation, other than the company car, which, as you know, made me sick. And by the age of six I was beginning to notice that other girls had rather nicer things than I did, which was making me a little sick too. And I couldn't afford to get much sicker. Mum, possibly to compensate for Dad's extravagant streak, was a fierce critic of the 'throw-away society', as she called it, and this meant she bought second-hand and No Frills brand from Franklins supermarket whenever she could. The second-hand uniform shop at primary school, tucked away in an embarrassed little shop at the back of the school hall, became Mum's second home once we started school. And for some reason, the worst of my second-hand school uniform at primary was the second-hand socks, probably because they were brown, a faded dull and dreary brown, like our lawn, not the deep brown of Babs' eyes. I thought we had quite enough dull brown in the fake forest as it was. Evidently the school didn't agree. And these sad and saggy, second-hand, faded brown socks became the symbol for me of all that was sad and saggy about my situation, compared with the situation of most other girls at school, who at least got to wear *new* socks.

In particular, my sock envy was focused on the upright, unfaded and cleverly clinging brand new socks worn by my best friend, Jodie Crane. Jodie was my best friend *despite* her socks, obviously, and despite her mother being a veritable fan of the throw-away society who made a point of never putting her daughter in anything other than shiny brand new everything, including socks. When they were slightly worn, out they went and in came a new, even clingier pair than the first. I yanked up my faded, saggy brown socks and told them to get a grip, but I couldn't blame them when they refused, slumping back down around my ankles in sad, faded defeat. They had already been through primary school once, possibly twice, they did *not* want to go through it all over again. I understood *and* sympathised, but it didn't help.

Then one day a total sock calamity! Jodie showed up wearing brand new *white* socks. What was the meaning of this! They're not the uniform! I was totally speechless when I saw Jodie's slim ankles in those crisp white socks and couldn't even bring myself to ask *why*. I had been doing quite well at school to that point, despite my sad sock situation; I was even tied first with another girl (not Jodie) to get to the moon first when Mum brought Nana into our class for Education Week (at least there was one) mid-year. It was 1972 and the moon was all the rage. But my motivation wasn't the moon, which we reached first by making the least number of mistakes in dictation each week. I wanted the tall cylinder of jellybeans that stood next to a smiling yellow moon, as well as the most gold stars lined up next to my name on the star chart that hung on the wall beside it that were the prizes for getting to the moon first. But even though spelling was not a particular strength of mine, if the reward had been new socks, white or brown, there wouldn't have been a contest. I would have beaten Neil Armstrong to the moon. But after Jodie showed up with her brand new crisp white socks and nobody told her she had to go back to brown, and the second-hand uniform shop didn't even stock white socks so I knew my chances of getting a pair were slightly worse than my chances of getting to the actual moon first, that tall cylinder of colourful jellybeans and golden stars lost their appeal and I sunk back into a sad brown slump, just like my socks.

'How come you've got *white* socks?' I finally built up the courage to ask Jodie after several days of being blinded by envy and the glare of those bright white socks in the summer sun. 'Mum got them for me,' was the depressingly blameless answer I got back that did nothing to calm my raging sense of injustice. So much for *best* friends; without any sock solidarity what was the point? But with Jodie it wasn't just the bright white socks. Everything about Jodie and her whole family was bright white and gleaming compared to everything about me and my family. So there was not much point crying over the socks, for they were merely the bright white tip of a very big and bright white iceberg of advantages. So after a while I stopped. But I never stopped envying Jodie.

* * *

The Cranes could not have been more different to my family had we come from different planets, their planet being Earth; our planet being one where nothing is ever thrown away (for starters). Jodie's father worked for 20th Century Fox and for her seventh birthday he hired out a theatre to put on a private viewing of *The Sound of Music* for Jodie and her friends. I had to wear a hand-me-down dress that was too big for me and years out of fashion, because it came, like a lot of our non-school clothes, from the Thompsett girls; daughters of one of Mum's friends, who were all naturally much older than us. When the von Trapp children got their curtain dresses I felt a bit better about my baggy second-hand dress until I saw the girls dancing in their curtain dresses and they didn't even look second-hand! Jodie, of course, had a brand new dress for her party.

I don't remember what I did for my seventh birthday; probably went to the beach and got stung by a bluebottle, which happened a bit. At least it wasn't a brown bottle.

Jodie's parents, like everybody's parents, were about twenty years younger than Mum and Dad. Jodie's father, who was a surf lifesaver when he wasn't arranging private viewings of the latest film for Jodie's birthdays, was exactly twenty years younger than Dad and looked even younger still, because Dad *wasn't* a surf lifesaver and didn't wear his age as well as Mr Crane did. On Saturdays, when Dad was in the library trying to save the Third World, Mr Crane was in the surf at the treacherous Long Reef Beach trying, and often times succeeding, in saving lives. I suppose they had *saving* in common, Dad and Mr Crane, but they were rather different sorts of saving and rather different sorts of dads. Just as Mr Crane probably didn't even know where or what the Third

World was, Dad barely knew where or what the surf was and would have had less chance of saving anyone in it than Mr Crane had of saving the Third World, despite him not knowing where to find it.

Mrs Crane was *only* sixteen years younger than Mum, and because Mum wore her age better than Dad, the mums didn't look quite as different as the dads. They did, however, have very different views on the virtues of the throw-away society, as mentioned; and on a few other things too. Jodie lived in a two-storey house in Careebong Road, just around the corner from us, with an in-ground pool that her parents had had installed soon after they moved in. Mrs Crane managed a jewellery shop in Brookvale mall and this was one of the reasons why they could afford the pool and other luxury items, such as new white socks. Mum disapproved of this arrangement. Mum had very firm views on married women working, views shared even more firmly by Dad. Their view was that married women should *not* work except in an emergency, and Mum did not think a pool qualified as an emergency. Much less did brand new socks. So this was quite a difference between the two mums. As it turned out, an emergency of the sort that did qualify in Mum's eyes, if less so in Dad's, would befall our family before too long.

Another difference between Mum and Mrs Crane was that Mrs Crane sunbathed topless by their pool and Mum *didn't*, and not only because she didn't have a pool (or a bikini). As a result of this difference I had never even seen Mum's bare boobs, at least not that I could recall, but as I was invited over to swim in Jodie's pool on a fairly regular basis, being Jodie's *best* friend, and Mrs Crane supervised our swimming lying topless on her back on the sun lounger, I became very familiar with Mrs

Crane's boobs. I couldn't tell you if Mrs Crane's boobs were any *better* than my mum's boobs, but they were certainly more seen. Jodie told me, when I asked, ever so discreetly: 'Why doesn't your Mum wear a bikini top?' that her mum wanted an all-over tan. I was pretty sure my mum didn't want one of those.

I was lucky I got to swim in Jodie's cool pool; unlucky when I didn't. It was a tricky situation, really, because Jodie didn't seem to have any system for deciding when I should be invited and when I shouldn't. The afternoon sun at its hottest, when we walked home from school together and I made all sorts of hints about the lack of quality viewing on TV that day, was no guarantee that an invitation to swim in her cool pool would be forthcoming. Sometimes she invited Beth Fahey over for a swim instead, possibly because Mrs Crane had a limit to how many children she could supervise topless. Jodie and Beth were friends too, but not *best* friends, I didn't think. Beth went to a different school. Other times she seemed to invite no-one, or people I didn't know, which amounted to the same thing, and I'd end up having to invite Beth over to watch *Scooby Do* on TV to commiserate with her about not having a pool either.

Once, commiserating with Beth was not enough. It was a very hot day in the summer holidays and the Cranes were away, leaving all that cool, sparkling blue pool going to waste, which seemed like a terrible shame. I think I must have inherited something of my mother's dislike of waste. I knew their expected return date, and just before they were due back I built up the courage to help myself to their pool. I couldn't go alone, I was not yet eight and Beth was out, so I decided to ask Mum. When I put the idea to her I added that Mrs Crane had said we were welcome to use their pool while they were away, which she may well have done. It was not impossible. I had a vague notion she had said something of the sort, but I might have dreamed it, though my dreams tended to be nightmares. Either way, Mum agreed. Being English, Mum felt the heat and got sick of driving us to the beach, especially in the summer holidays when it could be a daily affair. She was always complaining that the car was a 'furnace' when we got back into dear old, not-air-conditioned Deirdre, to drive home from the beach, our bare legs sticking to the seats, the steering wheel too hot to touch, feeling altogether hotter when we got home than when we left, often with a bluebottle sting or two to show for our troubles.

So a swim in the Crane's pool right round the corner was a very tempting idea indeed. Tim and Babs were at home too so they had to come with us, which made a nice party of four. Being the *best* friend, I led the way and showed everyone into the pool area through the wrought-iron side gate that was another source of envy for me. Wrought iron was so pretty and so fashionable. Our gate out to the pipe was plain old, worn-out wood. They had a pool, we had a pipe. They had wrought iron, we had wood. What was a green-eyed girl to do?

The pool, sparkling and stretched out luxuriously in all its bright blue glory under a proud and powerful sun, looked as inviting as ever, if a little wary of the unexpected visitors. Mum told us not to make too much noise and to begin with we didn't. She took a cooling dip in the pool before lying back on Mrs Crane's sun lounger. After ten minutes we were making as much noise as we liked, as if it was our very own pool, and having convinced myself that it was our pool, I couldn't help thinking how much more fun it was swimming in the pool without Jodie, because when she was there it was harder to imagine it was my pool; harder, but not impossible.

After not much more than ten minutes Mr Crane's face appeared at the rumpus room door that opened out onto the pool, with an expression of 'What the hell's going on here!' on his sun-tanned, lifesaving face. Evidently there'd been some mix-up with the dates. I could only apologise profusely and would have done, if it had been my job to do so. Instead I stared wide-eyed with humiliation while Mum leapt up off Mrs Crane's sun lounger and stood dripping pool water all over the place, in her old-fashioned swimsuit (thankfully not topless), trying to explain about the invitation. From the look on Mr Crane's face he knew nothing of any invitation. We hurried out of the pool then and stood by, dripping with guilt – or at least I did. My only consolation was that Dad wasn't with us. For once I was glad of the Third World.

After that I pleaded with Mum for us to get our own pool, feeling the moment couldn't have been better to make my case. 'Please, Mum, *please*,' I begged and pleaded. 'It would be so much fun! You'd love it. We could stay in all day. You could get your own sun lounger. Please, Mum, *please!*' I went on at every opportunity, telling her how perfect our back lawn was for a pool and reminding her of what a pain the bindis were and what a *furnace* the car was driving back from the beach. I had learnt that word, 'furnace', and thought it might be a good moment to use it. 'But where would the boys play cricket at Christmas?' Mum said, most disappointingly, disregarding my furnace entirely.

'The *front* lawn!' I ejaculated, rather too quickly, as it suggested I didn't really care two cents for the Christmas cricketers. Because the fact of the matter was that our front lawn was not a realistic option for cricket or much else. It was big enough, bigger than our back lawn, but it was completely public, unfenced and sloped into the bargain. A stray cricket ball could have ended up in the Fahey's Christmas pudding if we'd played Christmas cricket on our front lawn. But I wanted a pool so bad I wasn't going to let the Fahey's Christmas pudding put me off.

'The boys play footy on the front lawn!' I said when Mum pointed out the deficiencies of the front lawn for cricket. This was true. They did. However, these boys were not *our* boys and Mum and Dad rather preferred they didn't play footy on our lawn. The boys who helped themselves to our front lawn for a game of footy whenever they felt like it were some or all of the seven Schrouten boys who lived across the road and didn't have a lawn of their own. *They* had a pool. This liberty used to drive Dad mad, and not only because they were uninvited. Worse, they'd call out 'Hi Mark!' if they saw him watching through our oversized front windows, instead of Mr Jones, which was the ultimate affront. The Martian boys next door also regularly helped themselves to our front lawn, climbing the liquidambar tree in the corner to catch cicadas. When Dad would see a lanky limb protruding from the upper leaves, knowing none of us were lanky, he would again be incensed, saying to Mum: 'Haven't they got their own trees to climb?' So our front lawn was a great use to our neighbours but a pain in Dad's neck and next to no use to us, and so it would ever be. Mum saw through my desperate attempt and said we could not afford a pool anyway.

Never mind. I would dig my own pool in a corner of the

back lawn, leaving enough room for the Christmas cricketers, who could break an ankle stepping in it for all I cared. Mum surprised me by taking my pool project half seriously, even though I was only eight. She couldn't help me dig the hole – we only had one spade – but she did find me a black plastic sheet from under the house to line my pool with that only had a few spider holes in it. Blue would have been better, but Mum said she didn't think Franklins sold No Frills plastic sheets in blue, and I had no reason to doubt her. She knew the No Frills range pretty well. She helped me gather the largest rocks we could carry from out by the pipe, and after pinning the plastic sheet down I dragged the hose across the lawn and filled my pool with water.

The ground must have been a *bit* dry that summer and those spider bites a bit bigger than I first thought, because the water disappeared straight through the sheet and into the ground quicker than you could say: 'Fool's pool.' But having come this far, half breaking my back digging a hole barely big enough for my bottom, I was not going to be put off that easily. I rearranged the plastic, found some heavier rocks with Mum's help, and tried again. Eventually the pool filled with water that was not entirely brown and I got into my cossies and into *my* pool, the parts of me that would fit in at least, and felt a certain satisfaction that only those who build their own pool with their bare hands can feel. And my bottom was definitely cooled.

But after a few weeks of refilling my pool and sitting in it now and then, making Babs sit in it too, by herself because it wouldn't fit both our bottoms at once – though we tried – Mum suggested that perhaps it was time to pack up my pool, to give the hole time to heal before next year's Christmas cricket. So that was the end of my pool project.

* * *

For her job, Mrs Crane made frequent trips to Singapore to buy jewellery for the shop in Brookvale, as well as all sorts of wonders for Jodie. Jodie had her ears pierced before any other girl in Australia, I think, and when velvet tops came in, she definitely had more of them than any girl in Australia. She told me they were much cheaper in Singapore than in Australia. This didn't help. Jodie had eight velvet tops by the time she was eight, one for every colour of the rainbow, plus two different pinks and blues. I had one velvet top. It was red. It probably should have been green. Jodie's velvet tops were arranged in a neat and colourful tower in her white-painted built-in wardrobe with sliding, gliding doors that ran along one whole wall of her bedroom that she shared with *no-one*. She had a younger sister, Kylie, who was seven-and-a-half years younger than her and had her own room too. I don't need to tell you the colour of my wardrobe or that I had to share it, and the room, with Babs.

That summer, when I was eight and Jodie was nine, because she was five months older than me, Mrs Crane decided to take Jodie with her to Singapore, possibly to buy more velvet tops. She only had two blue and two pink tops; perhaps she needed two of *every* colour. I would have been gripped with an envy even more powerful than my pool, sock and velvet-top envy combined to learn that Jodie was going overseas on a plane, if not for the fact that, as fickle luck would have it, I was going on a plane that summer too. I was not going to Singapore to buy earrings and velvet tops with my young hip mum, mind, but to Perth to visit my Uncle Walter and his family with my Nana, who was 88 and had a crook hip. Still, it was a trip away and I got to fly in a plane for the first time, just like Jodie. I was extremely excited.

I needn't have been. 'Our flight was very exciting but there was too much mustard on the bread', was the opening line of the first letter I wrote home from Perth, summing up the level of excitement of the whole trip, but for a few exceptions. Uncle Walter's youngest child, Louise, was eighteen and the only one of their three children still living at home by this time. We bonded a little. She used to take me out in her car and get me to buy cigarettes and Cherry Ripe chocolate bars for her from the local milk bar. At eight this felt like a definite step up in the world, even if I didn't approve of her choice of chocolate bar. Why have fruit with your chocolate if you didn't have to? I accepted a piece of Cherry Ripe even so, but declined a cigarette. Actually Louise was only joking when she offered me a cigarette, which I found pretty funny, until she showed me her supply of unopened cigarette cartons under her bed. Why send me out for cigarettes if she already had more packets under her bed than the whole milk bar had? I couldn't work this out and was left to wonder if these trips in Louise's car meant we were friends or not.

Nana and I shared a small room and because it was summer and didn't get dark until long after we went to bed, I had to watch Nana getting undressed. I didn't *have* to, but I found that when I tried to avert my eyes, without looking too pointedly at the wall in case Nana was offended, my eyes would turn themselves back in her direction. Some nights I successfully pretended to be asleep, but other nights, trying to stare up at the ceiling, one eye would stray sideways, pulling my neck round with it. I had never seen a girdle before and found its proportions and strange dangling straps somewhat unsettling. Nana had bird-skinny legs but was quite round about the middle, contrasting attributes that were somehow emphasised when she was in her girdle and nothing else.

I think the night girdle might have been the reason I decided one day in Perth, after agreeing to go with Nana for a walk that I would not go for a walk with her after all, and would stay back at the house to do handstands in the garden instead. The look of disappointment on her face, as she tried to get me to change my mind, standing at the bottom of Uncle Walter's driveway, I have never forgotten. I felt so mean I almost changed my mind back again, but Nana walked so slowly and Uncle Walter had a sunken lawn that was great for handstands, that I said sorry again and ran back to the house. The other factor in the equation of whether or not to go for a walk with Nana was my brand new underpants. I had chosen these underpants for Christmas that year and they were so much prettier than the hand-me-down ones we got from the Thompsett girls, I felt compelled to show them off as much as possible, even if no-one was looking but me. Sometimes Auntie Josie, Uncle Walter's wife, watched my handstands from her kitchen window and told me that she didn't think my new underpants, which had tiny little holes in the centre of the flowers, were suitable for hand-standing. This made hand-standing all the more thrilling, with the danger of incurring Auntie Josie's disapproval. I had to take my thrills where I found them.

In the New Year we all drove south to Albany, all six Burkes and me, the only Jones. Nana and I shared a motel room and on our first morning she took me down to the shop next to the motel and let me choose a whole bag of lollies. I was happy enough to walk with her for that! Back in the room we finished getting ready for our day out, me eating my lollies while Nana brushed my hair and tied it back in a loose ponytail that soon fell out, because she didn't have the strength to tie it tight enough, but I didn't mind. I had my lollies. Whatever excitement Jodie was having in Singapore was nothing to this!

Nana had a funny way about her and could often make me laugh. When I was younger she used to hold up a finger (not the rude one), and keep it there with such a deadpan face, saying: 'Don't laugh' until that was all I could do. I'd crack up every time and would not be able to stop once started, long after she took the finger down. I was *much* too old for that trick now of course, but something she said that morning made me laugh and when I did I inhaled a large boiled lemon lolly straight back into my windpipe. It lodged in the back of my throat like a rock. This was *not* quite so funny. I couldn't breathe – at all. I lurched forward, pulling away from Nana and her brush to bend over coughing as hard as I could to try to dislodge the lolly, but it wouldn't budge. I spun round towards Nana, pointing at my throat, trying to say 'stuck', without great success, and seeing Nana's soft old face widen in a most uncharacteristic panic made me panic all the more. Nana banged on my back then with the hairbrush as hard as she could, which only hurt a little and I knew wasn't nearly hard enough. And when the lolly remained stuck, and I saw her face turn to an even deeper panic, I knew she couldn't help me.

Nana was telling me to cough as hard as I could but I was

already doing that and it wasn't working. There was no water supply in the room and in a frantic state now, not knowing what else to do, I flung open the door and tore out of the room, running for my life, with no time to make it to Russia. We had used the communal toilets once the night before and I thought I remembered where they were so I ran in that direction and found them, with an aluminium tub and long-spouted tap just inside the door. I pounced on that, finding some extra strength to turn on the stiff tap, and scooped as much water as I could into my mouth, tipping my head back without swallowing in case the lolly lodged further down. I coughed out with as much force as I could over the sink but still the lolly stayed stuck, hard and stubborn as a rock. I hadn't taken a breath for what must have been more than a minute and my head felt like it was going to explode.

I didn't know what else to do and tears were running down my face, which must have been blue. I looked wildly around for help but there was no-one around. Having no other option, and shaking with panic, I forced myself to repeat the same procedure of scooping water into my mouth, throwing my head back to get water on the lolly without swallowing, then lurching forward over the tub and coughing for all I was worth. I remember finding something extra to cough with that time, a fierce, desperate determination, knowing it was my last chance to live...

Miraculously, like a nugget of pure gold, that stubborn lemon lolly shot out of my mouth and landed with a life-saving clunk in the tin tub. I drew the best breath of my life then, and panting with relief, leaning on the edge of the tub for support, I turned to see Nana come in through the bathroom door, tears of relief in her soft old eyes.

***

Perhaps the three years of ballet I had done by that stage saved my life that day. All that pulling up had to have strengthened my diaphragm and given me a more forceful cough, not to mention strengthening my will to live.

Indeed, against the odds, and a physique that was still far from ideal for ballet, I was going from strength to strength in the dance studio, getting Honours for my first two RAD (Royal Academy of Dancing) grade exams, and being chosen to lead the dancers on stage in Northside's end-of-year concert in my second year. It was a production of the *Four Seasons* in which the girls in my year were dancing as blue and brown birds. I was chosen to lead one of the two lines of little birds in alternating colours coming onto the stage, one from either side, each with a yellow beak stuck on the top of our balaclava hoods. I had several little birds following me and had to set the timing for everyone's arm flaps up and down, and for our feet to rise up onto tip-toe and down into *plié*, up, down, up, down, all the way until we met the other line of birds coming the other way to form one straight alternating blue and brown line across the front of the stage, ideally without a collision. It was quite a responsibility – having to look to the audience and smile all the while, hoping that my line of little birds was doing the same.

It was no effort for me to smile on stage, but the little bird leading the other line on stage did not always remember to smile. In fact she looked a bit worried, I thought, with her yellow beak stuck on top of her pretty bluebird hood, as she approached from the other side. Why she looked so worried when *she* got to wear the bluebird costume and I had to wear the brown, I did not know. Maybe when you've got eight velvet tops of every colour of the rainbow and some, getting to be a blue bird instead of a brown bird is not such a big deal. Because the other lead bird in that concert was indeed Jodie. She had started ballet at Northside shortly after I had, and was doing quite well too. And as envious as I was at the time of Jodie being chosen to wear the bluebird costume, with every other advantage she seemed to have over me, I bet she doesn't still have her bluebird costume, the way her Mum threw things out to make way for the new. But I still have my brown bird. And being brown it has preserved rather well, brown being rather better, I should think, at hiding the dirt.

Chapter 6

Of mice, men, money and mayhem

Mum, it's fair to say, had what I believe some people consider an English approach to housekeeping. *Hands-off* might be another way to describe it. She had grown up in a house with a live-in maid, which might have contributed to her 'English' approach. Also, the space she had to work with in our house was rather uninspiring and time was in fairly short supply. She much preferred to be out in the garden, typing long chatty letters to her friends back in England, keeping her daily diary up to date, reading or playing the piano she'd hauled all the way out from England. Mondays were spent at the tennis club improving her back-hand. When Babs started school she joined the volunteer squad of canteen ladies for half a day once a week, all of which cut into her housekeeping time.

When the housework simply couldn't be put off, she could be found out on the front lawn, sitting on a mat, legs stuck straight out, head down, pitch fork poised, seeing to the paspalum. Mum had a thing about paspalum; dust and grime, no, paspalum, yes. Even if it had grown *inside* the house I think she would have seen to the paspalum. Her diaries record hours and hours of time spent in a single day on paspalum eradication, especially on the front lawn, which seemed to grow paspalum as its chief function. Often the paspalum was the only green on the lawn, as if it had sucked out all the green from the grass – which it probably had. And although I didn't much like paspalum either, when it was the only green on the lawn and took up so much of Mum's time, I couldn't help thinking it might not be worth all the trouble.

The exception to Mum's English approach to housekeeping was when the Van Leeuwens came over for bridge. The Van Leeuwens were *not* English; they were Dutch and, as such, they did not have an English approach to housekeeping. Mum would go frantic with a duster and vacuum and polish before bridge evenings with the Van Leeuwens, almost to the point of neglecting the paspalum. Unfortunately, the Van Leeuwens only came round for bridge every fourth Friday.

Fortunately, on the other hand, dust doesn't kill you. It can be bad for asthmatics, yes, but I had my ballet to rely on now, so there was no need to worry about the dust on my account. And indeed no-one did. Rather, in 1974, with the housekeeping situation becoming more and more English by the day, we decided to embrace the mayhem and acquire two mice, one cat, and a young boy from El Salvador called Paolo. Paola didn't add to the dust, exactly, because he was only in photo form. But he did add something to the general mayhem in being our World Vision-sponsored child who stood on the piano, with a perpetual scowl on his face, as if he was not entirely happy about the arrangement either, and I couldn't blame him. The cat was called Chico, which means 'little boy' in Spanish, as Mum told us. So there was a Spanish theme to the additions to our household that year. Why, I couldn't quite tell you. Sometimes you just have to go Spanish.

So now we were English *and* Spanish. Also we were American, because we called the mice Mickey and Minnie, as they were, naturally, male and female. Within the first year we had 35 *more* Americans in the house, as well as the Spanish, which was a few more multinationals than we'd bargained for. Even Mum's high threshold for mayhem seemed to have been breached with a total of 37 mice and emergency measures were taken to separate the males and the females, and a second, much larger cage bought for the females and their latest litter. The local pet shop took a few mice off our hands and Jodie took two; two males of course. The Cranes would *not* be making any mice.

It could have been worse; Tim had wanted a dog. Babs and Mum had wanted the cat. I'm not sure who wanted the mice; definitely not Dad, who was not a mouse or a cat or a dog person, though he had wanted Paolo. I don't recall wanting any animal or any child from El Salvador, particularly not one that scowled all day and was the person Dad, and sometimes Mum, turned to from then on, to remind us how lucky we were and how much worse off than us some children 'like Paolo' were. Paolo's clothes were too big for him and his bare feet were dirty. He didn't look *that* much worse off than us.

* * *

It turned out I was allergic to animal fur, so it was just as well Babs was the animal lover, not me. Unfortunately, this animal allergy wasn't diagnosed until all our animals were dead (I did not kill them). In the meantime I scratched my green eyes red and my pink throat raw whenever I had hand-to-eye contact with the cat or mice until I looked like Minnie the albino mouse with her red eyes and white fur, more or less the colour of my hair. I wheezed too, but that could have just been the asthma. Ballet wasn't a miracle cure, though I did breathe much easier in the studio, where there were no animals; unlike at home, where there were approximately 30.

There may not have been any animals of the four-legged, furry-backed variety in the studio, but that year there were several dwarfs. Fortunately I was not allergic to *them*. Indeed, I was one of them. A professional full-length ballet of *Snow White and the Seven Dwarfs* was put on at the brand new Seymour Centre in the city that year and although I was still not built for ballet exactly, it turned out I was rather well built for the part of a ballet-dancing dwarf. Mrs P clearly hadn't anticipated *that*. In fact, being shorter than average, a bit stocky and with an oversized head, I was almost purpose-built for the part of a dancing dwarf. Not that other girls with less ideal attributes, such as Jodie, who was tall for her age and entirely in proportion, weren't also cast as dwarfs, because they were. In fact there were three casts of seven dwarfs, with one understudy in each cast, so 24 dancing dwarfs in total, chosen from dance schools all over Sydney. Still, I felt I was the most convincing of all the dancing dwarfs, even more so than the three boys who were also cast for the part.

I was extremely pleased to be cast as a dwarf, not least because I got to wear a beard. I had never worn a beard before. It was not altogether comfortable wearing an elasticated beard, but when I pulled on my beard and positioned it under my bottom lip, instead of under the chin, as all the other dwarves wore theirs, it hid my pointy chin. At this age (nine), I had decided that my face was much too big and my chin much too pointy. If only I could have worn the beard *all* the time. At school I was starting to be teased for a few of my physical oddities. One girl I had never spoken to before, who was in the year above me, had come up to me out of the blue one day to ask: 'Why is your face so flat?' I hadn't known my face was flat before this, probably because it's hard to see your profile in the mirror, especially when you don't have one, but I started to worry and wonder about my flat face after that.

Another group of kids at school liked to chant 'Sally Jones has no bones' whenever I appeared. I wanted to prove to them that I *did* have bones, but I didn't know exactly how to do this. I probably should have pointed to my chin: 'What's *that* if not a bone?' I could have said, but I wasn't quite that cool or confident. Instead I said: '*You* don't have any bones' before departing at a pace for the nearest shadow, while trying to hold my pointy chin up without drawing attention to it, which was not so easy to do. A beard might have given those kids something *else* to think about. I might have no bones, but I did have a beard.

The only trouble with wearing the beard under my lip on stage was that while dancing it would continually slip up into my mouth, and when you're a dwarf in the middle of a dance in front of a paying audience, you can't just pull your beard down whenever you feel like it. So I ended up dancing with a mouthful of beard and when Mum brought everyone, including Auntie Robin, in to watch one of our performances, nobody could recognise which dwarf I was, which was disappointing because I was definitely the best one.

The other thing about getting to dance as a dwarf in a professional ballet production was that we were paid. I was happy enough with the beard *not* to need to be paid, but everyone, including the understudies, was paid for rehearsals as well as performances. I can't remember exactly how much it was in total, but I think it was something between $50 and $80, which was quite a bit of money back then for a nine-year-old. A Paddle Pop from Mr Whippy cost 20 cents at this time, for instance. With my dwarf money I could have bought all Mr Whippy's caramel Paddle Pops, which was tempting. Caramel Paddle Pops were my favourite. But instead, all the dwarfs opened up bank accounts, except for Jodie, who already had one, and I deposited my money therein, enjoying entering 'Dwarf' and the sum of money next to it in my bank book.

My little blue bank book was made of paper and not much bigger than my hand, but what it lacked in size and strength it made up for in quantity of pages and empty ruled lines to fill. Once I'd filled one line it seemed I had an obligation – to the book – to fill more. So I saved my $1 Christmas money from Nana and $2 for my birthday that year. And when that still left too many empty lines and pages I decided to start selling the boysenberries I picked with Babs out by the subbo end of the pipe. Babs wasn't keen on going door-to-door selling boysenberries, so I went alone. I arranged the plump, dark purple berries, the plumpest, purple-est berries on top, into the plastic punnets that Mum saved for me, and went round to the monstrosities in the subbo, figuring that there was more money for berries at that end of the street than at ours. I knocked on doors, waited for someone to come to the door, then asked: 'Would you like to buy some fresh boysenberries for just a dollar?' I knew to call them 'fresh' and to make the price sound cheap, which it wasn't really. I also knew not to tell them that I picked the berries from the pipe just behind their houses, which meant they were really *their* berries. My strategy worked and I sold several punnets, putting the money in the bank and making a separate entry in my little blue bank book for each punnet sold.

Mum thought this was very enterprising and said, 'Perhaps you're going to grow up to be a successful businessman like your great-great-grandfather' – meaning David Jones, and business*woman*, but they didn't have that word back then. I knew what she meant. I thought perhaps I might want to become terribly successful like my great-great-grandfather, but I wasn't particularly excited by the idea of selling boysenberries for the rest of my life. Dad didn't say anything to me about selling the boysenberries, and I got the feeling he disapproved of the activity and of my little blue bank book too.

After making money from the boysenberries on top of the dwarf money I started to earn a reputation in the family as 'the one who saves'. Babs, although only eight at this time, already had a reputation for letting money slip through her fingers, and Tim, who had started a paper run, didn't have a reputation either way. His money was his business. Before I could deposit my money in my bank account up at our local Arndale shopping centre I kept it in my ballerina jewellery box in the drawer under my bed. Nobody knew it was there except for Babs. One day I discovered a whole dollar, in two brand new silver 50-cent pieces, had gone missing. I knew Babs had taken them. 'Give me back my money!' I screamed in her face when I tracked her down in the kitchen. She smiled sweetly and said: 'I didn't.' Meaning she did, clearly. 'Give me my money *back!* I know you took it!' I screamed even louder, shoving my open hand, palm up, under her nose. She shook her head and repeated, 'I didn't.'

'I'm telling on you!' was my next cry of outrage before I stomped off in search of Mum.

I found her in the laundry doing the washing, and told her the sorry tale. 'Babs took my money and won't give it back! You have to make her give it back! It's *my* money!' This was fairly clear, I thought, and was a little disappointed by Mum's failure to show the appropriate outrage. Babs had followed me into the laundry and Mum turned to ask her, quite casually, if this was true: 'Did you take Sally's money, Babs?' Babs, with her big round brown eyes and butter-wouldn't-melt-in-her-mouth expression, smiled sweetly at Mum and shook her head. Never was there a clearer expression of guilt! But instead of telling Babs to tell the truth and give me back my money, when I turned to look at Mum I could swear I caught her sharing a sly smile with Babs. It was very difficult not to smile when Babs smiled, admittedly, but what about my money!

'Perhaps you lost it, Sal, or spent it,' was the next thing Mum said in her cheerful voice, busy scooping No Frills washing powder into the measuring cup, clearly without the slightest concern about Babs being a thief. Stealing is a crime, isn't it? I was fairly sure it was. Stealing from your big sister must be the worst sort of stealing there is, and when your mother doesn't care, and is even on the side of your little sister liar thief, it is surely the very worst of the very worstest of crimes of all.

'I *hate* you!' I said, with feeling then, and I wasn't looking at Babs, before I tore off out of the laundry in floods of tears.

When Dad got home from work, after I'd been in the bedroom on my own for hours, half starving to death, Tim came to get me and tell me that Dad wanted to talk to me. I found Mum and Dad in close conference across the dining table at the other end of the kitchen from where I stood, clinging for support to the stove, with Mum in tears. I knew I'd done it now.

'You ap-p-p-pologise to your m-m-m-mother for sp-speaking to her the way you did, Sally!' Dad positively roared at me, stuttering and trembling with rage. He had a big voice, Dad, despite the stutter, and because he didn't often use it, it was all the more terrifying when he did. I mumbled a half-genuine 'Sorry.'

'That's not good enough, Sally! You say a proper sorry to your mother. You don't know how lucky you are to have a mother like yours!' Dad went on roaring and stuttering, till I started crying with a confusing mixture of shame and anger and began to feel like I really did hate them both now. 'Sorry, Mum!' I mumbled, with slightly more feeling, before running back to my bedroom for a night without dinner. Why didn't anyone care about *me*? I wanted to know. And what about my money? I never saw it again.

* * *

Mum let us wander far and wide in those days, further than the other mums did. And despite my mixed feelings about the fake forest, I liked to roam and explore as far as I could, which is how I came across the wild boysenberries in the first place. When Babs wasn't out of favour I took her with me, because she was better than no company. Sometimes a friend from school would come round and we'd go off for miles into the bush that surrounded us in just about every direction.

There was an area of particularly dense bush without tracks about a mile from our house that we got to by walking down into the bottom of the Subbo, along a dirt path beside one of the new houses, over a rocky creek behind that, then across a hardly-used oval. That was my favourite place to go bushwalking. One day I took Babs with me and we discovered a waterfall about twenty minutes in, if we walked in the right direction, listening out for the water that was never much more than a trickle but was amplified in the quiet. That became our very own waterfall and we returned to it often with a feeling of great adventure every time. Once, we talked the Fahey girls and our brothers into joining us and took bread to toast over a fire that we made on a cave floor looking out twenty-feet or so above the waterfall. It was completely stupid to light a fire in the bush at our age, all under eleven, but the boys took charge and seemed to know what they were doing (Tim was a scout), and no bushfires were started that day.

But another time, when it was just Babs and me and one of her friends from school, Kellyanne, we met a snake at the waterfall. It was unfortunate that Kellyanne was with us that day, as she was particularly afraid of snakes and had been saying the whole way: 'What if we see a snake?' I, of course, had assured her that we definitely would not.

'Snake!' Kellyanne screamed, being the first to spot it, before leaping backwards out of its path and into a corner that she couldn't get out of. Babs leapt with her. They were both backed into a corner, leaving me out in the open, on my own – with the snake! I looked down to see a python-thick, 2-metre long, improbably green snake slithering over the rocks and shallow water at the base of the waterfall, not more than a couple of inches from my long second toes, dangerously exposed in sandals. I remained calm. I couldn't move.

'What are we going to dooooooo?' wailed Kellyanne, as she and Babs stood clinging to each other up against the steep rock face and I, closer to the snake, stood wondering the very same thing. But as Kellyanne appeared to be asking *me* what we were going to do, after the initial freeze of panic, my mind started to work towards an answer. After a short pause to collect my courage I said in a coarse whisper so as not to alarm the snake: 'Move slowly and quietly *that* way when the snake turns to go the other way. It'll be all right. Snakes can't see behind them.' Kellyanne must have been reassured because she followed my instruction, as did Babs, and not too many seconds later, I followed, gradually picking up speed to then chase the others up the rock face, sure there was a bright green snake chasing me.

There wasn't. We got away and never met another snake on our travels, at least not of the reptile sort, and even went back to the bush after that, though never with Kellyanne. Indeed it was not on our bush wanderings that we met with the creepiest of dangers. Rather, it was in our very own street, almost right outside our house.

One Sunday afternoon, Beth and I were walking along our street when we heard a man's voice call out: 'Girls!' We looked around but couldn't see anyone. Then we realised the voice was coming from a man lying underneath a parked car on the side of the road, his bare arm waving to us. 'Could you come here for a minute?' the man said when he saw us looking, beckoning us over. I went over. He had nothing on but a short white towel. I thought this a bit odd, but it was summer time and boiling hot as usual and I decided it must be Mr Parker come in a hurry from his pool to fix something under his car. Not many minutes went by in summer that I wasn't imagining people getting in and out of their pools. Beth decided no such thing.

When I went over and crouched down to see what the man wanted, I looked back to see Beth standing on the verge as far back against the wall of the Parker's house as she could get, her eyes full of alarm. 'It's just Mr Parker under his car,' I wanted to say to Beth, but she was too far away. 'Scaredy cat Beth' was my next thought, even though she would have been barely eight at the time. I was the one who should have known better, being nine. But I wasn't even wary, much less scared, possibly due to the Parker house being only a few doors down from ours, or the fact that I had recently saved my little sister and her friend from a very scary snake.

The man (who wasn't Mr Parker) told me he had a mozzie bite on his lower leg that he couldn't reach and asked me to scratch it. I knew a thing or two about mozzie bites – naturally – and feeling sympathetic, scratched his leg, thinking it was quite a reasonable request, as he clearly couldn't be expected to reach down to his lower leg while lying on his back under a car. It was a bit unpleasant scratching his hairy leg, but still assuming it was Mr Parker, and trying to be neighbourly, I endured. Somehow, scratching a leg with a name to it was less strange than scratching a nameless leg. Names are important.

'Can you scratch a bit higher?' the man under the car asked next, and I did this too, wanting to make sure I scratched the right spot as I knew how annoying it was when you missed the exact itchy spot. While I was doing this Beth appeared next to me to take up her post nearer the man's ankles, and to pass me the tools he now asked for from the toolbox he had carelessly left too far for him to reach. I was grateful to have her company, though as the elder of us, I found her too slow about getting the man his tools and to my shame, proceeded to chivvy her along to be quicker about it.

Then higher again the man wanted me to scratch. He really was getting us working for him. I didn't want to scratch any higher up his leg, underneath the short towel, but I was committed now. I had said I would. And I felt kind of sorry for Mr Parker having to get some kid to scratch his leg. How dim can you be! I scratched higher up his leg ...

After I had scratched as high as I was going to scratch up under the towel, as far as I *could* scratch, and saw that Beth was looking very uneasy now, I said that we had to go. But then he asked if we could go round to the back of the car to look underneath it on the pretence of checking to see if he'd fixed it properly. It was only then that I began to be a bit suspicious, as surely he didn't think I knew anything about cars. Still, my childish confidence and naivety, as well as my sense of obligation and curiosity kept me complying with his requests and I duly went round to the back of the car, crouched down and looked underneath. Beth did not. She stood to the side, and then began backing away towards her side of the street...

I was not so much struck by the car at that point, but by the man's great big white feet sticking up and beyond that a pink elephant I was so embarrassed to see – mostly for *his* sake – that I finally lost my confidence and felt the need to leave. But thinking the man didn't realise how exposed he was, I troubled to explain: 'I can't tell if it's fixed or not; I don't know anything about cars,' by way of an apology, before running home as fast as I could. My more sensible, younger friend was already gone.

Later on, after we'd seen a police car parked outside the Fahey house for some time and the man's car had long since gone, I told Mum and Dad a bit about the man under the car, guessing, at last, that he was the problem. I didn't tell them the whole story, which now seemed much too strange to tell them about. I was expecting the police would soon come over to our house to ask me about the man under the car. I thought I could tell them and was almost looking forward to it, feeling important to have the information the police needed, though I wasn't going to tell even them about the pink elephant. But the police never came to our house. Their car left and soon afterwards Mrs Fahey came across to talk to Mum and Dad. They talked quietly with their heads bent over, sat close together around the dining table, so I couldn't hear what they were saying. I think Babs and Tim must have been sent to their rooms but I was allowed to stay in the living room, just not to hear what was being said.

In the end nobody asked me anything or spoke to me about the man under the car at all. But Beth must have told her mum enough because after Mrs Fahey left, Mum and Dad were very subdued and Dad kept giving me this disappointed look that made me feel like *I'd* done something wrong, which I suppose I had. They didn't know what to say to me, I guess, but I badly wanted someone to say *something* about it, because I didn't even really know what had happened.

The man was known to police for similar crimes in the area and was eventually caught. Mrs Fahey got the call from the police. Beth told me.

Chapter 7

Too many teeth

By the time I was ten it was decided, by those who decide about such things, that I had too many teeth. Something would have to be done. It was the pointy chin that was the problem. Also my adult teeth were fairly big and square, not pointy like my chin, which didn't help. In short, my teeth were all wrong for my head, which was hardly surprising, really. I was clearly an odd fit for a variety of things.

Our family dentist worked out of a building in Forestville, the next-door fake forest to ours. Real forests don't have anything to do with dentistry. Real forests have perfect teeth. His name was Boyle and, in my opinion, his name was a good fit. Boyle wore a Cheshire cat grin on his massive round face and a pair of giant blue-tinted glasses that were *almost* effective in hiding the pleasure he seemed to take in his work. After sticking a long pointy needle of perfect pain into my tender ten-year-old gums, he practically climbed on top of me, pinning me to his chair with an elbow in my ear to get the leverage he needed, for his silver pliers, glistening with glee, to then set about wrenching out my terrified tooth that had barely shown itself above the gum.

The anaesthetic was never strong enough and the pain of extraction was beyond belief. My hands would instinctively grab hold of Boyle's arm to try to stop him, until he had to get the nurse to hold them down. Mum, meanwhile, sat outside in the waiting room reading the women's magazines, avoiding the housekeeping tips, at a safe distance from the terror.

On the fourth tooth – I had four adult teeth removed, with a separate appointment for each tooth, presumably to drag out the torture – I fainted in Boyle's chair, in a triumph of will that wiped that Cheshire cat grin off his face. While I was out cold Mum was hurried in from the waiting room to find out what *now* was wrong with her high-maintenance daughter. When I came to she was standing beside the spit bowl looking worried and irritated in equal measure, with Boyle telling her, somewhat alarmed, he'd never had anyone faint in his chair before. I guess that was *my* fault too (I did have a history of fainting).

Being dragged back to consciousness by Boyle repeating my name over and over, like some kind of torture all of its own, to meet his giant face and insect eyes hovering about an inch above mine, was almost enough to make me faint a second time. To cap it off, he hadn't even got the tooth out, it was still clinging, trembling and terrified, to the gum and I was going to need another long needle and industrial-strength pliers to finish the job. Still, it's important to have the right number of teeth.

By the time it was Babs' turn for the dentist's chair, laughing gas had been introduced to dentistry, which meant she not only escaped the preliminary torture of a long needle injected into tender young gums, but she came home from the dentist's still laughing, saying it was fun. The only consolation was that I figured Boyle couldn't have been enjoying himself half as much.

I had another terrifying toothy experience around about this time: watching *Jaws* at the tender age of nine, effectively all alone in a darkened room and before the rest of Australia – so without spoilers. As things stood, I could have done with the spoilers. I hardly knew what a shark was before I saw *Jaws*. It was the occasion of Jodie's tenth birthday and Mr Crane had arranged a private viewing of the film before its public release. I might have been unafraid of crocodiles once, but by this stage I was not in general terribly confident in the company of large toothy creatures that could, and would, given half the chance, eat me. It didn't help that as Jodie's best friend I was sat up front on the beanbag closest to the screen, with Jodie on a beanbag more than an arm's reach away and her other friends, including the even younger Beth, somewhere a million miles away behind us. Also, they played the film after dark, with the lights out, downstairs in their rumpus room that was situated right next to the lapping pool, its friendly sparkling blue water by day turned, by night, into a sinister (potentially shark-infested) blackness. And because the Cranes didn't feel water-based fear (*they* didn't have to) I felt, as Jodie's best friend, I had to at least appear to be enjoying myself in a similarly fearless fashion. But just in case Jodie *did* feel fear having a giant, man-eating, or rather, woman-eating shark within arm's reach, she had her mother and father close by, watching the film somewhere in the darkness behind us. I was all alone in my beanbag. Where were my parents when I needed them? This was, as ever, a good question.

Although I generally went to great lengths to pretend I was a cool customer in front of the Cranes, once the film started and that stupid girl went into the water at night and her useless boyfriend tripped on his trousers and was not going to save her, all bets were off. By the time the girl was clinging to the buoy with the deep black water all around her, terror in her eyes and possibly no legs, I was trembling with hysterical fear, my feet snatched up out of the water that lapped all around my beanbag, with a dark fin circling, bobbing all alone in shark-infested waters with nothing to protect me but a few stupid beans.

'You're not *scared* are you, Sally? Not a big girl like you?' said Mr Crane from the darkness behind me. I don't know where he got *that* idea from.

That was my best friend's tenth birthday party. I can't recall what I did for my tenth birthday, except that I didn't go to the beach. No-one in Australia went to the beach that summer, except of course for the Cranes. When they asked me to go with them to the big wave Long Reef Beach where Mr Crane was a lifesaver, I told them I had to go to my nana's to visit Uncle Horrie's ghost. Uncle Horrie was Nana's brother who had died in her spare room a few years earlier and continued to occupy it with a thick grey haze that could not, I didn't think, be fully explained by the dust and sun. I was a little wary. But I would take Uncle Horrie's ghost over *Jaws* any day.

Actually, I didn't mention Uncle Horrie to the Cranes; they were already sceptical of this excuse of having to go to Nana's of a Saturday that I whipped out every time they invited me to Long Reef Beach, first in fear of the waves, then the sharks. Mrs Crane didn't think it was 'natural' for a girl my age to have to go to her nana's every Saturday. Adding Uncle Horrie would not have improved that situation any. But I couldn't get out of every trip, so some Saturdays, even after *Jaws*, I felt obliged to go with the Cranes to Long Reef Beach and be carried out on Mr Crane's shoulders to take on the biggest waves in Sydney, whereupon I closed my eyes and prepared to die by shark, or tsunami, whichever took me first. It didn't help that Mr Crane had told us that part of *Jaws* had been filmed off the coast of Australia.

Somehow I made it to my tenth birthday. And instead of a party to celebrate achieving double digits, I 'celebrated' by giving up Mum's homemade lemonade in a bid to lose weight for ballet. By this stage I had moved on from my earlier addiction to pink milk, to a stiffer, more grown-up drink, which I became even more addicted to than the milk. And this drink *was* stiff. You could practically stand a spoon up in the greenish gold syrup that was ninety-nine parts sugar water and one part citric acid. There was no actual lemon in it. So in other words, at nine, I was addicted to sugar and acid, which was possibly a slight improvement on my addiction to pink milk as far as my asthma went, but was likely even worse for my weight, because of the huge sugar content and the fact that I drank it by the gallon. And by this age I was starting to notice that I didn't look enough like a ballet dancer and wanting to do something about that. And like a true addict I knew I couldn't just cut back on my almost 2-litre-a-day habit, but had to give it up entirely. Having some experience with turkeys, I knew I had to go cold turkey on Mum's lemonless lemonade.

But it wasn't easy. One of the simplest, not to say sweetest, pleasures of my childhood was racing home from school of a baking hot afternoon, powering up the steepest part of the pipeline that was tricky to balance on and high enough that you'd break your legs if you slipped off, to drop and slide down the side of the pipe outside our gate, legs all a-tingle with the hurried landing, charge in through the gate and across the lawn, to fling open the flyscreen door and pounce on the canister of ice cold lemonade kept in the fridge door. I was always first to the lemonade and downed almost the entire litre canister without taking a breath, before rushing to refill it from the 5-litre container stored in the second fridge – which by this stage was not only for Dad's back-up grog. It was quite a sacrifice giving that up.

I think most of my motivation for this first sacrifice (there would be others) was down to a girl in my class at school called Kim, who was petite and pretty and also did ballet, though not at Northside. Our teacher, Mrs Mann, made quite a fuss of Kim's ballet, asking her how she was doing on a fairly regular basis, knowing I did ballet too – because I made sure to tell her – but never bringing the subject up with me. Unfortunately, by the time I'd lost my lemonade weight, which was almost a stone in three weeks, I'd moved to another class, so Mrs Mann never saw my transformation into someone who could pass, at a push, for a budding ballerina.

But Mrs P *did* see. One day in the studio she did one of those double-take head swivels when she seemed to suddenly notice my dramatic weight loss. 'You're looking very slim these days, Sally. Good girl,' she said, with a distinct note of surprise in her voice, as if I looked like an entirely different person, not just a slimmer one. I was happy with entirely different, and Mrs P's approval was all the motivation I needed to stay off the lemonade for good. Before long, Mum stopped making it; evidently Tim and Bab's thirst combined did not warrant the effort. It's a wonder the Australian sugar industry didn't go out of business too.

* * *

All the while I was busy losing weight and teeth, Dad was working away to save the Third World. To that end, in 1976, ten years after he launched his noble mission, he had finally completed 90,000 words on the subject of how to end poverty in the world's poorest countries and was ready to send the manuscript off to publishers overseas – just as soon as it was typed up. Dad, a deeply impractical man incapable of operating anything more mechanically complicated than a ballpoint pen, had handwritten his treatise with that faulty left hand, which turned out not to be as hopeless as once feared. But, as neat as his left-handed penmanship was, it was not neat enough for academic publishers who expected a typed copy. So it was just as well that he married a typist. Still, typing 90,000 words plus almost as many footnotes on a tired old mechanical typewriter, a relic of the war, as was Mum's typewriter brought out on the ship from England, was never going to be a speedy process. And because my ballet by this stage took up more of Mum's time than anything else, this would quickly become *my* problem.

If I might just briefly explain: Dad suffered ongoing guilt

about his inability – on account of his bad back – to do any of the 'manly' jobs around the house, like mowing the lawns, taking out the garbage, washing the cars, digging holes and generally fixing things that broke (which was just about everything). Until Tim was old enough to take over some of this work, Mum did most of it, which, to be fair, was another reason why she neglected the housekeeping and chose the lawn locker on *Temptation* instead of an electric Hoover, for instance. She needed somewhere to house her tools. And once Dad needed her to type up his book as well, although this was hardly a 'manly' task, his guilt and frustration took on such epic proportions that he had to take it out on someone. I was the obvious target. I see that *now* ...

I should probably clarify too that Dad's back injury was not a Basil Fawlty kind of war injury. It was rather more real than that. Once, when we were quite young, his back seized up completely and Mum had to call for an ambulance, which arrived just as we did, in a taxi from Nana's, to see Dad being taken down our steep driveway, crouched on all fours, a white sheet over him like a tablecloth, his face grim in concentration, as he struggled to hold on to the stretcher angled at 45 degrees, along with his dignity. He did not entirely succeed. He was in hospital for several weeks after that, getting intensive physiotherapy just to be able to stand up and walk again, and seriously contemplated having an operation to try and separate his compressed vertebrae that had only a 50 per cent chance of success. If it failed it would cost him the use of his legs permanently.

He never got the operation and eventually recovered most of his mobility, but after that he had to avoid lifting anything heavier than a pen in fear of another seizure. As he could not do much to improve this situation, he looked for other ways he might take the pressure off Mum. Getting me to stop ballet seemed to go to the top of his list of strategies in this regard. In truth, Dad didn't ever like me doing ballet, describing it as a 'selfish, frivolous pursuit, too focused on appearances', and looked for any excuse to get me out of it, or so it seemed to me.

Not knowing what frivolous meant exactly, though I knew it wasn't good, I focused my resentment on the 'selfish' part, which seemed particularly unfair seeing as I was dancing in order to breathe, wasn't I? I was. I even went as far as to draw up a 'Selfishness Survey' to take to school and ask my friends and people I only vaguely knew, because I only had three friends and I needed lots of people to prove Dad wrong, to rate how selfish they thought I was on a scale of 1 to 5. Although a couple of kids I asked clearly didn't understand what 'selfish' meant, apparently assuming it was a good thing and giving me the maximum five, the overall result was a healthy, neither selfish nor selfless 2.5 that I proudly took home to show Dad. That was when he told me, 'It's just as well there's not another one of you in the world', which seemed a bit harsh, considering the overall survey result.

But he had a point. By my fifth year of ballet, the year he needed his book typed, I had classes almost every weekday afternoon, as well as weekend private lessons prior to exams and rehearsals for the end-of-year concerts that started well before the end of the year. This meant a lot of driving for Mum, though there was much carpooling done between the ballet mums (and occasional dad), as well as sewing of costumes, with Mum making most of my dance costumes herself, except for the tutus.

She even offered to take the minutes for the fortnightly meetings Mrs P now ran on Monday nights to help manage her ever-expanding school, which had become, by this stage, the top ballet school on the North Shore. It was somewhat inconvenient that only a year after I started ballet, Mrs P had moved from the cake studio close by to a larger studio in Belrose, another 20 minutes' drive away. Neither did it help that Mrs P was not the most punctual person in the world and lessons often ran so late that when Mum was on pick-up duty she could be out for well over an hour, waiting for our class to finish and then dropping the other girls home.

'You'll wear your mother out!' Dad would bellow at me whenever Mum was kept out late or engaged in something ballet related at home. Mum would say cheerfully: 'It's fine, hon, I can manage. Don't worry.' Which it was, and she could – but he didn't want to hear that, whether it was true or not, and wouldn't let it go. Although I wasn't the only one who took up Mum's time, Tim and Babs had after-school activities too, from the time he started needing his book typed up Dad became increasingly resentful and complaining about my ballet, which filled me with increasing resentment and did not improve relations between us, until we stopped talking to each other almost entirely and the ballet battles began in earnest.

*　*　*

Extracting my excess teeth to the point that I passed out was only phase one of the too-many-teeth operation. The surviving teeth were all wrong too. More pain would be required. I got braces on my teeth at the optimum time for having your mouth filled with chunky black metal: when you're about to start high school.

No-one else I knew got braces at this time, instead *they* all got boobs. I would have much preferred an operation to fix my crepe crisis (zero boobs) situation than my crooked teeth, but, as ever, I was not in charge.

As far as I was concerned, I was already up against it in the looks department without adding braces and subtracting boobs. I was still eleven when I started high school and I looked even younger than that. My hair, always a problem, had taken an even stranger turn in recent years, becoming frizzy for no apparent reason. Or perhaps the No Frills shampoo that I used without conditioner – nobody told *me* about conditioner – explained the frizz. Either that or my hair had taken fright from the repeated attacks by screeching magpies dive-bombing my head on my way home from school, to pluck out as many of my already depleted tally of thin white hairs as they liked. And all the while Jodie walked beside me, with her much thicker, darker blonde hair, entirely unscathed.

It was also possible that the fist-size clump of knotted hair I discovered at the nape of my neck one day that Mum had to cut out with her giant dressmaking scissors – who knew you were supposed to brush *all* your hairs? – might have given my hair something else to get worked up about. Indeed there were many possibilities.

To make matters worse, I decided that the best thing to do with my frizzy-frazzled hair was to wear it tied in two frizzy bunches, like cheerleading pom-poms, either side of my already oversized head, possibly indicating that it was not only my hair that was slightly frazzled by this stage. What with being short for my age and one of the youngest in the year, with *Ugly Betty* braces on my teeth and a chest as flat as a crepe, this frizzy, little-girl hair-do completed the picture of a child totally unprepared for high school, least of all the rough-as-guts state co-ed high school I was zoned to go to, thanks to a recent rezoning of school boundaries.

Jodie, of course, was in a completely different situation. She had all her hair. She also had boobs and straight white teeth, and at twelve could have passed for sixteen. Next to her I looked like her much younger sister who had missed out on all the good genes. Or perhaps the second twin, who had failed to thrive from birth.

But never mind all of that. The uniform at this rough-as-guts high school that Jodie and I were both zoned to go to included bright white socks. What could possibly go wrong wearing bright white socks?

Chapter 8

The toughest girl in school

As it turns out, bright white socks can't save you from the miseries of high school. In fact, this might be an understatement in my case...

The high school that Jodie and I were to attend, was not the local Forest High just across the road from our primary school, the school that Michael Hutchence, future lead singer of INXS, was at that very time attending, but Killarney Heights High, a 20 minute bus ride away that was not then, and never would be attended by anyone famous. And you will soon see why. The other problem with this zoning change was that it meant Jodie was my *only* friend at high school because just about everyone else I knew from primary was zoned to Forest High. And although Jodie was my *best* friend, she was also the best looking girl in our year and standing next to her I couldn't help feeling that my physical deficits multiplied. I was Robin to her Batman (at best).

If you can picture a dark blonde Cleopatra, that was Jodie –

at twelve. And sure enough, when Jodie walked through the gates of Killarney for the first time it was like she was walking onto a yacht. Sailors swarmed. The boat rocked with gossip about who this gorgeous goddess of a girl was, and in all the clamour to find out I was knocked overboard and left to drown. Nobody even threw me a life ring. It probably would have been simpler for everyone if I had drowned, but I think my frizzy hair bunches acted as some kind of floatation device and I survived, but barely, my first day at high school.

Jodie and I weren't put in any of the same classes, which was probably safer for all concerned, but at morning recess and lunch, I looked for my only friend and found her in the centre of a crowd of cool kids, all of whom looked older than they must have been, unless they had repeated several years, which was not impossible. At Killarney, as I quickly learned, everyone was assigned membership in one or other of four distinct social groups: the Toughies, the Brains, the Dags or the Freaks. If you wore glasses you were a Brain; if you played in the school orchestra you were a Dag; the Freaks were a slightly more varied bunch, united by one or another physical oddity, such as severe acne or excessive height; and to be a Toughie, the top group, you either surfed or knew how to wear a bikini and look cool on the beach watching the surfers, sometimes during school hours.

Even at twelve Jodie knew how to wear a bikini. This was a fact that seemed to have been ascertained on her first day at high school, although she was not wearing a bikini on that particular occasion and we were some distance from the beach – even if we were at sea – and so she was immediately recruited into the Toughies. And this was the group I found her at the centre of on that first day at Killarney and dared to approach, taking frizzy bunches, a crepe-flat chest and metal-braced teeth where they had never gone before. I was not exactly welcomed into the Toughies, it's fair to say. With my various physical oddities, I could have been a Freak several times over. But as best friend of the girl who *was* welcomed with open, groping arms by the Toughies as their natural queen, I was granted grudging rights to hover on the margins of the Toughies, like a groupie Toughie, doing what I could to compensate for my abundant lack of Toughie assets.

Unlike Jodie I could *not* wear a bikini to save myself and for that reason repeatedly declined her invitations to spend the weekend with her and most of the other Toughies on Long Reef Beach – the toughest of Sydney's beaches, as her father before her had proven. I would still rather go to Nana's and hang out with Uncle Horrie's ghost. But as all the Toughie girls shaved their legs and I could just about do that, I seized a razor from Dad's bathroom drawer and promptly got rid of the three or four hairs on my legs. I took up smoking behind the basketball wall at lunchtime, with most of the other Toughies in my year, making a quick study of how to hold a cigarette to maximise its cool look, not between two extended fingers, which was for sissies, but in a cage of fingers crouched over the cigarette that when you dragged on it, burnt a hole in your palm. What were a few cigarette burns to show my loyalty and gratitude to the Toughies for letting me stand in their reflected cool glow and take the shine off that glow by my own abundant uncool? Nothing. Indeed it was not nearly enough.

Anyone can shave their legs and suffer a few minor burns, and being so far behind the other Toughie girls in the all-important boob and beauty departments, I had to find other ways of looking 'tough'. I could not take up surfing, as brother Tim had done in a bid to get in with the Toughies in his year. You couldn't just surf your way into the Toughies, as Tim found out to his cost when the Toughie boys in his year went to the trouble of having T-shirts made up with 'Tim Jones surfs' printed on them and wearing them in PE class as their way of saying there is more to being Tough than surfing. Also, girls didn't really surf back then. They were more like surfie accessories. On top of that, there was my abiding fear of big waves and sharks to consider. Indeed, I would probably have preferred to take my chances with a bikini than a surf board.

Fortunately, it didn't quite come to that. Instead I went all out to prove my 'toughness' in the classroom. In PE I sat down on the concrete floor in the canteen that doubled as a gym during our warm-up star jumps, against my dancer's better judgment that knew the benefit of a good warm-up, to show solidarity with my new Toughie friend, Karen White. Karen was rather overweight for a Toughie girl and although she had an impressive bust, she was somewhat on the margins of the Toughies, rather like me. Well, sort of. I was more on the margins of the margins. But Karen didn't hold this against me too much, and in exchange for her tolerance I did what I could to show solidarity with her. So I sat down during star jumps, ignoring our teacher's shouts of 'Get up!' and my own rather cold bottom.

Karen, it's fair to say, had a little more in the way of insulation in that department than I did, and probably in the way of true toughness too, in not caring that we were driving our teacher mad, even if our teacher was called Mrs Payne and lived up to her name. When Mrs Payne tried to physically drag Karen to her feet, she stayed put for as long as she could and so did I, feeling slightly stupid, with all the other girls star jumping around us, but not wanting to let Karen down and happily feeling myself toughening in the process, especially in the posterior region.

In cross-country, which brought on my asthma and threatened to knock Karen out with her own boobs, I oftentimes led the charge of disobedience, cutting across the oval instead of running round it a trillion times under a merciless sun. Mrs Payne always caught us but it was still worth it, and on lunchtime detention I got to recover the loss in fitness I might have gained in completing the cross-country course by not smoking. For my asthma, it was a win-win.

In English class, Karen and I sat together and talked the Toughie talk until we ran out of things to say and drove *that* teacher, Mrs Chalmers-Lang, mad, too. On my report card that year, Mrs Chalmers-Lang wrote in a loose, fast hand that suggested an emotion approximating rage: 'If Sally would only stop talking!' That was *all* she wrote, indeed, along with a somewhat sad grade. I was not exactly proud of that grade or comment, as English had been my best subject in primary. I'd even won a copy of *The Lion, the Witch and the Wardrobe* for my efforts one year and raced to the library to borrow the rest of the books in the series and spend that summer totally absorbed in Narnia, dreaming of friendly fauns and proper forests and almost forgetting about the pool we didn't have, while checking and re-checking the back of our old brown wardrobe for a possible portal out. But that was before it became imperative to look tough at all times. It was also before it became acceptable at school to make us study a book (*Lord of the Flies*), about a bunch of boys running riot on a deserted island, killing each other. I could not understand Mrs Chalmers-Lang choosing such a boy book for us to read, nor how it was that the boys in the book essentially got away with murder when I didn't even get away with cutting across the oval to save my own life. Meanwhile at home that year I was secretly reading *Anne of Avonlea*, having, for obvious reasons, already enjoyed the first book in that series, *Anne of Green Gables*, showing my true, not-so-tough colours.

In Latin class I sat next to a true Toughie. Her name was Eliza and after I met her that instantly became my new favourite name. I thought Eliza Chadwick was hands down the toughest girl in school and bragged to Tim: 'I sit next to the toughest girl in school.' In truth, Eliza only sat next to me in Latin class as a last resort when other Toughies were away or she came in late to class and the seat beside me was the only one free. Eliza looked and even sounded like the actress Ellen Barkin, with that same raspy voice that made her seem years older than she was, but was most likely due to the number of cigarettes she smoked. Whenever we smoked at lunchtime we smoked Eliza's cigarettes. For some reason she always had cigarettes. I think her parents let her smoke, even though she was only twelve. But no-one – possibly including her parents – messed with Eliza Chadwick and to impress her I would, and did, go to considerable lengths in Latin.

This was no great loss to the world, as I was not particularly motivated to pay attention in Latin class anyway. Our teacher, Mr Hunt (who we called Grunt or Grunty), was a keen smoker himself and routinely arrived late to class in a cloud of thick grey smoke coming out of his ears and nose. Through the open door we'd see him take his last long drag on his cigarette before flicking it over the railing of the mezzanine floor into the lunch quad below and walking into the classroom exhaling the contents of his lungs all over us. It was not a great start.

Grunt was not a young man, indeed Latin may well have been his first language, and his hair matched exactly the colour of his exhaled smoke, adding to the effect of a smoke explosion when he entered the classroom. His face, by contrast, was the colour of the setting sun, a bright pink-purple-orange that suggested smoking might not be his only pleasure, and his breath confirmed this. I never got the impression that he particularly *enjoyed* teaching Latin to our class and it's fair to say he passed that lack of enthusiasm onto his students. What I'm trying to say here is that I don't think I can be entirely blamed for devoting much of Latin class to trying to impress Eliza rather than conjugating verbs.

On one particularly slow morning, when I was standing up the front of the class facing the blackboard on detention for some talking-related misdemeanour, a not uncommon occurrence, I decided I was bored of being on detention and it wasn't achieving the desired effect of impressing Eliza. When I snuck a peek round at the class I saw she had her pen up and her head down. This wouldn't do. After looking around at the limited resources I had at my disposal, with Grunty standing almost next to me but facing the class, I seized a handful of chalk dust going to waste in the chalk holder, and turning back round to face the class, making sure Grunt was occupied and Eliza was watching, reached my arm up over Grunty's head – he was not a tall man – and let the chalk dust rain down upon his grey woolly hair. It was a harmless act really, as Grunty would likely not have known the difference between chalk dust, dandruff or residual ash, if he noticed anything at all. And it definitely cheered Eliza up. She smiled and raised her eyebrows, which was acknowledgement indeed of my success, as she was a cool customer whose eyebrows were not raised for much. And at least Latin class wasn't a total waste for me that year. I learnt to carpe diem.

Seizing the day in Latin class also got me an invitation to Eliza's thirteenth birthday party a few weeks later, which scored me points with my fellow Toughies *and* with my sceptical brother, who had rolled his eyes and laughed in open scorn when I'd told him I sit next to the toughest girl in school. Now who was laughing? Now I was going to her birthday party, so there was no denying we had a connection, even if Tim continued to maintain that Jodie was the only reason Eliza was friends with me. Jodie was, just incidentally, also invited to Eliza's party.

It was a sleepover party and Eliza's bedroom was in the attic. Of course it was! I had been wondering where the toughest girl in school would sleep, not being able to imagine her in a regular girl's bedroom with flowers and frills and bunks (as we had – the bunks and flowers, not so much the frills). And sure enough, there were no bunks or frills or flowers in Eliza's attic room. Eliza had a double bed tucked under a sloping gable roof in a huge elongated room, practically the size of our whole house. Even Jodie had to envy *that*, I thought, with some satisfaction, though Jodie wasn't the envying type. But really I was too much in awe to envy Eliza her attic room and rather felt privileged to be able to stay in it even for one night with all the other Toughie girls; seven of us in total.

After we had the party in their double garage, smoking and watching Eliza drink bottles of beer in front of her parents while listening to the 'toughest' sort of music I'd ever heard, the sort of music you couldn't, or didn't if you knew what was good for you, dance to, we finally retired to that roomy attic to get changed into our pyjamas and nighties and sit on that comfy double bed, chatting. Actually the other girls chatted while I gazed out Eliza's picture-book window beside her bed, enjoying a private *Anne of Green Gables* moment, imagining myself an orphan taken in by Eliza's parents, who had no other children and were more than happy to let me live in their roomy attic with a *triple* bed if I wanted, until I was rudely interrupted by a rather distracting turn in the conversation: 'No tits I can understand, but no pubes? That's just sick.' It was Eliza speaking in a voice of pure disgust for the total *Freak* she had run into somewhere, apparently without her clothes on; a girl our age without tits *or* pubes!

'Sally doesn't have any tits.' This was the next thing said, in a voice of undisguised scorn, by one of the other Toughies. I don't remember which one, possibly because at that moment I was concentrating all my energies on maintaining a calm exterior against some difficult odds. 'But she's got pubes, right? You've got pubes, haven't you, Sally?'

It was Eliza again. This time staring straight at me from an uncomfortably close distance, in a voice that suggested that should I be found to *not* have the vital hairs, I had no business being at her party, sitting on her luxurious bed, talking with all these normal, healthy girls, and may well be tossed out that picture-book window to a fitting end.

I have mentioned I think that I was quite fair-haired at this time, and indeed that I struggled to maintain a decent number of hairs on my head and legs. Also, that I was younger than just about everyone else in my year and was, at this point in time, still very much twelve. All these factors pointed to the regrettable reality that to my name I had not one single pubic hair. No mistaking it, because I regularly checked.

Eliza wanted an answer, as did the other girls, including Jodie, who were now all staring at me at close quarters with matching Toughie expressions on their matching pretty faces.

'Mhmm,' I managed to mumble, doing my best to form an expression of 'are you kidding me, of *course* I have pubes!' on my face, backed up by much vigorous nodding. Miraculously, Eliza and her fellow pubic warriors backed down, but that didn't stop me spending the rest of the night lying wide awake, convinced that at any moment now I was going to be subjected to a pubic inspection with a torch – there were torches present. I wasn't, but ever since then I have suffered an intense disliking for the word 'pubes', followed closely by the word 'tits'.

* * *

In ballet you don't need pubes, boobs *or* tits to get ahead. In fact, some might consider these attributes, so essential at high school, liabilities in the dance studio – especially boobs. Indeed I remember one girl at Northside having to give up ballet because her boobs grew so big, seemingly overnight, that she lost her balance entirely and could no longer do *allegro* work without risking injury to herself and possibly others dancing nearby. She was a talented dancer and it was really quite a shame and not funny at all when she had to admit defeat and hang up her dancing shoes, although I'm sure she went on to do very well at high school.

At twelve we were seniors at ballet and that meant having to take ballet more seriously. One of the ways we took ballet more seriously was by not wearing any underpants underneath our stockings and leotards, as underpants, bulkier things back then than they are today, were thought to spoil our line. The RAD regulation leotards for seniors are black, but as seniors, unlike the juniors, we were allowed to wear any colour leotard in class, and often did. Unfortunately, for some of the girls — namely all the seniors except for me — they could not wear pale-coloured leotards without a certain lumpy, squiggly effect showing down below.

I envied their pubic hair even so, but didn't let myself wallow in this envy. Instead I bought myself an all-over rose pink Lycra unitard that fit me like a second skin to embrace my smooth, fuzz-free body, wearing nothing under it but my thinnest pair of stockings. If you've got it, or haven't got it, as the case may be, flaunt it.

Indeed, for all my insecurities about my looks at school, and the doubts expressed earlier about my build being all wrong for ballet, since giving up Mum's lemonade and losing quite a bit of weight, I had gained a substantial amount of confidence about my physique for ballet. This was partly due to the fact that by some deeply ironic twist of fate, Dad had passed on to me a set of almost purpose-built dancers' legs. His legs were disproportionately long, with just the right amount of sway back to extend the line of the leg. I also had a full, 180-degree turn-out at the hip, which is the right amount of turn-out you want for ballet. If I had inherited Mum's shorter, less swayed back and turned-out legs instead, I may well have had to give up ballet too. Short legs were almost as bad for ballet as big boobs. And a lot of girls did give up ballet before it started to get serious, including Jodie, who had given up before starting high school. I can't remember why exactly, but it was clearly the right decision for her. If only I could have given up school.

That first year of high school (1978) I took my Pre-elementary exam, which is the first senior RAD exam and much more difficult than it sounds. It is the first exam that requires pointe work and there is nothing simple about learning to dance *en pointe*. Fortunately, I mastered it with relative ease, partly thanks to my sway back legs that made it easier to lock my knees and balance while standing on the tip of my pointe shoe. Also I had a high pain threshold. I don't need to explain why.

I scored the top mark in Sydney for my Pre-elementary exam that year, from an examiner who was sent all the way out from the Royal Academy headquarters in London. And as a result I was asked, along with another girl from Northside, who had done extremely well in her Elementary exam, to demonstrate the syllabus to the RAD Teachers' seminar that was run for the Australian teachers by the London examiner. This was an honour indeed, to be selected to stand alone at the barre in the centre of a grand old hall, a former wool storage warehouse in Kings Cross, with perhaps 60 pairs of eyes focused solely on me. Dad's legs didn't let me down and Mrs P, who sat among the circle of teachers in the front row, smiled and seemed proud. At least I thought she seemed proud until it was the turn of the other girl to demonstrate her syllabus and I got to see what a proud Mrs P really looked like.

Tegan Cole – the other girl – had recently joined Northside

from a school further up the northern peninsula, where her talent had been spotted and it had been suggested she move to a school that could better develop those talents. That school was Northside. Mrs P seized on Tegan and her talents from the moment she joined us and I was knocked off my perch as the most promising dancer at the school. Mrs P made no secret of the fact that Tegan was her new favourite. Tegan was nearly two years older than me and in the class above, so we were not in direct competition in the classroom. But competing in ballet eisteddfods, which also became a feature of the ballet year for seniors, we were often in direct competition in open-age categories. When we were, Tegan always beat me.

I couldn't blame Mrs P for favouring Tegan. If my legs were built for ballet, Tegan's everything was built for ballet. And on top of a perfect physique, she had a classic face for ballet. She looked like Audrey Hepburn – or Margot Fonteyn, the best ballerina of all time – with small, dainty features and contrasting large luminous black-brown eyes, pale skin and thick, dark, wavy hair. Better still, everything of Tegan's was in proportion. My long legs meant that my body was disproportionately short, which created a slight stockiness about the torso. I also had long legs and short arms. Tegan's legs and arms and body all matched. Her Audrey Hepburn head was also just the right size for her body, whereas my head was a couple of sizes too big for mine. To round off Tegan's perfection, she even had boobs, just the right size boobs to give the V-neck of her leotards and tutus a purpose. I was almost more jealous of those boobs than of anything else of Tegan's, except for her long lean arms, her thick dark hair, perfect-for-ballet face and, not to be forgotten, phenomenal dancing talent.

Never mind. When the comparison became too depressing for my green eyes to cope with, there was always school to fall back on. My social success at Killarney was progressing at a pace. From about the third week I had developed a crush on one of the Toughie boys, a boy called Simon, who had surfie-blond hair with a muscly build and, in appealing contrast, sad dreamy blue eyes and a gentle voice. Now I know what you're thinking: *she's* dreaming. And indeed you are not wrong. I *was* dreaming. Simon was ever so slightly out of my league. Indeed with braces and without boobs, I didn't even have a league at high school. And Simon was pretty much King of the Toughies in our year and had his pick of the Toughie girls, almost all of whom, as explained, were beautiful and well built. Dancers' legs were not going to be enough to win Simon.

For a while I accepted this and merely admired him from a distance. But after the occasional encouraging smile sent more or less my way from him, which may or may not have been a trick of the light or meant for the girl standing next to me, I began to think there might be some hope. Part of the reason for this was the fact that, unlike most of the other Toughie boys, and all the best looking ones, Simon had not yet dated Jodie, which suggested he might be looking for something other than extreme physical beauty in a girlfriend. He himself resembled, to an uncanny extent, Sylvester Stallone in the movie *Rocky*, except a blond, blue-eyed version.

Having seen *Rocky* for my twelfth birthday, and been particularly moved by Rocky's attraction to Adrian, who was not a classic beauty – though she did have lovely long dark hair, white teeth and boobs – I decided it was not impossible that I might become Simon's Adrian, and he, my Rocky. We had exactly the same colour hair, Simon and me. Not Adrian and me. Adrian had the same colour hair as Rocky. So you see, it all made perfect sense, just like in the movies.

But more than a year went by without our matching hair leading to anything more than the occasional smile exchanged across a crowded quad at lunchtime, if indeed even that. Then Simon announced he was having a fourteenth birthday party at his house on a Saturday night, and all the Toughies were invited, even me. Hurrah! This was my chance. The only *slight* catch was that we were encouraged to bring a partner and Simon had invited a girl from a private school. So now I was competing with the posh girls as well as the Toughies at Killarney. This was not good. Who was this posh mystery girl anyway, and what did she have – apart from boobs, probable beauty and poshness – that I didn't have?

There wasn't anyone else other than Simon who I liked at Killarney, or, more to the point, anyone who had even noticed I existed, at least as far as I could tell. I was not exactly experienced in the romance business, unlike virtually all the other Toughies, not least of all Jodie. Jodie, of course, had a date for Simon's party lined up. Since starting high school, she had never been without a boyfriend. She'd even had a pregnancy scare at the end of our first year, when all the Toughie girls had stood around at lunchtime, speaking in worried whispers about Jodie's late period, while I, supposed to be her *best* friend, had listened in, wondering what a period was and being surprised to learn that Jodie had ever had one. So much for *best* friends; I knew nothing. All I could gather was that Jonno, the most physically mature Toughie boy in the group who looked about twenty, and a park after school, had been involved. But no details were provided and I was not able to put the park and periods together without asking the sort of questions I feared might expose my total ignorance of all things parks and periods, indeed pregnancy too, although I did know a thing or two about pregnant mice (unlike Jodie).

But Mum hadn't told me anything about periods or parks. A pair of bulky underpants (from those wretched Thompsett girls), with a huge pad the size of a boogie board stuck inside them, had mysteriously turned up in my underwear drawer one day, and remained there, ugly and unexplained, ever since. And the only date I'd been on, if it can be called a date, had not been in a park. Mum had set it up with the son of a friend of hers, and this boy, Peter, had taken me into the city to see *Amityville Horror* (his choice). I had not seen much of *Amityville Horror* that day but not because Peter had distracted me with his hands or lips. *He* was completely absorbed in the film. I was covering my eyes in abject – if slightly affected – terror.

Then on the train home he had gone to the trouble of making me feel even more stupid than usual, which was not easy to do, by asking me to guess the name of each approaching station, about eight in total, and when I failed to guess it in every single case, having never travelled on that line before, he delighted in telling me what it was and having it confirmed when we got there. He was some kind of train-station-naming expert. Who knew? The fact that he was from Melbourne made this stunt slightly more humiliating, as it suggested he knew Sydney better than I did, at least as far as the train stations went. The best thing about that date was that Peter went back to Melbourne soon afterwards. I found out later on that the name of the next station is signposted on the previous one. I was even more stupid than I thought.

My first 'date' did not bode well for subsequent attempts, or the likelihood of there ever being any. And sure enough, the week of Simon's party arrived and still no date. Then in Woodwork class that week, the elective I had chosen over sewing because hammering seemed more fun than hemming, and also because I'd have a better chance of being in Simon's class, which I was, while lathing my swan-shaped paper-roll dispenser, someone behind me suddenly said: 'Sally!' It was a boy. This much I ascertained without looking round as there was only one other girl in the class and she was away sick that day. I turned around, hoping it was Simon, but saw instead two of his friends who I barely knew. Just about everyone was a friend of Simon's.

'Craig wants to ask you to Simon's party,' one of them said, most surprisingly, as I didn't know Craig any better than I knew either of them. 'He likes your hair,' one of them added, 'but he thinks you've got a big nose from the side,' chimed in the other, followed by a hearty snigger from both.

I should probably explain something here before we go on. Towards the end of my first year of high school, after seeing the abomination of my frizzy bunches in the class photo, I convinced Mum to take me up to Hair 2000, the new trendy salon opened up at our local Arndale shops, to get my first proper haircut. The cut got rid of the frizz and split ends – of which I apparently had some kind of extreme case – thickened up my hair with cunning layers, gave it shape and style, and all-round improved my hair out of sight. The trendy young hairdresser told me I must *not*, under any circumstances, use No

Frills shampoo and should *always* use conditioner, and with Mum standing right beside me when she said this, there was to be no argument. This made a big difference too. When my hair grew out, a slightly deeper blonde too, it was, without wanting to brag, quite nice. So this explained Craig's compliment about my hair.

Craig's other comment, about my side-on nose, was not so easily explained. Up until then I had not been aware I had a big nose from the side, as one wouldn't be if not told. Craig did me a favour there. But given the previous observation about my abnormally flat face, it was a little hard to make sense of, unless the extraordinary flatness of my face made my nose *look* big from the side. That was a possibility.

Whatever the case, I immediately added big-nose-from-the-side to my list of physical deficits and promptly adjusted my angle to be standing face on to Craig's emissaries, instead of side on. I may have adjusted my hair too.

Craig himself, it might also be pointed out here, was not exactly Brad Pitt, or even Sylvester Stallone. He was skinny, with long, lank, uninteresting brown hair that hung down over his face so that I couldn't exactly say what he looked like. He was, however, an old friend of Simon's going right back, as I understood it, and so, although I had never spoken a word to him directly or properly seen his face, this friendship with Simon made him interesting to me.

'Is this a joke?' I asked the two boys, still sniggering about the side-on nose, knowing Simon and Craig, who were both in that class, were standing at a bench somewhere behind me and not wanting to turn around in case they were laughing too. If it wasn't a joke, I was going to accept the invitation, despite never having spoken a word to Craig and not knowing what he looked like. I was not fussy, indeed. I was not fussy like my German great-grandmother who had once turned down an invitation from the future King of England (Edward VII), also delivered by emissary, when she was sixteen and strolling along with her mother beside the Rhine River and he – an actual prince – had sent an emissary to ask if she would care to join him in his carriage. She would not care to, said her mother on her behalf, on account of the future king's reputation as a ladies' man. And fair enough too, although it was perhaps a *little* fussy. I was not quite that fussy.

'Nup,' was the succinct answer I got from Craig's emissaries to my question about whether or not his invitation was a joke, and although not entirely convincing, as they were still sniggering when they said it, it was enough for me and I accepted the invitation. I then returned happily to my lathing, being careful to hide my big-from-the-side nose behind my hair, without risking my long hair getting caught in the lathe, which could rip my whole face off, leaving nothing but the nose – with my luck.

Before the party on the Saturday night, there was a frog to be dissected in Science class. I hated Science, it's fair to say, and it hated me. I had no aptitude for it whatsoever. I could hardly even look at the slides of cell clusters on the overhead projector without feeling sick, just for something completely different, and Science seemed to have an awful lot to do with cell clusters. The thought of dissecting a frog was even less appealing than looking at slides of cells and I had been dreading frog dissection ever since it had been announced earlier on in the year. I had grown a few frogs from tadpoles in my younger day and apart from the gore of an animal's insides close up, which did not appeal at all, I felt a fondness for frogs that made the idea of slicing one open even more repulsive.

But then Simon showed up at my elbow and changed all that. Suddenly frog dissection seemed the most exciting, indeed romantic prospect ever. Frogs have a romantic connotation, don't they? They did that day.

We were dissecting our frogs in pairs and for some totally fairy-tale reason, Simon chose to share *my* frog. He could have had any frog but he chose mine.

'So you and Craig, eh?' were the first, somewhat regrettable words my frog prince spoke to me, as we stood close together preparing to make the first incision in our upturned, rather suggestively splayed frog. 'I guess so,' is all I could say in answer, wishing my handsome frog prince would change the subject, as I watched, mesmerised, as he sliced open *our* frog top to bottom, the tanned, flexed muscle in his forearm at such close quarters, I felt rather sliced open too. It's fair to say I was not altogether concentrating on the frog. When I reached forward to pin back the frog's skin either side – the least I could do – our arms brushed and my hair fell forward into the frog, which was not planned exactly, but should have been, because Simon then held back my hair for me, which practically pinned me to the spot, much like the frog, not wanting to move in case the spell was broken, even though I more or less had my face in a dissected frog. It was the most romantic moment of my life.

Then I fainted, face first into the frog. No, I didn't. But I might have done and probably *should* have done, because I feel sure Simon would have caught me up in his strong arms, just in time, rather than let me fall face first into the frog. And *that* really would have been romantic; a story to tell our grandchildren indeed.

* * *

Dilly, our new second-hand Datsun hatchback, white on the outside and black on the inside, drove Jodie and me to Simon's house in Killarney Heights the Saturday night following the frog prince episode, and Mrs Crane's much slicker, unnamed golden Torana was due to pick us up at 10.30 pm, four hours later. It was not ideal to be arriving at Simon's party with the most beautiful and popular of the Toughie girls who, sitting next to me in Dilly, in a gold and white striped boob tube, short black denim skirt and exotic Chinese-symbol dangly earrings, recent arrivals from Singapore, vividly reminded me of this fact. But it was better than arriving alone. I had practised kissing *someone*, who may or may not have looked a little bit like Rocky, on my pillow the previous night, and in my pastel pink flared jeans and blue crepe-crisis-disguising, off-the-shoulder, loosely fitted cheesecloth top and cork-heels, I felt more or less prepared.

'Jodie; hi!' said Terry, a hardcore Toughie friend of Simon's, who greeted us at the door, his eyes fixed firmly on Jodie's boob bump all the while, completely ignoring me. 'Alan is going to be glad to see *you*. He's downstairs!' Terry added enthusiastically, as we walked in and he led Jodie towards the spiral staircase descending down to the right, having said a passing 'Hi Sally' to me. I loved spiral staircases, as you know, and wanted to follow, but I didn't much like Terry *or* Alan, nor did I want to be accused of tagging along, so I resisted the lure of the spiral staircase and left Jodie to her Toughies, following the sound of voices coming along the hall instead.

At the end of the hall I found Simon standing behind the kitchen bench top with Lana, a girl I knew from ballet, preparing appetisers together, just like husband and wife. This was unfortunate.

'Lana!' I said, about ten times louder than I needed to, so that the adults gathered in a room behind the modern open-plan kitchen turned to see if there was something wrong. Simon was surprised Lana and I knew each other (from ballet) and this surprise at least covered for me for a bit, while I did my best to adjust to the fact that I knew Simon's private-school girlfriend and she was the ravishingly beautiful, tall, slim, dark-haired, almost-nothing-like-me, Lana. I was also a little disarmed by Simon's blue eyes that I had never seen look so blue or so directly at me, as they did fleetingly when I arrived.

One way or another I had forgotten all about Craig. But when Simon and Lana started whispering to each other over the appetisers I remembered him all at once and was suddenly extremely keen to see him. 'Is Craig here?' I asked, with a little more urgency than I would have liked. 'Na, he can't come,' said Simon. 'He just phoned to say he is sick. He said to tell you he's sorry.'

Holding back tears was never a specialty of mine, so I think I need to be congratulated for more or less managing to do so at this critical moment, as I stood there in front of Simon and Lana, stupidly stunned and genuinely disappointed by the news that Craig wasn't coming, and worse, by how casually Simon had seen fit to tell me. I considered asking for Craig's number to ring him and beg him to come, but I was yet to speak a word to him, or him to me, and he might actually have been sick. Also, I was having trouble speaking.

I had to get out of the kitchen. Remembering the spiral staircase with a rush of relief, I turned without having said anything to the news about Craig, and took off in that direction, feeling Simon's pitying stare burning into my back.

Downstairs I found a rumpus room almost exactly like Jodie's, with a bar cubicle in the centre, dark-painted concrete walls and beanbags everywhere. The lights were dimmed, but I could clearly see Jodie sitting in Alan's lap on one of the corner beanbags, busily pashing. I'd never seen Jodie kissing before and I was struck by how good she seemed to be at it. Then Alan, mid-pash, caught my eye and gave me a very stern look. I realised I was staring. Could it get any worse? It could.

I pushed past the various pashing couples in beanbags, and at least one standing behind the curtains that might have been doing more than pashing, and headed out some sliding doors to a small courtyard. Eliza was out there smoking away, surrounded by a crowd of people, one of whom I knew was her steady boyfriend, a senior three years older than her, but they didn't look out of place together. She nodded over at me and carried on smoking, blowing perfect smoke rings, and talking in that sexy raspy voice. I considered asking her for a smoke, knowing how cool smoking made me look, but we were not really friends anymore. It was a long time since the chalk dust incident, and I hadn't done much to impress her since, and she'd probably figured out I didn't even have any pubic hair either.

I looked round for Karen before remembering she said she wasn't coming. In desperation, I moved ever so discreetly in Eliza's direction to eavesdrop on the conversation, while pretending to study the dusk sky that had nothing in particular to recommend it. Someone in Eliza's group said Simon and Lana were busy on the floor of the bar cubicle 'getting to third base' and didn't want to be disturbed for anything. This was approximately the very last thing I wanted to hear at that point and it sank the last of my hopes for any kind of romance happening at that party – if not ever.

Before long, I found myself back inside, doing my best to avoid the bar cubicle, though I would have liked to refill my TAB from the bottle on the bar top. Holding an empty glass in my hand was not improving my image of being all alone at a party with nothing to do. I spied a cake and knife on a side table, a safe distance from the bar cubicle, and pounced on it. Saturday was now my only cake-eating day and the cake looked good...

It is only after I cut myself a generous slice and eat it in a hurry that I realise it is the birthday cake and Simon was probably supposed to be the first to cut it. Oh well; *he* is busy. The birthday message on top is almost intact.

No-one is dancing. The music is going to waste. This won't do. Music is supposed to be danced to, not *kissed* to. 'Come on, people! Let's dance!' I don't say this, but I consider saying it. I am pretty good at dancing to almost any music but I can't dance on my own. Can I? I decide I can, even though it's not quite my taste in music, something from Neil Young who all the Toughies were getting into at the time, while I was still stuck on ABBA. 'Dancing Queen' is *literally* my song.

I dance a while to 'Old Man', impressing no-one with my expressive hands and arms, then decide dancing on my own to Neil Young's 'Old Man', surrounded by kissing couples and at least one couple getting to third base, is a little too sad even for me. I have to get out of the kissing room. There's a door to one side I hadn't noticed before and I open it, thinking it might be a bathroom I can hide in for an hour or two, but it's a poolroom full to the brim with boys. 'Hurrah! I am not the only one without someone to pash!' is my first thought. And my second: 'Maybe it's not too late for me after all.'

The boys in the poolroom do not seem overly pleased to see me and when I go in anyway, I realise I know most of them and none are likely to want to get to know me any better. Two are Craig's emissaries from Woodwork class and Terry is another. I know he is going round with Helen from school, yet another gorgeous Toughie, and I am quietly pleased to know that I am not the only one who has been stood up. Helen must be at a gym comp. She is a gymnast.

'Where's Craig?' one of his former emissaries asks, and all the boys playing pool and some of them standing round, have a good chuckle about that.

'He's sick,' I say, a little under my breath, as I realise they probably know better. Still, I bravely ask to have a turn playing pool and they don't tell me to get lost outright, so that is something, even if they do make me wait through two more games before they let me join in.

It is unfortunate that when I do get a turn to join in I discover that pool is not quite as easy as it looks – I have never played pool before – and every time my ball oh-so-narrowly misses the hole, I can't help letting out a squeal of frustration, even after Terry tells me to 'quit squealing'. I must not be my usual relaxed self.

Eventually I end up on my own, outside on the grass on the

front lawn, in the shadow of a high hedge, commiserating with the stars, and waiting for Mrs Crane's Torana to show up and put me out of my misery. People start leaving on foot and parents arrive to collect others. They walk up and down the garden path, lit by a night light, and I watch them, unseen from the shadow of the hedge. I have a plan for when Mrs Crane arrives, which depends on her going inside to collect Jodie first, as the other parents have done. Then I will sneak inside after her and pretend I've been inside all along. Hopefully Jodie won't spoil it by coming to the door. I haven't seen her all night. She's probably *still* kissing Alan.

But it's not Mrs Crane who arrives next. Instead the front door opens and Terry and Simon come out. I haven't seen Simon since the kitchen and my heart skips several beats to see him now, walking up the front path, his sun-bleached hair shining under the night light. Terry heads out the gate and Simon turns round to walk back down the path, head bowed, hands in pockets, quite alone. I briefly wonder where Lana is then push that thought away. I don't want to think about Lana. I am free instead to study Simon's face without fear of being seen. There's something thoughtful, even sad about that beautiful face, I think, wishing he would turn this way a little so I could ...

'Sally?' Simon says, turning towards me, as if he'd read my thoughts exactly, peering into the darkness. 'Is that you?'

I thought I was invisible. I don't want him to see me like this, and yet, if he *did* decide to walk across the grass to find me in the shadows I would not be altogether sorry.

'Hi!' I manage, jumping out of the hedge shadow a ways, as I watch, disbelieving, Simon walk across the grass through the night straight towards me.

'What are you doing out here?' he wants to know, understandably, but in a voice that is kind not scornful. I can just make out his smile. *He's* not wearing braces. Standing in the darkness with Simon so close and his voice so kind, is almost too much for me and I'm practically holding my breath trying to avoid a proper flood of tears. For I have in fact been crying, just a little, if truth be known, and would not need much more emotional tumult to tip me over the edge into full-blown melodrama, which wouldn't do, not for a Toughie. Not for Simon.

We stand in the silence a while, Simon patiently waiting for an answer, as I look down, avoiding his smile.

'Just waiting,' I manage, but barely. Then, after another silly pause, 'for Jodie's mum,' I say, a quiver of emotion betraying my voice. There's another wait then and I hear Simon breathing heavily and shifting his feet in the grass, looking down and then looking up again. I can see his bright white hair, the same as mine, which was probably what gave me away. I want to apologise, to make things less awkward, and even to suggest we go inside, but I can't speak, and my body wants to stand in the silence with Simon.

'You know', says Simon finally, in a voice lowered almost to a whisper: 'Craig's an idiot.'

A frog croaks.

Chapter 9

Sentimental Saturday

'Right, said Fred, climbing up a ladder with his crowbar gave a mighty blow, [two, three, four] he's in trouble, half a ton of rubble, landed on the top of his dome ...'

THIS IS DAD OF A SATURDAY NIGHT, NOT CLIMBING UP A ladder but singing, and sometimes dancing along, as far as he could, to the *Sentimental Journey* program on the radio. If he got carried away enough, there he'd be, in front of our oversized front windows, the Faheys, Gravillies and Schroutens free to watch from across the road as he jigged up and down, rubbing the sides of his head, sending his grey comb-over flying off at a steep lean in the wrong direction, as if it was trying to find some other head to cling on to. And who could blame it? Mum, who was obliged to keep Dad company of a Saturday night, being rather more aware of the neighbours than he, would be slunk down on the settee, sipping a slow Cinzano and soda, one glass to Dad's three of cask wine, tapping a supportive toe, trying to convince herself this was all perfectly normal, and when that failed, whipping out her knitting needles and beginning a rapid knit, purl, knit.

'Right, said Fred' was a regular feature of our Saturday nights, being such a firm favourite of Dad's that Mum, in a weak moment, had made a recording of it in case it wasn't played and Dad couldn't cope. After the *Sentimental Journey* program of hits mostly from the 1940s played earlier on in the evening, in crackling tones that evoked fond memories of simpler times (the war), Dad then began on his favourite records. *Dance the Greek Way*, which was recommended by our neighbours the Gravillies – who were Greek – was another firm favourite, as was *The Best of Kenny Ball*, with particular enthusiasm shown for 'When the Saints Go Marching In', blasted out on a deranged trumpet. *The Merry Widow*, which was usually the last record to play, I think was more Mum's favourite than Dad's.

While Dad danced – his own way – to these various old-time tracks, we three, having been dispatched into the master bedroom with the TV, revelled in a night of not-so-sentimental American crime dramas, enjoying our only night of TV without the risk of Dad coming in and telling us to 'turn the ruddy thing off!' Indeed, the disappearance of the TV from the living room was a big part of Dad's merriment of a Saturday night (along with Fred, Kenny, the Greeks and the grog), as he hated the ruddy thing with a passion. The disappearance of his children behind a closed door didn't hurt either.

Dad went out of his way to avoid the TV. Apart from the cricket, the British comic duo *Morecombe and Wise*, *Fawlty Towers* and *The Sullivans*, an Australian World War II drama series, which he enjoyed, or at least tolerated, he had no time for

TV and strenuously resented all the time we spent watching it – except on Saturdays. During the week, especially on non-grog nights (Mondays and Tuesdays), Dad would come home from work and invariably yell, before barely in the door, 'Turn the ruddy thing off!', unless Mum could hold him off at the door and persuade him to let us watch to the end of the program.

She did not hate TV indeed, and wanted as much as we did to find out what happened to Hogan or Gilligan. If the Fahey girls were watching TV with us, which happened quite frequently, he'd be angrier still, yelling at them to 'Go home, you lot!' the minute he walked in the door. To avoid this unpleasantness, Beth got good at listening out for Dad's footsteps on the driveway and when she heard them, leaping up off the settee to announce, with the greatest urgency: 'Mr Jones is home!', before grabbing Jan and scrambling over the back of the settee and out the back door before Dad could appear in the front window.

But sentimental, ever so slightly sloshed Dad, singing to 'Right, said Fred' and dancing the Greek way (as far as a going-on-60-year-old drunk Anglo-Australian with a bad back could), didn't mind how much TV we watched; indeed the more the better. And because of this our Saturday nights at home were, especially for me, happy occasions, even more fun than Saturday nights spent out at friends' parties. While strains of Kenny Ball's enthusiastic trumpet could be heard coming from the other end of the hallway, reassuring us that Dad was otherwise occupied, we three could be found in Mum and Dad's room, revelling in an evening of uninterrupted crime fighting, courtesy of *The Six Million Dollar Man, Wonder Woman, Charlie's Angels, Hawaii Five-O, The Streets of San*

Francisco and *Rockford Files*, to name a few of the mainstays that provided a steady soundtrack of bionic running, gunfire and screams to give Kenny's marching saints a run for their money.

And when Saturday nights became my only eating night, as they did before long, I enjoyed this routine all the more. Making regular dashes to the fridge in the ads, I'd often bump into Dad going for the cask wine, eyes moist with merriment. And he'd be in such a good mood he'd call me 'Sal' and ask how I was going, the ballet battles seemingly forgotten for a night; a temporary ceasefire called. I'd be as relieved as he was by this pause in hostilities, and make sure to say I was going 'well' not 'good', because I knew he was a stickler for that *well*, even on a Saturday night. And all would indeed be well between us.

Only occasionally Dad got a bit *too* sentimental of a Saturday night, like the time, when we were quite a bit younger, before bunks, when he came charging into our bedroom with a full glass of wine and did a somersault across my bed – fortunately not with me in it – crashing his legs into the narrow strip of wall beside the window, just missing the glass. I remember thinking: Dad must be pretty happy to do a somersault, having hardly ever seen him so much as bend his back in any direction before. I was also impressed he didn't break his wine glass, though most of the wine did end up on my bedspread. Fortunately, it was an old bedspread from the Thompsetts, of the sort that could absorb any number of stains without looking any worse. But he might have broken the glass – or the window – or his back.

Saturday nights at other people's houses, I discovered that year, were not quite so sentimental. One Saturday night away from home, not long after Simon's party, Jodie invited me to her mother's 40th birthday. Jodie greeted me at the door of her house, wearing something new from Singapore: a green and white batik sarong, though it was only spring. Jodie always dressed as if it was summer. Perhaps it was for her. I had on my same pale pink jeans, blue cheesecloth top and cork wedge heels that I'd worn to Simon's party, not so much because the outfit had been such a runaway success on that occasion, but more because it was my only 'smart' outfit.

'You've *gotta* see this!' Jodie said laughing and snatching my hand up as she hurriedly led me round the corner to her parents' bedroom. I stayed standing awkwardly in the doorway of a room I'd never been in before, and preferred to keep it that way if possible, to watch Mrs Crane dive on top of a life-size cardboard cut-out of a man, who wasn't Mr Crane, lying stretched out on their double bed, kissing and caressing and generally showing her extreme affection for the cardboard man.

'Sally! Don't you just love this man! I *love* this man!' Mrs Crane cried out to me, getting up and laughing hysterically with her group of friends who were in the room with her, before diving back on top of the cardboard man again. As I did not know who he was (he turned out to be Neil Diamond), I didn't exactly know what to say, or where to look, and could only offer a faint smile. Then Mr Crane turned up beside me and I was even less at ease with the situation. 'Don't worry about her, Sally; she's a crazy lady,' Mr Crane said, as Mrs Crane threw herself back on top of the cardboard Neil Diamond, kissing and carrying on, and I thought to myself: 'Perhaps my mum and dad aren't so crazy after all.'

We moved downstairs to the rumpus room and Mrs Crane

took Neil Diamond with her. There was a spinning disco ball, which was something new for me, and a room full of people dancing, mostly to Neil Diamond music, and even though Mrs Crane was dancing with the cardboard Neil Diamond, holding him close, and Mr Crane was rolling his eyes at her, I felt more comfortable to be dancing, and began to see what Mrs Crane saw in her cardboard man. But that only lasted a few minutes before Mr Crane came up to me and shouted above the music, 'You look so grown up tonight, Sally! I hardly recognise you!', which kind of spoilt the disco mood and made me feel self-conscious about my dancing, even if I had just had my braces off and was feeling a little more grown up than usual.

On another Saturday night, I stayed over at the house of one of the Toughie girls from school, a girl called Teresa who I hardly knew, but because she lived in the same street as me we thought it would be a good idea to have a sleepover. I think it was more her idea than mine. During the night at Teresa's house, lying in our separate single beds in her room, while I struggled to get to sleep after an awkward dinner with her family when no-one spoke and her father sat opposite me looking like Herman Munster with an unnaturally tall forehead, Teresa suddenly climbed out the bedroom window and disappeared into the night. After that I definitely couldn't sleep, left alone in a house full of particularly strange strangers. I never did like *The Munsters*. I considered climbing out the window after her and running all the way home, but I was afraid of the dark and Teresa might wonder where *I'd* gone, if she ever came back.

When she did finally return through the same window, about two hours later, she climbed straight back into bed, turned to face the wall, and went to sleep without a word. I was glad to have her safely back, but didn't get much sleep that night wondering where she had gone to and how come she was so much braver than I was about the dark. In the morning I found out. I asked her where she'd been and she told me she'd been with Jonno having sex at Forestville Primary School, which explained it. Apparently she did the same every single night, whether she had someone sleeping over or not. At least it wasn't personal.

I didn't go back to Teresa's after that. But I did understand now why Jonno looked permanently sleepy at school. He had to walk from his house in Killarney to collect Teresa in French's Forest, about three miles, then to Forestville for certain other exertions, then back to French's Forest to drop Teresa off, then back to Killarney, every single night. I almost had a newfound respect for him. He was only fourteen, after all, even if he did look twenty. I was still thirteen and still confused about periods and parks. But at least I didn't have to feel so bad about being scared of the dark, as Teresa clearly was too or she wouldn't have needed an escort.

Yet another Saturday night spent away from home that educational year added to my appreciation of how other people lived. It was another sleepover situation, but this time we would be sleeping in a tent, so there wouldn't be any climbing out of windows. This was a shame, because I would have been prepared. But never mind. Sometimes it's better *not* to be prepared. The occasion was Lana's fourteenth birthday party and it was an all-girl party, as Simon and Lana had broken up not long after his party. I know what you're thinking, but I'm afraid that wasn't the case; I didn't have anything to do with their break-up, at least as far as I knew. Lana refused to discuss it, as did Simon.

Lana went to the girls' school in St Ives, the North Shore's poshest suburb, and all the other girls invited were from that school. I was the only ring-in from ballet, and a little surprised to be invited. Lana was obsessed with Olivia Newton-John or 'Livvy', as she and just about everyone else in Australia called her, and her party had a *Grease* theme. We were all told to come dressed as *Grease* girls, but not as Livvy. Lana was to be the only Livvy. And she was Livvy *after* the transformation. She wore high heels, tight black leather pants and off-the-shoulder black top, custom made for the occasion, while the rest of us were in T-shirts, full skirts and sneakers. Fortunately I still fitted into my old turquoise blue character skirt from the RAD grades, as I didn't have any other full skirt and didn't need to stand out any more than absolutely necessary.

Wearing these '50s costumes, with Lana as the sexy Livvy, strutting out front, with cigarette and sunglasses, we went parading round the streets of Terry Hills where Lana lived, another posh suburb, the Australian equivalent of Beverly Hills, with wide, quiet streets lined with shiny new monstrosities. We rocked the quietness, singing: 'You're the one that I want, oo-oo-oo, honey' at the top of our voices. After that we went back to Lana's very own monstrosity and sat on her bed in a room completely lined, walls, door *and* ceiling, with *Grease* posters. There, while the other girls talked and sung some more, I gazed enviously at Lana's ensuite, thinking, of all the things missing in my life, that really takes the cake.

After a swim in Lana's in-ground pool, during which I stayed underwater as much as possible, doing handstands to hide the ongoing crepe crisis, hoping I might impress the other, better endowed girls, with my perfectly pointed feet, we had a barbecue, which allowed me a few delicious moments in my element before it was time to repair to the large blue tent that had been set up beside the pool. Because that's how much room there was in Lana's back yard, enough for a full-sized pool, large tent *and* barbecue.

I had been looking forward to sleeping in a tent. I loved camping, as a rule. Once a year Mum took us camping in the Blue Mountains with her friend Beryl, who lived up there and knew everything there was to know about camping. Provided I slept on my side and not flat on my back, which made me vomit, I was very happy in a tent. I even cried and carried on when our camping trip was rained off one year, refusing to leave until Auntie Beryl collapsed the tent on top of me. It only ever rains in Australia when you pitch a tent.

In Lana's tent, however, it didn't rain. Instead, as the blue light began to fade she announced it was time for 'pashing practice'. Pashing practice? I was not entirely sure what that was. But then Lana gave a good demonstration with one of her friends, rolling together on the tent floor, their faces glued at the lips, so I was clearer after that. 'You can do this if you want to,' Lana said then, coming up for air to put a hand over her lips before seizing her friend again and repeating the performance, this time with a hand over her mouth, though in the fading light it was difficult to be sure the hand stayed in place.

Although I was used to watching people kiss by now, I felt distinctly uncomfortable watching Lana and her friend 'practice pashing' on the tent floor, and did not relish the prospect of having to find a partner to do my practice pashing with, for this was clearly a compulsory exercise, although it didn't quite fit with the *Grease* theme, I felt. And why did Lana need pashing practice anyway? Hadn't she pashed Simon enough to be an expert in the art? I had certainly imagined she had. Altogether I was feeling confused and a little unprepared, it's fair to say, and once again would have appreciated some warning. I could have at least practised on my pillow.

The other girls, who all knew each other, seemed rather more prepared than I was and started coupling up and rolling around on the tent floor too. I had a terrible feeling this was going to be Simon's party all over again, where everyone else coupled up and I was left standing on my own, squealing. But as Lana had invited an even number of girls – probably the reason I was invited in the first place – when the others coupled up, there was one small girl, with a pained expression on her face, left standing. Greatly relieved, I edged a little closer to this girl, whose name I couldn't remember, and bravely asked: 'Do you want to do it with me?' And when she didn't exactly say no, though she didn't exactly say yes, either, I moved a little closer again, deployed the optional hand, as did she, and got to it. We were both a bit too nervous to remember to get on the floor, so we stayed standing throughout. Still, all things considered, I think we managed quite well. Nobody disqualified us, at least. It might not have been *exactly* what I had in mind for my first kiss, but it was a start.

* * *

The first typed copy of Dad's book, all 90,000 words plus countless footnotes, that was sent off to a publisher in America that year, got lost in the mail. It was the only typed copy, other than the carbon copies, which left something to be desired in the way of quality. Also the corrections that Mum had made with Liquid Paper to the top copy had not come through to the carbon copies. If the original copy didn't show up, touching up the top carbon copy was going to be a painstaking operation. Why a photocopy of the best copy hadn't been made before it was sent off to America is not entirely clear, but it probably had something to do with Dad being the least practical man in all of Australia. Also the expense of photocopying 90,000 words plus footnotes for Africa in the late '70s would have been considerable, although one less trip to Prouds jewellers would have probably covered it.

When Dad was notified that his precious manuscript had gone missing in the post, it's fair to say he did not remain calm, nor did Mum, thinking she would have to type the entire thing again, a process that had taken more than six months. Indeed the whole house went into a panic, as 'Dad's book' was by this stage almost as much a part of all our lives as it was of his. Dad, already riddled with Mum-related guilt, would not hear of Mum retyping the book from scratch, so the carbon copy it would have to be. So when he wasn't at work, or she on the road, driving me hither and thither, they spent long hours together finely weeding out the mistakes and doing their best to touch up the carbon copy with a combination of typewriter, Liquid Paper and pen.

My timing, as ever, was off, because this frantic recovery operation took place at the same time we were preparing for our end-of-year concert at Northside, our first full-length ballet. We were putting on *Thumbelina* and I was dancing the important roles of lead beetle and solo stork. This meant extra rehearsals to be driven to, as well as extra sewing for Mum. And at one point, at the height of Dad's book panic, I found myself standing in the living room in my orange stork stockings and white leotard while Mum sewed feathers onto my bottom and bust (crepe) regions, a task that could not be done while Dad was at work, alas, because I was either at school or ballet at those times and I had to be inside the leotard for Mum to get the position right on the feathers.

That his mission to save the Third World, already seriously delayed, was being held up further by me and my stork feathers, was clearly too much for Dad and after pacing to and fro, casting stony looks in my direction, as I tried to look gainfully employed while dressed as a half-feathered stork, he finally yelled: 'Is that absolutely necessary when there is so much *else* to be done? Time is of the essence, love. I really think you're going to wear yourself out! Can't *she* do that?' Unfortunately *she* couldn't, and it *was* absolutely necessary. A stork must have a full flotilla of feathers.

Just before the carbon copy of Dad's book was about to be sent off to America and *Thumbelina* was about to be staged at Kuringai College in Lindfield, Dad got word from the publishers that the original copy of the book had finally turned up in the mail, only two months late. As good news goes this wasn't the best, but it could have been worse. The painstakingly touched-up carbon copy could have just been sent – or gone missing in the mail too – and as that wasn't photocopied either, we would have really been in a pickle; those 90,000 words having to that point taken Dad fourteen years to write. Another consolation was that *Thumbelina* was a great success.

Unfortunately, the good news ended there. For soon after this Dad's right retina snapped and he was told he needed urgent surgery to save the left eye if he was to avoid going blind entirely. He was rushed into Sydney Eye Hospital and prepared for surgery that same day. We took time off school and Mum drove us in to see him right before the operation. He was dressed in a long white baggy gown that made him look even older in the glare of the white hospital ward where we found him. There were other people visiting patients in the ward and I was embarrassed they were looking at us and thinking we were not quite normal. Then Dad, in his old-man smock, grabbed Mum and kissed her goodbye so hard on the lips, like I'd never seen him do before, and that looked all wrong to me too – drawing on all my kissing experience, of course – that I had trouble not yelling out: 'Let her go!'

The operation to save the left retina was a success and the danger of Dad going completely blind was averted. But nothing would be the same for us after that. Dad would have to take extra care of his one working eye, go for regular check-ups and be sure to read and write with good lighting, preferably daylight. He would not be able to drive at night anymore, nor would he be able to keep his job at Nestlé. Dad was going to have to retire. He was fifty-nine and we were fourteen, thirteen and twelve.

This was a total disaster for the family. Dad's job at Nestlé was our only income and it was a pretty good one, even if it didn't always seem like it. There was talk of having to sell the house, which was still mortgaged. But much worse than the question of where we were going to live was the question of whether or not I would be able to continue with my ballet.

The ballet battles between Dad and me had increasingly become about the expense of ballet, which apparently was more than the expense of Tim's various sports (soccer, cricket, tennis and surfing), and Babs' horse-riding combined. Babs had tried ballet, piano, and various other more expensive after-school activities but hadn't liked any of them. Was that *my* fault? It wasn't. I was allergic to horses anyway. More to the point, I needed ballet to breathe. But when Dad told us that 'some sacrifices' were going to have to be made after he retired I knew he was talking about my ballet. And I wasn't wrong.

On the Saturday afternoon that followed Dad's last day of work in the July of '79, he called a formal family meeting to tell us about our 'changed circumstances'. The living room furniture had been arranged so that we could sit facing each other, the parents on one side and the children on the other. This gave me the impression of being on the wrong side of the meeting, the side having to make the sacrifices. 'As you are aware,' Dad began in the formal tone of speech he favoured when sober, 'our circumstances have changed considerably and some sacrifices are going to have to be made.' He followed this by telling us 'There's nothing to worry about; everything is going to be all right'. He was avoiding our faces, mine in particular I thought, by glancing at a piece of paper that was not entirely steady in his hand and stuttering even more than usual as he spoke, which did not exactly make me feel like everything *was* going to be all right, far from it. I glanced at Mum for reassurance but the look she gave me, a grimace more than a smile, did not help. Dad told us then that the pension he had taken from Nestlé, instead of a lump-sum payout, would be a smaller, weekly sum that would continue for the duration of Mum's lifetime so that Mum would never have to go back to work or worry about money. He was clearly proud of this and became emotional when he said it. I didn't exactly know what all this meant, but had the distinct feeling it was not good for me.

'Everything is going to be alright,' Dad repeated, which really didn't help, 'but some sacrifices are going to have to be made in the short term.' This is when I knew for sure I was in trouble, because Dad glanced briefly up at me when he said that and when I looked over at Mum again she couldn't even manage a grimace. Dad said he was not going to look for another job because he was expecting to hear back from the publisher very soon with good news about his book and then he would have to give lectures on his book overseas and our financial situation would be much improved. In the meantime, changes were going to have to be made – as he kept saying. He looked straight at me then and I thought I saw a smile tease the corners of his mouth. I tensed up like a coiled spring and when he said: 'Sally,' (not Sal), the certainty of my fate hit me like a death sentence, the coil sprung, and I leapt out of my seat, before the hammer could fall, and screamed, 'I am not giving up my ballet!' then charged off down the hallway to lock myself in the bathroom and burst into a biblical, or should that be balletical (I know it's not a word), flood of tears.

When no-one came to the door after more than an hour had passed, I knew I was right about what Dad had been going to say and became almost terrified at the prospect. I couldn't believe Mum would really go along with Dad and make me have to give up ballet after all the time and effort I'd put in and how well I was doing (all things considered). I honestly could not imagine life without ballet. Everything was going to be *all wrong* if I had to give up ballet.

After night fell and I couldn't hold out in the bathroom any longer, I unlocked the door as quietly as I could and crept round the corner into my bedroom, happy to find it empty. From the familiar sounds coming through the wall, Tim and Babs were watching *The Six Million Dollar Man* in Mum and Dad's room next door. And from the other end of the hall I could just hear Mum and Dad's *Sentimental Journey* program playing on the radio, thankfully not 'Right, said Fred', but still cheerful enough to make it seem as if nothing had changed *for them*. Lying under the covers on my top bunk, staring at my 'Where there's a will there's a way' poster of a mouse pushing an elephant up a hill, I determined to run away if I really did have to give up ballet.

I had quite a bit of money saved in my little blue bankbook – more than $200 – and I thought Mrs P would help me. Maybe I could pitch a tent in the garden of her house in Belrose, within walking distance of the studio. Surely *she* wouldn't want me to give up ballet, even if Tegan was her favourite. I didn't have a tent, mind, but I thought Auntie Beryl might lend me one if I asked nicely. It would only have to be a small tent. I imagined all the extra practice I could get living so close to the studio and almost felt better. And with those, somewhat soothing if ever so slightly impractical thoughts, I eventually cried myself to sleep, to the not-so-sentimental sounds of gunfire, screaming and bionic running coming through the wall.

Chapter 10

Running off to join the ballet

The following year was a year of firsts and lasts. It was the year I won my first blue ribbon at the City of Sydney Eisteddfod, dancing my 'Bolt of Lightning' demi-character in the open-age category, wearing a silver lycra unitard that included a balaclava and gloves, a costume that prompted the adjudicator to write on my report card, 'a lovely physique for ballet'. Even if this comment was probably down to the balaclava making my head look smaller and the gloves making my arms look longer, it was a most encouraging comment and another fine first indeed. Also, that year was my last at Killarney because at the end of it, at the age of fourteen, I left school to study ballet full-time and take my School Certificate by correspondence. So instead of having to give up ballet and running away from home, I gave up school and ran away to join the ballet. How this miraculous turn of events came about I am not entirely sure, but I have a few theories.

Not long after Dad's 'changed circumstances' speech,

Stanford University Press, the publisher he'd first sent his book to, the ones who had lost track of it in the post for a while, and who had initially used the phrase *when* we publish' in their earlier communications with him, after almost a year of waiting, eventually got back to Dad with a letter of rejection. This was Dad's first rejection letter; it would not be his last. So Dad's book was not going to save us after all. Nor would it save the Third World, at least not yet. The only reason this wasn't the final nail in the coffin for me was that my fees for that ballet term had already been paid. Also, when Mum saw my face the morning after the speech, when I emerged from my room looking like a bantamweight boxer after a fight with a heavyweight, refusing to talk to her other than to ask for Auntie Beryl's phone number, I think she suspected I might be planning to run away to the Blue Mountains, where Auntie Beryl lived, which was probably a bit further than she would have wanted me to run to, if not far enough for Dad. So there was no more talk, for the time being, about sacrifices having to be made.

Then, instead of *me* running away, after the rejection letter came and with my ballet future still hanging in the balance and Mum telling me evasively 'we shall see' in response to my pained enquiries on the subject, Mum and Dad were the ones who ran away, to their favourite old-English guesthouse in Bowral, for a ten-day break, leaving us in the care of Nana, who was 93 and had recently fallen off a bus and broken her hip. But never mind, she'd been given a new hip and in our early to mid-teens, we three were more or less capable of looking after ourselves. Carpooling favours were called in because Nana couldn't leave the house on account of our front and back steps being too much for her new hip. Also, she had never learnt to drive and even if she had, Dad had relinquished his company car when he retired and had taken Dilly, now our only car, to Bowral. While Mum and Dad played golf on the sprawling greens that surrounded their English guesthouse in Bowral, with Mum doing Dad's driving because the swing and twist was too much for Dad's back, back in the fake forest we muddled through, with Mrs Fahey assisting with the shopping and me helping Nana with the cooking by making a mountain of cream profiteroles, having recently learnt how to make choux pastry in Home Science class at school. Nobody went hungry at least, although Nana did find the chewy choux pastry a bit tough on her false teeth.

Then, after Mum and Dad returned from Bowral and Nana went home in a hurry to Queenscliff, we got a horse. No, this was not so that if Nana ever returned she would have a way of getting to and from the shops, although *that* would have made some sense. Rather, the horse was a birthday present for Babs' thirteenth birthday. But there seemed to be some kind of rush on getting the horse because it turned up when Babs was still very much twelve. In hindsight, I think what must have happened to change our changed circumstances so far back the other way so that rather than selling a house we bought a horse, was that Mum must have done some pretty fancy driving up in Bowral. And using the horse as leverage, she must have talked Dad into letting her go back to work part-time as a secretarial temp to pay for the horse and any other incidental extras, such as my ballet. It must have been some pretty fancy driving indeed, because Dad held as firmly as any man ever did to the principle that a gentleman does not 'let' his wife go out to work for anything, not even a horse. What also helped, I suspect, was that I won a $250 scholarship from Northside to substantially cover my ballet fees for another year.

Still, it does seem a *bit* strange that we got a horse at that precise point in time and in such a hurry, given that we were already struggling under the weight of five people, one cat, two budgerigars (Babs' tenth birthday present) and several mice, without adding a horse to the mix. But Babs apparently had her heart set on something bigger than a budgie, and Mum probably needed something as big as a horse to shift Dad's firm views about working wives – and dancing daughters. So it all made a kind of sense when you thought about it for a long, long time.

There were, however, you might or might not be surprised to hear, a few *slight* teething problems with the horse. On account of the hurry we were in to take delivery of our horse, the appropriate accommodation had not quite been arranged on the day of purchase and so, for the time being, the horse would have to live with us on our back lawn. Just as well we never got that pool. Still, our horse was a large specimen – when Babs said she wanted something bigger than a budgie she wasn't kidding – and our back lawn, while the perfect size for a pool, was not quite such a perfect size for a large horse. But never mind. Duc, short for Ducati, pronounced 'Duke', not 'Duck', Babs did not want a duck, as was the name of our new stallion, would not be staying long ...

This was just as well for the Smalls, our new next-door neighbours. For as luck would have it, they moved into their house, on the other side of our house from the Martians, the very day Duc moved into ours, and when their heads poked up over our shared fence their expressions suggested they were not altogether pleased with the new addition to our family, being fairly sure that when they had last inspected the house there had not been a horse over the next-door fence. They were right. Nonetheless, there was *now*. And while he was there, we were having our own battle trying to keep him from Mum's prized azaleas, which he had taken an instant and unexpected liking to and which Babs feared might be poisonous to horses, as a surprising number of plants are. Evidently this, as well as a *few* other things, had not been thought of before we took delivery of the horse. We would have to learn as we went along.

Not being able to keep Duc from Mum's azaleas while we were asleep, it was decided that the best place to tie Duc up for the night was to the pipe beyond the back fence. There was quite a bit of wild grass out there for him to eat, without danger of poisoning, we hoped, and he might give it a good trim into the bargain, appears to have been the thinking. And although the rope, or rather string, that Mum retrieved from under the house to tie Duc to the pipe with was not *quite* long enough to go all the way round the pipe, all that wild grass should keep him happy for at least twelve hours, probably. In the meantime, with our horse more or less safely tied up somewhere out there in the darkness, it was time for a family rubber of bridge before bed.

Duc arrived on a Friday and Friday at our house was bridge night, come what may. Wild horses couldn't keep us from our Friday night bridge. For when the Van Leeuwens weren't available to play bridge with Mum and Dad, we played as a family, because naturally we had all been taught to play bridge as a matter of priority, it being such a vital life skill.

But sure enough, while developing this vital skill that Friday night before heading off to bed, Duc at some point realised he was free to leave and did, so that the following morning, when we went to check on our horse, he was nowhere to be found. For a person as opposed to the throwaway society as Mum professed to be, it was quite surprising that she had effectively thrown away a horse. Her diary entry for that dramatic night records what happened thusly: 'Tim and I made a Small Slam in no trumps!!' followed by 'Duc gone!!!' It is clear from the number of exclamation marks used that Mum had her priorities right at least, using one more exclamation mark for the runaway horse than for the Small Slam in no trumps. For those who don't play bridge it might be necessary here to point out that 'no trumps' is the hardest bridge suit to play and a Small Slam means you can only lose one trick, so it's no small thing to achieve, contrary to its name. Still, neither is a runaway horse a small thing, not least a large runaway horse, and discovering Duc missing in the morning was a big slam drama indeed, especially for Babs. Some years earlier, on our way to school, Babs and I had witnessed a terrible accident on the ever busy Warringah Road highway that Duc could reach from the pipe in a couple of minutes if he headed downhill, when a red setter dog had run out onto that highway and been hit by one car after the next, its red fur like feathers flying everywhere, its eyes filled with a wild terror as it kept trying to scramble to its feet between cars before finally finding its feet and dashing past us, like a red ghost.

I don't know if Babs was thinking about this that morning, but I was. And if Duc had gone in that direction, directly downhill from where we'd left him, we were all in for a whole lot of misery.

Mum got smartly on the phone to call the police, not knowing who else to call about a missing horse. When the police said they hadn't come across a horse lately, Mum and Babs jumped into Dilly and took off on a wild horse chase around the neighbourhood, leaving Dad at home to man the phones. This arrangement soon presented a difficulty in the form of Tim's Saturday inter-club cricket match. Dad was supposed to drive him to the match but with Dilly otherwise occupied looking for a horse, this was not possible. Tim was loath to miss his cricket match, being the team's chief all-rounder, and Dad was loath to make a call to one of the other cricketing parents to come and collect him, wanting to keep the phone free in case someone called about a horse, and not having an altogether clear idea where Mum kept the numbers of the other cricketing parents anyway.

Fortunately, Dilly returned just in time for Dad to hurry Tim to his cricket match, but unfortunately, without a horse. Babs was in tears, naturally, and I tried to think of something big-sisterly to say to reassure her, and found myself completely at a loss. Animals were not my specialty. I think I said something about the difficulty of losing such a large animal and the likelihood of him turning up sooner or later. I'm not sure this helped, as Babs then took to the phone and spent some time ringing her friends to tell them to keep a look out for her horse.

Not long after she got off the phone the police rang back to ask: 'Have you lost a horse?' Mum, who answered the phone, said that we had, and they believed her. What a relief! The only delay then was waiting for Dad to return with Dilly so that Mum and Babs, with me tagging along for the ride in case I could be of any more vital assistance, could make haste in Dilly to the horse pound where Duc had ended up, after someone who knew such places existed had somehow delivered him there, miraculously uninjured. On the way, a quick stop had to be made at Discount Saddlery to purchase a lunge rein, hooks and chain, the bare essentials for keeping a horse tied up, as Babs and Mum *now* knew.

Being a small Datsun hatchback, Dilly could not be expected to accommodate a large horse, so Mum and I came home in Dilly while Babs rode Duc home from the pound along the edge of *two* busy highways. She wore a hard hat lest Duc, the runaway horse, bolted again and she, the twelve-year-old novice rider, fell off. The odds were not good. She *didn't* fall off, however, and full credit to her for that. She was doing her bit to keep the Joneses up too.

Then after it was decided that even with the best lunge rein, hooks and chain in the world a horse could not be safely secured to the pipe, the Faheys were called upon to take a turn at looking after our horse on their back lawn, which was slightly larger than ours. It was good of the Faheys to take care of our horse, seeing as they'd had no inkling that morning when they woke up that there'd be a horse in their backyard when they went to sleep that night. But perhaps because Dad had driven Mr Fahey into the city every weekday morning for the past eight years, they possibly thought a few nights with a horse in return for this favour was a fair exchange. We told them it would only be a few nights.

And it wasn't too many more nights – and days – than that, before a more suitable paddock was found on the edge of the fake forest, in another wishfully named placed called Oxford Falls, where Duc could be kept, in theory at least, for the relatively modest sum of $23 per week, plus feed. As Mum had just celebrated her first paycheque of $73.24 for a day and half's work, this arrangement seemed fairly affordable, provided Mum continued to get regular temping work, I continued to win scholarships to cover my ballet fees *and* the horse agreed to stay put in the paddock.

On this last point, alas, Duc did not agree. Somewhat predictably, Oxford Falls proved too good to be true, and within the first week Duc escaped from his paddock into the neighbouring paddock to eat, not azaleas this time, but something called crofton weed, which is in fact poisonous to horses. Unfortunately, it seemed we had acquired a horse that did not entirely know what was good for it. The keepers of the paddock refused to take responsibility for keeping Duc *in* the paddock, and away from the weed, suggesting instead that Mum call in a bulldozer to dig up the weed so he wouldn't be tempted to get out of it (the paddock). But having even less experience with bulldozers than with horses, if that were possible, and worried about our limited funds stretching to bulldozing, Mum imagined a simpler solution would be to buy a few sturdier paddock posts and enlist the help of Dad one fine Wednesday morning when she wasn't at work to hammer those sturdier posts into the ground.

A bulldozer was soon called in.

* * *

Overall it's fair to say that Dad was not coping too well with our changed *changed* circumstances, including the arrival of the horse. As mentioned, he did not cope well with distracting noises and Duc had proven to be one big distracting noise. But worse than the noisy horse (and his total failure to get his difficult daughter out of ballet), Dad was struggling with Mum going back to work. Besides the damage to his principles, on a practical front he was struggling to adjust to the domestic side of things. Being at home on his own most days of the week, he felt obliged to do something towards the preparation of the dinner. But when he tried to peel a potato with the assigned implement, step one of the meal-preparation challenge, he found the knack eluded him entirely, possibly due to his left-handedness. Possibly. Mum, meanwhile, was struggling to get her typing speed up to scratch on an electric typewriter after 40 years on a manual. If neither of them overcame their respective challenges it was not going to be only a large horse that starved. Fortunately, Mum did succeed and potato peel doesn't kill you. But it was touch and go for a while and Dad didn't help the situation any by venting his frustration on the unsuspecting woman from the temping agency who regularly called of a morning to offer Mum work and more than once got Dad instead, telling her: 'Mrs Jones is not available for work today. Please do not call her for the rest of the week!'

Altogether it was a bit of a wonder we ever managed to make ends meet and keep a horse stabled, fed and poison-free that year. But we did manage it, more or less, and after a while Duc *and* Dad and the rest of us adjusted to our changed *changed* circumstances and life pressed on.

In particular, I pressed on dancing, and, as mentioned, even started winning. I won a second scholarship in 1980, this one worth $500, which was almost enough to cover a year of full-time tuition. And that was how it came about that I was able to leave school at the end of the year. Still, it was a wonder I managed to talk Mum into letting me leave school at fourteen and an even bigger wonder she was able to talk Dad into it. I can only think Mrs P, with her Russian powers of persuasion, helped persuade Mum, and Dad had given up by this stage on ever getting me or anyone else to do anything he wanted, if he couldn't even get a potato peeler to peel a potato.

Mrs P had only recently started her full-time school and was keen to recruit dancers to it. She had also persuaded Tegan's mother to let Tegan leave school to study full-time ballet while doing her Higher School Certificate by correspondence, which would have helped my case too.

Leaving school to study ballet full time, from my point of view, of course, was a dream come true. The fact that I *still* had no boobs at the age of fourteen and three-quarters was reason enough to leave, especially as the senior uniform I would have had to have moved into the following year consisted of a see-through white blouse that could not, under any circumstances, be worn without a bra, and a bra could not, under any circumstances, be worn without boobs (they didn't have padded bras for girls in those days). And I think if it hadn't been for full-time ballet I would have had to contrive some other reason to leave school before it was time to move into that brutal blouse.

It was also the case that for at least a year I had been taking more and more time off school for ballet, including leaving French class early every Wednesday afternoon to catch the bus to Belrose for pas de deux class. It was a pity it had to be French class, as French was one of the few classes at Killarney I almost enjoyed (along with maths and cooking), but the pas de deux teacher, Mr Rubin, was not a big man, and he personally requested my presence in his class, as I was the smallest and easiest to spin and lift. So what was a girl to do? I had to go where I was most needed. And pas de deux is a French of sorts.

Then something happened at school that left no doubt in my mind, if there had been any doubt, that it was time for me to leave Killarney. After Simon's party, things between us had gone from about eight on the awkward scale to ten, at least from my point of view, with ten being the most awkward. He and Craig talked with each other at lunchtime, with me standing in the near vicinity, as near as I felt I could get without crowding them, and neither of them ever said anything to me. Craig never apologised to me for not coming to the party and Simon never mentioned the idiot comment. Occasionally I caught Simon looking my way with something approximating interest, but it seemed a long way from the closeness of that night at his house, if closeness it had been. Perhaps I'd imagined the whole thing. I figured he knew I fancied him – subtlety was *not* my strong suit – and perhaps regretted the comment, maybe worrying it would get back to Craig. Or else he'd forgotten the whole thing and I'd misread the signals in the first place. I was hardly an expert in such matters.

By the third year at school I had drifted away from the Toughies, including Jodie, and most of the time hung out at lunch with my friends from maths class, Dags, Freaks and Brains the lot of them. I don't know if anyone noticed my drift or cared if they did, even Jodie, but what happened one lunch time suggested I hadn't been entirely forgotten by the Toughies. I was standing in the quad with my maths mates over by the library, almost as far from the canteen where the Toughies hung out as you could get, when one of the girls in our group who was facing me said: 'There's a Toughie guy heading this way. He looks like he means business. A friend of yours, is he?' They all knew I had certain historical affiliations with the Toughies and found this somewhat amusing. For a happy second I thought it was Simon finally come to his senses, for I still hadn't forgotten Simon – indeed I never would – but when I turned to see who it was, I saw, in the brief second or two he allowed me, that it was not Simon but Terry, the guy who'd told me to quit squealing in the pool room, striding our way with a distinctly 'business-like' expression on his face. Before I could answer my maths mate, something even more surprising happened. Terry picked me up off my feet and proceeded to cart me back across the quad like a sack of potatoes.

This was *not* pas de deux. With pas de deux there's always a warning before you're lifted off your feet. And the way Terry picked me up and carted me across the quad, with my bum practically dragging on the ground, because he was not trained in the art and I was protesting loudly, telling him to 'Get lost!' and 'Put me down!', while squirming to break free, was about as much like pas de deux as French. Indeed it was the most humiliating and awkward moment of my life, which was saying something. He had two guys with him, who were providing a kind of shield either side, which might have been why no-one stopped us or said anything as we passed through the busy quad towards the canteen: three burly fifteen-year-old boys carrying a not-so-burly fourteen-year-old girl, struggling to break free. Even my maths mates let me be carted off without saying or doing anything to intervene. Perhaps they thought this was what Toughies did all the time. It wasn't. This was another first indeed, at least as far as I knew. What it was all about I had absolutely no idea.

'Get lost, Terry! Put me down!' I repeated but with diminishing firmness, when it was clear he wasn't going to get lost or put me down and the sound of my own squealing was making me feel like a total Dag. We hurried through the covered canteen area and rounded the corner to the boys' toilets, which were above the canteen, up two flights of stairs. Still no-one stopped us. Once we started climbing the stairs, going up sideways, with the other guys carrying a leg each and Terry now holding me under the arms, my anger and awkwardness changed to something closer to fear, try as I did not to show it. I had never been anywhere near the boys' toilets and preferred to keep it that way. Alas, this was not the case.

Because of the way Terry was holding me under the arms my dress was riding up and my undies were showing. I tried to tug it down but I couldn't reach, and Terry's mates had a good chuckle about their colour, which happened to be red. Terry told them to shut up and they did, his voice sounding like the bark of an aggressive dog. It sent a shiver down my spine and I shut up too. A number of guys squeezed past us as we climbed the stairs sideways, taking up most of the width of the stairwell, but none of them seemed to even notice anything unusual about a girl being carried up to the boys' toilets. Until one did, a senior who stopped to ask: 'What's going on here?' But even though Terry was younger and smaller than him, when he told this guy to: 'Get lost. It's none a'ya bloody business,' he did, hesitating only slightly before continuing his journey down the stairs.

It must have been pretty obvious I was not happy about the situation, though I didn't have the guts to ask for help directly, which was stupid. But when that guy disappeared down the stairs I became properly scared as we approached the top step and the sound of deep male voices bouncing off the concrete walls and floor sounded like roars. I had entered the lion's den.

Suddenly Simon appeared on the top step, standing to one side, looking down at me, a calm expression on his face, not saying anything. What was *he* doing here? I couldn't believe it. I was not happy to see him. Instead I had the distinct impression he had been waiting for us; it was too much of a coincidence otherwise, wasn't it? I couldn't look at him and turned my head the other way, never to look back. He and Terry spoke quietly to each other as I remained stretched out and exposed at their feet. Why didn't he just tell Terry to put me down? My anger rose up to overtake my fear.

Perhaps it was a coincidence after all and Simon did save me that day, but it didn't feel like it. After he and Terry had had a few words in private, I was dropped, not put down with any care, but dumped onto the concrete stairs, my legs only fractionally ahead of my top half so that I tripped on the second step and nearly fell, and but for my dancer's training would have fallen, in front of Simon. My legs were shaking when I finally regained the use of them and stumbled again before finding my dancer's feet to fairly fly back down those stairs out to the welcome brightness of the quad, as fast as a bolt of lightning.

* * *

Years later, when we were all in our twenties, I found out that one of the Toughie guys in our year had felt so guilty about all the kids he'd bullied at school that he killed himself. Beforehand he tracked down these kids, now adults, and apologised to each of them for the way he had treated them at school. Apparently they were all quite forgiving, and told him not to worry about it. But he couldn't live with himself and left a note saying as much. It was not Terry or anyone else I'd had much to do with. It was Alan, Jodie's date the night of Simon's party.

* * *

My last day at Killarney was a Wednesday. On the Monday I had to meet with the school principal to say a formal goodbye. I had never been to the principal's office before or even spoken to him, and I was anxious that something I might say could jeopardise my leaving. I still couldn't quite believe I was actually getting to leave school to study ballet full-time, and the last days, so near and yet so far from this dream goal, were almost the hardest, as I could all but taste the freedom but didn't dare take a bite.

The principal's upstairs office looked out over the quad through a large window behind his desk. I guessed that explained why he, for one, hadn't seen me carted across the quad that day like a sack of potatoes. He would have been facing the wrong way. I probably should have said something to him or someone else about what happened that day. I don't know why I didn't exactly. But I guess it had something to do with feeling that nothing had really happened worth telling and embarrassment that whatever hadn't happened, hadn't happened to me. Also there was no-one I trusted enough at school any more, not even Jodie, who had briefly dated Terry, to tell it to. Perhaps it was my fault for ever having had anything to do with the Toughies in the first place; clearly not the right group for me.

The principal sat behind his desk asking me about my plans. I sat facing him, feeling somewhat awkward. I was trying to explain to someone who didn't even know who Margot Fonteyn was that my dream was to become the next Margot Fonteyn. I mentioned the Royal Ballet in England, to which he nodded, like that meant something to him. I guess I wasn't the only Australian who wanted to make it big in England. But we weren't exactly connecting. Then he surprised me by saying: 'You could be whatever you wanted to be, Sally.' Could I? Since when? Had he seen my science grades? I didn't know what he was talking about. Then I wondered: 'Is he trying to tell me something?' namely that I should keep my options open; that wanting to be the world's next greatest ballerina might not be my best option. I was so paranoid that I still didn't look like a ballet dancer I was prepared to believe that a man who didn't seem to know the first thing about ballet had the idea that I wasn't totally suited to it. The last thing I thought was that he meant what he said.

Not wanting to encourage him along that line of thinking lest he began to suggest alternatives that involved me staying on at school to complete my education, I only managed an awkward smile in response. Fortunately that was all he seemed to require and he let me go after that with a handshake and a good luck wish. I thanked him for that, I think, before exiting his office at a fairly dignified pace then picking up speed along the corridor to run down the carpeted stairs back out to the quad, almost as quickly as I had run down the stairs from the boys' toilets, feeling the principal might call me back at any moment to say he'd changed his mind.

On the last Wednesday at Killarney I excused myself early from French class as usual to catch the bus to Belrose for pas de deux class. However, I couldn't say the usual 'au revoir', because I wasn't coming back, so I said a simple goodbye in English to my favourite teacher and she replied in English too, making an exception to her 'speak only French in the classroom' rule. I appreciated it.

I walked through the silent and subdued school, feeling like the only person alive, out towards the front gate, smiling so hard I almost laughed out loud. At the front gate I turned back for one last look at the ugly cream brick and black steel-framed building, not unlike a prison, and because I was leaving it behind, felt a slight lift in my opinion of the place, but only slight. Then it was off down the steep descent of Starkey Street, picking up pace till I was all but running, as light on my feet as any runaway ever was.

Chapter 11

An Absentminded Professor en Pointe

Sometime between leaving school in the December of that year and starting full-time ballet in the January, I rubbed off my face in a chlorine pool, as if rubbing off the past to start afresh. It was possibly the world's first face peel, except that I didn't *mean* to rub off my face exactly. Of course, it wasn't my *whole* face that I rubbed off, just the top couple of layers of green-brown 'olive' skin to reveal a shiny, raw pink skin underneath. I had been in the pool for several hours and must have casually rubbed my face at some point while in the water, because when I finally went to get changed to go home I looked in the mirror – always a mistake – and found my face was a patchwork quilt of colours, which wouldn't do for my fresh start. So, after a brief pause to consider my options (there was only one) I hurried back to the pool, sunk down to the bottom to be left alone to my work and set both hands vigorously to work rubbing off the rest of my face. I apologise to anyone who was in the pool that day; I might have left rather a lot of motley old skin behind in the water. But it was all in a good cause, as when I returned to the changing room mirror I was happily surprised to see that my face was now more or less the one colour: pink.

The only *slight* problem with my new face was that when the pink faded, the off-white colour that emerged in place of the previous olive matched my hair colour exactly. This, according to my dance teachers, made my hairline disappear on stage when my hair was pulled back in a bun, as it had to be most of the time. From a distance, under the stage lighting, I apparently looked bald, which evidently did nothing to improve my head-to-body-size ratio, by effectively adding to the size of my head to reach alienesque proportions. Something would have to be done. As I could not change the colour of my face – *again* – or the size of my head, it was suggested by Mr Barnes, our immaculately groomed, contemporary-classical dance teacher who was particularly bothered by my bald alien look, that I dye my hair. I didn't mind this idea entirely. Although I quite *liked* the colour of my hair by this stage as it had deepened a shade or two on its prematurely-aged wispy white, I had always admired dark hair and Margot Fonteyn's well-defined blue-black hairline on the cover of her autobiography that was my ballet bible at this age practically made me weep with envious admiration every time I gazed upon it, and so I thought this might be my chance to get closer to my idol and achieve the classic ballet look.

Unfortunately, the immaculate Mr Barnes did not think black was my colour. My hairline was *not* Margot Fonteyn's indeed, hers being low and smoothly arched and everything you want in a hairline for ballet, and mine being high with a sharp widow's peak. If I dyed my hair black I would look like Eddie Munster, which was no great improvement on bald alien. Instead, Mr Barnes suggested auburn.

I did not exactly know what colour auburn was, nor did Mum, who had never dyed her hair on account of having a thick head of dark brown hair that didn't need dying – I got my hair, forehead *and* hairline from Dad. So when Mum and I went together to Franklins supermarket to look for hair dyes we were a little unsure, but pleasantly surprised to discover 'auburn' marked on the side of a box of No Frills hair dye. There was no auburn colour sample on the box, which was plain white with black lettering in the signature No Frills style. This made me a little nervous but Mum assured me that the coloured packaging on the other brands of hair dye was what you paid extra for and the dye itself is exactly the same. I could not argue with this reasoning, so No Frills auburn it was.

No Frills auburn turned out to be orange. They should really have put 'orange' on the side of the box, and perhaps a picture of the fruit, if they included pictures on their packages, which they didn't, because black and white fruit is depressing. When Mr Barnes and Mrs P together saw me for the first time with my No Frills 'auburn' hair, they were both rendered uncharacteristically speechless. This proved a most effective and efficient way of telling me I hadn't quite achieved auburn. When they did finally speak, the first thing they said in unison was: 'It will grow out.' Then Mr Burns said it will look better on stage. It couldn't look any worse. And as it was a permanent hair dye it wouldn't grow out for a while. Still, at least you could see that I had hair now, even if you rather wished I didn't.

The next Sydney eisteddfod was looming and I didn't especially want to be orange for that. I needed a new demi-character dance and orange hair narrowed my options somewhat. My winning 'Bolt of Lightning' demi-character, with the head-shrinking balaclava, would take care of the orange hair problem for the Junior Championship (12-15 years), but for the Senior Championship (15-22 years), which I was eligible to enter for the first time that year, Mrs P thought I needed something slower and with more character to provide a contrast with my new classical, which was fast, like my Lightning dance. Being short and now fairly skinny, getting skinnier by the minute, with the crepe crisis ongoing (and no wonder), I had fast, flashy footwork, and had been showing off this skill at eisteddfods for the past three years, to the point where I was in danger of becoming typecast as a speed dancer. And in ballet speed will only get you so far, especially in championships.

For the championships you performed two dances: one classical dance in a tutu to show off your technique, the other a demi-character dance that could portray almost anything at all – animals or elements, historical figures or fictional characters – provided the choreography kept within the classical genre and the dance was performed *en pointe*, at least for the girls. I was excited by the prospect of a dance with more character to it, fancying I had certain dramatic abilities, especially when it came to tragedy and melodrama. To this end I had for some time had my eye on Tegan's demi-character 'The Diary of Anne Frank', a beautiful slow and lyrical dance set to the most mournful music ever composed that was full to bursting with character and impossible to watch without being moved to tears. This was what I wanted to achieve and felt I had what it took to do so – I certainly made myself cry often enough. The orange hair would be a problem but I could wear a wig. In a strange coincidence, I was studying *The Diary of Anne Frank* in correspondence English that year and totally identified with the wilful, misunderstood and not entirely elegant Anne as if I was indeed Jewish. I started a diary. I shed tragic tears in the bathroom – for Anne. Now it was my chance to take her story to the stage and do justice to it as only someone who understood Anne like I did could. The fact that Tegan was disqualified from entering the Senior Championship that year having won it the previous year, with the help of that dance, made it all seem like it was truly meant to be.

Unfortunately, Mrs P (who was actually Jewish) did not agree and decided instead that I should be an absentminded professor – an obvious alternative. Still, I did not see it coming, unlike everything else that had ever happened to me in my life, and when Mrs P announced it in the studio I laughed, thinking she must be joking, then cried, knowing she wasn't (she was only *half* Jewish). Meanwhile, I wasn't entirely sure what exactly an absentminded professor was. All I really knew was that it wasn't Anne Frank. Indeed, as it transpired, what Mrs P had in mind for my absentminded professor was about as far from Anne Frank as a character could get. I was to be a dithering old man in glasses and a shabby grey wig, which would at least solve the orange-hair problem. Perhaps that was Mrs P's thinking. Alternatively, I wondered if Dad, who was essentially an absentminded professor in the flesh, had inspired Mrs P to choose such an unlikely dance for the Senior Championship for me, taking the 'senior' part a little too seriously, if you asked me. (No-one did.) I'd never seen an old man in a ballet competition before and never thought that particularly strange.

Fortunately, there was little time that year to worry about being cast as a bumbling old man instead of a heroic young girl. These things happen. The eisteddfod was not until September and in the meantime I was ever so slightly busy studying dance full time, taking classes in ballet, jazz, modern, pas de deux and character six days a week, and School Certificate Maths, English, French, Science, Geography and Cooking ('Home Science') by correspondence at night on Sundays and on the bus to Belrose of a morning, except for the cooking, which couldn't be done on the bus. It was not called *home* science for nothing. And apart from the cooking, which I became increasingly interested in the less I ate, and Anne Frank's diary, which I read and re-read obsessively, my correspondence studies generally suffered in competition with my dance studies.

By this time I had moved onto a strict breakfast-only diet, except for Saturdays, when I ate more or less whatever I wanted, whenever I wanted. This fairly drastic dieting regime was gradually instigated in response to Mrs P's Wednesday morning weigh-in sessions in the studio for all the full-time students, exercises in public humiliation that were not for the faint of heart or fat of thigh. I began by cutting out Tuesday night's dinner, then Monday, then Sunday, and by mid-year I was only eating dinner on Saturdays. Lunch followed a similar pattern. The system worked well and I lost enough weight for Mrs P to tell me one wonderful Wednesday that I didn't need to lose any more. The other girls hated me that day. It was one of the happiest days of my life, even if my drastic dieting didn't exactly make concentrating on my schoolwork any easier.

Somehow my reduced weight (37 kilograms) and low calorie intake didn't impact on my energy levels in the studio. On the contrary, I seemed possessed of an increased energy, as if dancing was feeding me in place of food – if I was a little shaky, with all that sacrificial virtue, come Friday. But in Tuesday's character class, with our larger-than-life teacher, Rita Dubovsky – an authentic black-haired, black-eyed Russian defector no less – for added inspiration, I set my red character shoes flying possessed of an energy that was downright patriotic. Rita's husband Marc played a frantic piano accordion accompaniment and with Rita calling out to me over the top of it: 'You huv ze Rrussian blud, Sarlly!' there was truly no stopping me. Home at last! No need to run for the hills ever again; the hills had come to me.

★ ★ ★

Mrs P was a more entrepreneurial dance teacher than most, and wanting to give her full-time students as much performance practice as she could, that year we also spent a good amount of time out of the studio. She called us the Sydney Youth Ballet dancers and booked us to dance in some of the most unlikely places all over Sydney. We performed in a proper castle that was tucked away in the bush, quite likely the only bush castle in the world, and on the cliff top above Long Reef Beach – where I had once feared for my life perched high on Mr Crane's shoulders – dressed as seagulls, for Mrs P's *Jonathon Livingston Seagull* ballet.

As real seagulls swooped by, eyeing us with suspicion, the cameras of the Australian Film and Television School filmed us for our records and their training; we didn't just dress up as seagulls and dance on a cliff top for the hell of it. We performed in a living room in Sydney's poshest suburb, Potts Point, for a select audience of potential fundraisers, the highlight of which for me was the *petits fours* served up afterwards that I could – and did – eat, the day being Saturday.

There were several performances *outside* the Sydney Opera House, on a shallow stage set up for the purpose, with the Harbour Bridge as a dramatic backdrop, and more seagulls eyeing us sideways, as well as at Manly Corso by the beach, with bronzed beachgoers cruising past in bikinis and board shorts, wondering what we were doing by the beach in our tutus and tights.

But my favourite, and possibly least likely, dance venue we found ourselves performing in that year was in the grounds of the Gladesville mental asylum, where we danced in bare feet, on the cool green grass, with the wind in our hair, watched by the curious inmates crowding at their windows behind bars. No need to explain why it was *my* favourite venue; green grass as far as the eye could see, and madness contained. If all Australia were like this, there'd be no need to run for the hills. Alas, it was only the mental asylum.

The reason we found ourselves dancing in the grounds of a mental asylum was not for the purpose of lending substance to the inmates' fantasies of garden nymphs, though that might have been a positive spin-off of the exercise, but to give the students of the Australian Film and Television School an interesting backdrop for their film. Specifically, to provide a backdrop for the duo 'Evergreen' set to an instrumental version of Barbara Streisand's song of that name.

Miraculously, I was one of the two dancers selected to dance 'Evergreen', though my green eyes might have factored into the selection (we wore green dresses). The other dancer was the dark-eyed Tegan. After filming the two of us dancing in the all-over green, with the rest of the company and inmates watching, the school's director decided he wanted to get some close-up shots of 'Evergreen' back in their studios. Reluctant to leave the green, I consoled myself that I'd likely find my way back there some day, one way or another.

In the Film and Television School studios in Ryde, Tegan and I donned our pointe shoes and ran through the three-minute dance several times in an attempt to achieve the best camera angles and close-ups. But something wasn't right. Mrs P, supervising the operation with her KGB eye for perfection, wasn't happy with the playback. We began again, one more time, and this time, while I was dancing my brief solo segment following Tegan's slightly longer solo, Mrs P whispered something to the director. Suddenly the main camera, mounted on a hefty trolley, was violently swung round to focus on Tegan, who was standing stock still, with her head bowed elegantly to one side. There the camera remained throughout my solo and on the playback it was clear why. There was Audrey Hepburn, her dark dreamy beauty accentuated by the pale green dress. Why would the camera ever leave her indeed? It was a wrap. Everyone was happy, even me; because you're supposed to dance as if no-one is watching you and now I didn't have to pretend. I should never have left the asylum.

* * *

As it turns out, you can only get so far as a ballet company without boys, and we dancers of the Sydney Youth Ballet (fourteen in total) were all girls. In the early eighties in Sydney, ballet-dancing males were not so easy to come by, so to improve our chances of attracting males to the full-time school and company Mrs P decided to move our base to the city. Our new city studio was located on the ground floor of the Sydney Institute of Technology building on Broadway in Ultimo, and once moved in, sure enough, we attracted several boys. Unfortunately, most of them were not dancers.

Having to use the communal bathroom facilities in the ground floor foyer beyond the studio meant that at frequent intervals throughout the day, dancing girls in skimpy leotards and tights were brought into close contact with male students who were not used to seeing dancing girls in their midst, with the inevitable result. I was safe, you'll be glad to hear, still looking younger than I was, with the crepe crisis ongoing. But many of the other dancers weren't so safe. Rather, within a few weeks of our move to the city several of the dancers had boyfriends and Mrs P considered perhaps we'd better retreat back to Belrose. Boyfriends were not good for the figure, you see, and the Wednesday weigh-in scales had followed us to the city, like the dancers' albatross that they are. These sessions had been weepy enough ordeals back in Belrose, especially for those dancers who had come from country towns out of Sydney and were living away from home for the first time, which was a fair few of them, most of whom claimed they were homesick, which was apparently not good for the figure either. But with boyfriends on board, these weekly weigh-in sessions became weeping melodramas of epic proportions. 'My boyfriend doesn't think I'm fat!' and 'I want to go *home!*' were frequently heard laments issued from atop the Wednesday weigh-in scales once we'd moved to the city. So the move was not a total success, though we did eventually attract two males to the company who could actually dance: Daryn and Nigel.

The move to the city also meant much more travel at either end of the day. The upside of this was that I now had a bus and a train ride on which to complete my correspondence work. The downside was that I had to get up at six every morning to properly enjoy my only meal of the day and make it into the studio by 8.15, to warm up for class at 9 am. There was never a spare seat on the 7.10 bus to Chatswood and completing schoolwork standing up on a packed, moving bus is not as easy as it sounds. With a total of two hours extra travelling time each day, Tegan, who lived further from the city than I did, gave up her correspondence studies shortly after the move. I would have given up too, but unlike the Higher School Certificate, which she had been studying, the School Certificate I was studying is compulsory. One battled on.

With some vital males on board and a few more females too, Mrs P decided to stage her first full-length professional ballet production at the end of that year, and chose *The Nutcracker*. This was to be performed in the grand old Regent Theatre (since demolished) on George Street, Sydney's main street, the street where a couple of decades prior my great uncle Sir Charles Lloyd Jones was sent off in a grand state funeral with thousands lining the street to show their respect. My George Street venture would be a slightly less grand affair, though thousands would come to watch us too, and Mrs P was bringing out a male guest artist from the Royal Ballet in London to dance the lead male role. So it would be a rather grander than usual affair for the company – and for me. Indeed I was going to be lucky to get any correspondence work done at all. With my fairy-like build and soloist status I felt I was guaranteed the lead female role of the Sugar Plum Fairy, especially since there were to be two casts, so I wouldn't have to compete with Tegan.

I had forgotten about Carlotta. Carlotta was a South African dancer who had joined us shortly after our move to the city. She was a particularly strong dancer on pointe, who was also quite petite, though not as petite as either Tegan or me. And fairies really should be as petite as possible, shouldn't they? Evidently not. Carlotta was cast as the second Sugar Plum Fairy, even though she had only recently joined the company and I had been with Mrs P since I was six, also quite a bit longer than Tegan. I thought this longevity and loyalty should count for something, and it possibly did a bit, but not enough. For Mrs P cast me as the third Sugar Plum Fairy, or the 'understudy', as she put it, though she promised me that if I 'rose to the challenge' I could dance the Sugar Plum Fairy opposite our famous guest artist from the Royal Ballet for one or two performances.

It was better than nothing. I rose to the challenge you can be sure. My correspondence work went out the window entirely (except for the cooking) as I threw myself into learning and mastering not only the part of the Sugar Plum Fairy but the various other dances I would be performing when not dancing the Sugar Plum Fairy, including the Waltz of the Flowers and the Snowflakes in the first act, and the Mirlitons and the Spanish trios in the second act. I was practically dancing in my sleep trying to master almost all the female dance parts in the entire ballet. Fortunately *The Nutcracker* score is by Tchaikovsky, a Russian, so I had an advantage there.

As our guest artist, Wayne Eagling, could not join us from London until the week before opening night, we rehearsed the main pas de deux with Daryn and Nigel. As there was no third male available, I had to watch these rehearsals and mark them out with my invisible partner in the background, waiting for a quick run-through with Daryn after Tegan had finished with him. Then, when 'Mr Eagling' arrived, I waited some more through their long rehearsals to have a quick run-through with him at the last minute.

Despite it being rushed, our run-through went well and Mrs P said I could dance Sugar Plum for the second matinee. This was only one performance, not two, and only a matinee, but it was a whole lot better than nothing and I was fairly beside myself with excitement at the prospect. Of course there was still the possibility that some debilitating injury or disfiguring disease might befall Tegan or Carlotta (or both) in the meantime. That was something to cling to.

Unfortunately, this did not happen. Tegan and Carlotta did not break anything or get sick for the duration of our ten-day *Nutcracker* season at the Regent. So that meant, for me, it was all riding on the last matinee performance, my big chance to dance the lead role in a major ballet, with a dancer from the Royal Ballet who had once danced with Margot Fonteyn, indeed. I was delirious with excitement. The whole family bought tickets to that matinee, even Auntie Robin. Even Tim, who had to take a day off his Saturday job at Manly fun pier to be there; even Babs, who found it difficult to go a Saturday without riding a horse. And even Dad, who still preferred to spend his Saturdays in the library and, if he could, to forget he even had a dancing daughter. Indeed even Nana, who was now 95. Everybody and everything was set for my grand debut as a fully-fledged ballerina dancing opposite a man from the best ballet company in the world. What could possibly go wrong?

What went wrong was that I got a tiny bit overexcited with all the build-up to my big debut and leapt the wrong way in the Spanish dance during the Friday night performance. When I came into the theatre the next morning, ready to run through the pas de deux with Mr Eagling on stage before the performance, I found my good friend Min (Melinda) with a worried expression on her face, telling me 'Mrs P wants to see you backstage' and showing me where Mrs P was standing waiting for me in the shadows under the stairs (like a troll), before leaving us in a hurry. This was strange.

'I'm sorry, Sally,' Mrs P began, without any kind of greeting, so that I knew something was definitely wrong. But in my wildest dreams (or rather nightmares) I could never have imagined what she was about to say next. 'I'm sorry, Sally, but I can't let you dance Sugar Plum with Mr Eagling today. You're just not ready.'

I didn't quite catch every word she said because I was truly in shock, and couldn't believe what I was hearing. My mouth hung open and I couldn't close it.

'You know you jumped the wrong way in the Spanish dance last night, don't you? Well, that won't do, I'm afraid. I can't have that. What if you jumped the wrong way in the pas de deux? I can't take that chance. You have to learn your lesson, Sally. You need to grow up.' Mrs P went on until I had no choice but to accept this was real. She meant what she was saying. I was not going to dance Sugar Plum.

But no; that simply could not be.

I began to beg and sob: 'Please, Mrs P, *please* don't do this. I promise I can do it. I ... I ... I've worked so h-h-hard. I won't let you down. I pro-o-o-omise.' I stuttered and spluttered as I pleaded with Mrs P to change her mind, standing there under the stairs, not caring what I looked like or who heard me. But Mrs P stood her ground, shaking her head and frowning at me as I begged and sobbed, the heavy stage make-up I had put on so carefully that morning in order to have plenty of time to rehearse with Mr Eagling now running down my face in thick black tears.

'No, Sally. Next time, perhaps; you have to learn your lesson,' Mrs P repeated, without sympathy, before walking off up the stairs to the dressing rooms, her feet overhead going clomp, clomp, clomp, as if stomping on my head.

When I realised there was no hope, I stood there under the stairs, limp with defeat and despair, before taking off at a run along the backstage corridor that was painted blood red to add to the drama, my tears making the walls bleed, then crashing back out the heavy stage door into the bright glare of the daylight, swearing I *hated* Mrs P and would never dance for her again.

* * *

Two and a half months earlier, the Senior Championship of the 44th City of Sydney Eisteddfod took place in somewhat less grand surrounds in a small theatre on the second floor of the

Teachers' Federation building on Clarence Street. I was number 38 of around 50 entrants. We danced our classicals first and I felt I had done what I could in my difficult up-tempo dance to show off my fast feet, musicality and 'dance quality'; the quality of dancing 'from the heart' that Mrs P prided herself on teaching her students. Mum took time out of her temping job in the city to come and watch my classical and said I got more applause than the other dancers before me had. This was not definitive proof I had danced well – ballet mothers could be a little bit biased – but I was encouraged anyway.

It was a long wait then to perform my absentminded professor through the remaining classicals and 30-odd demi-character dances before it was my turn. Mum went back to work in the meantime to return in good time to watch my professor. She had a special interest in that dance, having found the music for it herself, taping it off the radio one day, missing the beginning as she leapt up off the settee to press the record button, with the tape at the ready. Mrs P had asked her to find a suitable piece of music for an absentminded professor dance, not having time to do it herself and, somewhat miraculously, Mum had done exactly that, if not quite capturing the whole piece of music. But the lack of a clean beginning somehow added to the absentmindedness of the piece and although it was the most unlikely piece of ballet music you ever heard, with random clashes and crashes throughout and a wonky off-beat melody, it fitted the dance perfectly.

Still, I was fairly glad I would be performing this wacky dance in a disguise. And it was a thorough disguise. Along with my shaggy grey wig and thick-rimmed glasses, an old pair of Dad's with the lenses removed, I wore a grey stick-on moustache, a lab coat borrowed from the Martians next door, whose boys had all, sure enough, grown up to be science and engineering students, and to complete the picture, a white school shirt of Tim's and pair of Dad's grey trousers hoisted up and bundled together with one of his belts wrapped around twice. To this I added, with a little less consistency, a pair of black-painted pointe shoes, hoping the black would make them look a little less like ballet shoes and more like street shoes. The Martian boys had also lent me a rack of test tubes as a prop, clearly still feeling guilty about those contagious chickens, and these – the test tubes, not the chickens – were to stand on a desk in the front corner of the stage to be knocked over, preferably without breaking, as part of my absentminded act. I'd never had much success with test tubes in Science class at school, but perhaps I would do better with them on stage. Stranger things have happened.

Standing backstage, waiting for the adjudicator to ring her bell to announce she was ready for the next dancer, dressed as an absentminded professor, I was not feeling entirely confident. Not my usual relaxed self. The dancers backstage had laughed when they'd seen me dressed in character, in such a non-sneering way that it seemed they thought I had given up, which was a little off-putting. But I couldn't blame them; I didn't exactly feel primed for dancing gold.

The adjudicator's bell finally rings. My 'Absentminded Professor' is announced by the convenor and I cringe hearing how odd that concept sounds broadcast to a theatre full of ballet dancers, their teachers and parents, not to mention the all-important adjudicator. But there is no turning back now. I brace myself for the music to launch itself without introduction, relieved at least that the dance is not technically demanding.

When the first note sounds I lunge onto the stage *en pointe*, wobbling my head to the wonky music, stumbling along the diagonal to finish slightly off-centre. The audience chuckle immediately, which is a bit of a surprise and throws me a little. I should have been expecting it, but I wasn't somehow. Ballet eisteddfods are such competitive environments, especially at the senior level, that the last thing you expect from the audience is laughter, even when you're dressed in a grey wig and stick-on moustache. The laughter makes me want to laugh too, but I know I shouldn't; my moustache might fall off. I do my best to stay in character and maintain a level of composure as I carry on my wonky way and the audience's chuckling turns quickly to full-blown laughter. I am careful not to stare at the adjudicator's writing light glowing in the centre of the dark sea that is the audience; normally the focal point of your presentation. I have decided it would not do for an absentminded character to eyeball the adjudicator. Instead I fix my absentminded gaze somewhere off to the side, and bumble on.

The whole theatre is laughing now, even the girls backstage, who I can see watching me from the mezzanine level where the dressing rooms are, laughing with their mouths wide open. They really must be glad I've taken myself out of the running. I have to bite down hard on my tongue to stop from catching the laughter bug, while struggling to hear the music and remember my steps, which are carefully choreographed to *look* absentminded but are not in fact absent of mind, as it were.

When I fall to my knees and crawl under the old desk, knocking over the test tubes on top (not breaking them) and emerge the other side on my knees, with a befuddled look straight to the audience, I really can't hear the music for the laughter. The walls themselves appear to be laughing. It's a wonder they don't crumble and fall down. Nothing would surprise me now.

I am truly dancing deaf, doing my best from memory to shuffle here, stumble there, pausing with a troubled frown, trying to recall my last genius inspiration (tricky), all without clear musical cues, and feeling genuinely befuddled, which probably adds to the humour of the performance. But the audience has the serious giggles now and can't stop laughing whatever I do. I could probably do a strip tease and they'd carry on laughing. Perhaps that's not a good example. I am just about biting my tongue off trying to keep a straight face, as even the worry about having lost the music is not enough to make my situation seem anything but hilarious.

Somehow I make my way to the end of the dance that is marked, not by the last note of music, but by the applause that erupts over the top of the laughter that doesn't stop. I stop when I hear it and stand to face the audience, trying to stay in character with a genuinely befuddled look on my face. It is customary to curtsey at the end of your dance – if you're a girl. I just remember in time that today I am not a girl but an old man and should bow instead, which I do with my head at an absentminded angle, which produces more laughter and applause.

Finally, I shuffle off stage into the safety of the wings with some relief, as the laughter and applause continue behind me. 'That was brilliant!' the girls backstage say to me, practically pushing me back on stage to take a second bow. I shuffle back on, genuinely dazed, wondering if the world has gone a little bit crazy. Nobody ever takes a second bow in an eisteddfod and your competitors never tell you 'that was brilliant'.

Later on, after all the competitors have performed their demi-character dances, I sit in the packed auditorium in my tracksuit, my professor costume stuffed into a plastic bag at my feet, waiting with Mum and the other dancers, teachers and parents for the adjudicator to return with her decision. Nobody is laughing now. The auditorium has returned to its more usual strained, subdued hush, every single competitor hoping to win or at least get a place. The lights are dimmed and I can just make out Claire Novak, the frontrunner, sitting up the back. Claire is from the Queensland School of Dance, which always sends a strong contingent of dancers to the Sydney Eisteddfod. Why, I don't know; I guess they must not have their own eisteddfod. Claire was placed second in the Championship the previous year, second to Anne Frank. I didn't see her 'Dying Swan' demi-character this year, but I heard *it* was brilliant.

I wonder how the adjudicator is supposed to compare a dying swan and an absentminded professor. One dance is almost purely classical and the other almost purely character; neither is technically a 'demi' character. Carlotta, who is also entered in the competition, dances a 'grieving widow' demi-character. I'm not sure how that is supposed to be compared with my dance either. But her powerful well-trained technique, never before seen at a Sydney eisteddfod, makes her another definite contender for first. My dancing friend Min, as tall as I am short, is also a strong contender. With her long lean neck and arms she dances her 'Jonathon Livingston Seagull' demi-character, with a unique elegance and grace, qualities my dancing decidedly lacks. When I look over, I can see her in the auditorium sitting close to the front with her ballet-mad father – an artist from Venice, no less.

Up against these strong dancers, with their dramatic and moving demi-characters, as well as all the other dancers, most of whom I don't know, I can't help feeling that my function in the competition was to provide the light relief, not to be taken seriously. I sink down in my seat and cast a doubtful glance at the silly grey curls of the professor's wig protruding from the bag at my feet. Mum sits next to me, almost as anxious as I am.

Finally, the adjudicator stands in the centre of the stage with her assistant over to one side next to the table of trophies that forms a miniature city of golden skyscrapers gleaming under the stage lights. Dressed in all-over black, the adjudicator is almost as lean as the microphone stand she stands, poised, in front of, as she begins her address to the audience, now reduced to an agonising state of pin-drop suspense. The three 'honourable mentions' announced together go to Annabelle, one of the country girls from our full-time school, who has had consistent trouble with the Wednesday weigh-in scales, but has overcome much of that for the eisteddfod, and two dancers I don't know. I am happy for Annabelle. I did not want an honourable mention. Then Min gets fourth. When she stands to go up to the stage to collect her trophy, I can just make out her father smiling proudly, perhaps a hint of disappointment on his handsome face. Fourth is the first trophy, but the least of them. It's sort of winning and losing at the same time. I know, because I've been placed fourth before. I feel a bit sorry for my friend, but overtaking that is now the exquisite hope rising that there might be just room for me in the top three, along with Carlotta and Claire.

Then third place goes to a male dancer, a wild-card entry no-one seems to have heard of before and my heart sinks. Now I feel envy for Min, mixed with resentment that I didn't even get an honourable mention. Light relief indeed.

When Claire takes second – for the second time – my envy leaps to Carlotta. I can't believe she has beaten Claire Novak! I am the deepest green with envy of her. I am also close to tears. I know Carlotta is stronger *en pointe* than I am and I honestly can't believe she wouldn't have been awarded so much as an honourable mention at least. She must have won. Still, with the frontrunner out, everyone who hasn't been mentioned or placed yet is seriously hoping to win. You can feel the hope hanging like humidity in the air. Sometimes you can't pick the winner; why not them? I am no different to the rest of these hopefuls.

The adjudicator begins to introduce the winner. I am so strung out by this point that my hearing has shut down for all but the basics. I am concentrating on my number being called with a meditator's focus. But even that, when it does come, I don't hear. 'Ballet is meant to be entertaining, after all' is what Mum tells me later on the adjudicator said by way of introducing the winner. *She* heard that and would always remember it, because that was when she knew I had won. But I didn't hear it or even my number when it was called. Indeed, even when Mum sprang up out of her seat and cried: 'We got it! That's your number, Sal!' I didn't fully register I had won, and looked up at her from my seat, somewhat embarrassed at her public display of enthusiasm, which was rather out of character for her. She was not a typical ballet mum. I was glad the lights were dimmed.

Then it hit me: 'I *have* won! I have won. I have *won*! I have won the Senior Championship!' and with that bolt of lightning realisation I was consumed by such a dazzling white light of bliss that it blocked out everything else and I don't remember a thing that happened afterwards. How I managed to walk up to the stage to receive my trophy I'll never know. It's a wonder I didn't faint.

Chapter 12

My brilliant year

So I won the Senior Championship. Indeed, at fifteen, I was the youngest ever to win it, and the first to ever win it dressed as an absentminded professor. Who would have thought? Well, to be fair, I think Mrs P must have thought. That is, she must have had some idea prior to the eisteddfod that the adjudicator that year would be receptive to such an unlikely demi-character, unlike the adjudicator the previous year who had awarded the prize to one of the saddest dances ever choreographed, Tegan's Anne Frank, a very different dance indeed. And to win the Senior Championship two years running, as Mrs P had done, as well as getting a fourth and an honourable mention, proved she knew what she was doing more than most, as we were competing with dancers from dozens of dance schools across Sydney and other cities around Australia. The adjudicators each year were announced ahead of time and savvy teachers, I guess, took notice of their different dance backgrounds. The adjudicator for that 44th Eisteddfod had a background in dance theatre, a type of dance that incorporates comedy.

And so, when later on that year Mrs P smashed my heart to smithereens by telling me at the last minute I couldn't dance the Sugar Plum Fairy and in the heat of the moment I vowed I would never dance for her again, it was that bumbling professor and that dazzling white light of blissful victory that eventually brought me round, to open that heavy stage door again and walk back inside, past the fancy principal's dressing room on the ground floor that I would now not be using, and up those same stairs she had climbed so cruelly to the general dressing room to re-do my make-up, also in smithereens, and get ready for Snowflakes instead of Sugar Plum. However tough she was, and the Toughies of Killarney had nothing on Mrs P at her toughest, she was still, and always would be, boss of the ballet bliss.

Dad was drying the dishes when Mum and I arrived home late from the Senior Championship and didn't stop to come out of the kitchen to greet us at the door, as he would normally have done. Mum had phoned earlier, before the prize-giving, to say we would be late and to tell him to go ahead and eat dinner without her, something he particularly hated doing. And we had stayed even later than the time she had told him to expect us back, both of us basking in the bliss, so Dad was making his disapproval known. Disapproval of *me*, at least, not of Mum; he never disapproved of Mum.

It was after nine when we got home, so not terribly late, but it was a no-grog night for Dad, which didn't help. Tim and Babs were in their rooms. Mum rushed in brightly to tell Dad the good news, while I hung back in the living room, wary of Dad in this mood and not wanting to rub his face in my success. Sitting on the piano stool I could hear most of what was going on in the kitchen on the other side of a thin half wall, watched over by Paolo, who remained standing on our piano, grown up a few years now, wearing a suit jacket and long pants – clothes that were still much too big for him – and with the same disgruntled scowl on his face.

'She's the youngest ever to win the Senior Championship, you know,' I heard Mum tell Dad, in that slightly too-bright and breezy voice of hers that made me cringe a little for Dad's sake, followed by a mumble from Dad that I strained to make out, wanting to know if he was proud of me at all. There was the heavy crunch clunk then of what must have been a dinner plate being put away in the cupboard, slotted between two others. It made a resentful, scraping sound, as if speaking for Dad what he couldn't, or wouldn't, say with words. 'Why not leave the dishes, hon? They'll dry overnight. That's all I do,' Mum said then, repeating the same suggestion she had made to Dad almost every night since he took over the drying up following his retirement. But Dad didn't listen; tonight of all nights he needed those dishes to show that while *some* people were out till all hours dancing, keeping their mother out late after a long day in the office, others were slaving away.

Another clunk and scrape of a plate being stacked provided Dad's answer to Mum's suggestion; a good five-minute interval between that and the last plate. Dad was the slowest plate dryer in the business, it's fair to say, partly to give his hands something to do and partly to make a point of being busy, I always thought, but also because he was genuinely absentminded, with his mind wandering off to more abstract matters, such as economic theory, so that he forgot he was drying plates and began solving the world's problems until the plate in his hand practically screamed out for mercy: 'I'm dry already! *Please* put me down!' How ironic on this night of all nights, if that was in fact the case. Dad, of course, had no idea *how* I won the Championship, beyond his very general and unflattering idea of what ballet was (frivolous, selfish; too focused on appearances). He would not have even realised that his own clothes and old glasses had been leant to the professor project. Mum thought it better not to tell him.

After a while I went to bed, well before all the plates were dried but not before Mum got me to display my eisteddfod trophies and ribbons on the dining room table, which was clearly visible from the kitchen. It had been a successful eisteddfod for me altogether. I'd won second in the Junior Championship with my slower classical and 'Bolt of Lightning' dances; another second for my Russian character dance, for which Rita had expressed a certain black-eyed Russian rage that I hadn't won, and another first for 'Evergreen' in the open-age duo, trio and quartet section. The blue and red ribbons and tall golden trophies fairly swamped our small dining table and were still there standing proud in the morning, as was Dad, still refusing to congratulate me, though all the dishes at least had finally been dried up and put away.

* * *

Dad was in for a tough year. For the year after that Senior Championship win, excluding the slight setback of jumping the wrong way in the Spanish dance and missing out on dancing with Wayne Eagling of the Royal Ballet, would be a winning year for me. Indeed I would be back to jump the right way on that grand Regent Theatre stage and reclaim the spotlight the following year in the comedic ballet Coppelia, and with a dance partner who, as far as I was concerned, was even more of a prize than the royal Mr Eagling.

Meanwhile, I left schoolwork behind for the foreseeable future, gaining my School Certificate, even in Science, possibly due to having danced as a mad scientist that year. Indeed I was even awarded top in the year for Home Science, thanks to my growing obsession with food – the less I ate – and the fact that no-one at the correspondence school had ever tasted any of my cooking. But I didn't need to pass my School Certificate to be offered a job, as it turned out. Because almost immediately after the Championship win I got a call from the owner of the local dancewear shop, Ballet World, to ask if I wanted to work there on Saturday morning, without having to apply for the job. My reputation preceded me, and for once in a good way. I was offered $21 for three hours easy work fitting leotards and shoes to young aspiring dancers and happily accepted the job, adding the tidy sum (less the cost of a *large* Saturday cake from the local bakery) to my little blue bank book.

And it was in Ballet World at the end of that year, that I was first asked for my autograph. Young girls, with their mothers nearby for support lest they be overcome with awe in my presence – presumably – would tentatively approach to ask, with big starstruck eyes: 'Are *you* Sally Jones?' Although I was not altogether pleased to confirm that I was the owner of that tragically ordinary name, I did confirm that I was indeed Sally Jones and agree to sign their autograph books, if with the Russian version of my name: 'Saliana Jonoptonova'.

The following year (1982) I won the national Society of Dance Arts (SODA) Scholarship and was able to add $2000 to my little blue bank book, which couldn't quite cope with the third zero but we made do somehow. Technically, the SODA money was a scholarship held in trust for me to be spent on ballet tuition once my third Northside scholarship expired, so it was not quite mine to be entered into my bank book. But never mind; it's important to keep records of these things.

Straight after the scholarship win, before I'd scarcely had a chance to change out of my tutu, I was interviewed on 2CH radio by a reverend, the 'CH' standing for church. Why exactly I was interviewed for the church channel and in such a hurry I was never entirely sure. Sometimes it's a question of why not. And as to what I told the reverend in the interview, I am not so sure either. All I know is that when I heard the recording Mum made of the interview (later to be destroyed in a blaze of unexplained cause) I would have given the $2000 back to have it undone. I could scarcely believe how little-girl squeaky and *Australian* my voice sounded, not a hint of Russian in it, as I prattled on about wanting to go to 'Eeengland', that I vowed never to submit to a radio interview by a reverend again – and never did.

Dance Australia magazine wanted an interview too. And after that full-page article appeared with a photo I was recognised on the morning bus to Chatswood and offered a seat – by a middle-aged woman. This was a bit unusual perhaps, me being only sixteen, but still flattering. Mum always complained that no-one ever offered her a seat on the bus, and she was nearly 60 (we caught different buses). That said, I refused the kind offer, as I was quite capable of standing, no longer having to complete correspondence work. But the woman wouldn't hear of it: 'You must rest your feet!' she cried in protest, with a slightly demented smile, and so what was a girl to do? I sat down in her seat, leaving her, and many others more her age than mine, to stand and stare, or rather glare at me. Such is the price of fame.

Other days I rode into the city with Mrs P, who suddenly came forward with an offer to drive me into the studio of a morning. Despite the tension between us still, this felt like a privilege indeed to be riding alone with the boss of the bliss, even if she was the most intimidating person I knew and it was not the most relaxing start to the day. Nor did she go out of her way to pick me up at my house, but instead got me to wait beside the six-lane Warringah Road highway, and when I saw her car approach and slow, but not quite stop, I had to throw myself and my hefty ballet bag into the passenger seat. Just as well I had fast feet.

Depending on the speed of the peak-hour traffic, some days I had to run beside her car to get a running leap, rather like they do in the movies, except without any stunt training. And one time, after I'd had my four wisdom teeth removed (due to a superfluity of wisdom, no doubt) and my whole head had swollen to the size of an helium balloon so that I looked more like an alien than ever, when Mrs P pulled up to where I was standing on the side of the road, threatening to cause an accident, she hastily transferred the junk she normally kept on the back seat into the passenger seat so that I might be 'more comfortable' in the back with the extra room. I wasn't *that* much more comfortable, if truth be told, but I think she was. And fair enough too; any normal person with her head swollen to extra-terrestrial proportions would have taken the day off.

During yet another relaxing drive into the studio with Mrs P, this time when I was sitting in the passenger seat after my head had returned to its relatively normal size, she suddenly reached across and gave my upper arm an almighty pinch, not unlike the pinch I had received from my brother as a baby that had caused my fury faint. I did not faint this time, but I thought about it. With no warning and having little to pinch, still weighing less than 40 kilos, I did almost scream with the pain, and doubtless would have, if not for my very high pain threshold. I think she got the bone. But never mind. Mrs P said she was testing a new theory she'd just read about on how to measure excess body fat and I had passed the test. She pronounced me 'all right', so that was all right. Still, my arm stung for the rest of the day and I couldn't help feeling that pinch test was some kind of warning. However thin I got I remained particularly paranoid about my short arms not being lean enough for ballet. And now that I knew Mrs P was watching my arms, I would have been more comfortable in the back seat. Unfortunately, I didn't have any more wisdom teeth – or teeth at all, really – left to pull out.

Indeed Mrs P was invariably watching our weight. There was a small theatre within the Institute of Technology building called Turner Hall in which we staged modest productions for primary school students. One of these productions, *A Day in the Life of a Dancer*, began with us dancers standing at the barre in our leotards and tights, going through the steps of a regular class, with Mrs P narrating up front with a microphone, doing what she could to liven things up for the kids. During one of these performances Mrs P suddenly said: 'Do you see that girl there in the front, children; the one in the dark blue leotard? That's Sally. Wave, Sally!' I waved obediently, dreading what was coming next. With Mrs P you never knew. She continued: 'You should have seen Sally when she was your age, children. You would never have believed she could become a ballet dancer. She was such a chubby little thing, really she was.'

So *that's* what was coming. I sucked in my stomach until my internal organs came out my ears and thanked God I had chosen the dark blue leotard over the pink Lycra – I would never wear *that* again – as the children giggled and my fellow dancers on stage (including Tegan) sneered with pleasure to know my shameful, chubby little secret.

* * *

Building on the strength of our successful *Nutcracker* season – despite one of the dancers jumping the wrong way *once* – Mrs P expanded her reach further. Having been the Sydney Youth Ballet, that year we became the semi-professional Sydney City Ballet company, with funding secured from the NSW Arts Council, which was quite the ballet coup. Generally, Melbourne is regarded as Australia's ballet city, being home to the Australian Ballet Company, whereas Sydney is home to the Sydney Dance Company, which specialises in modern dance. But Mrs P didn't let that stop her. She was not Russian for nothing. She hired a ballet master to take the company on tour, an Egyptian man in his thirties called Hassan, as well as a new male principal dancer, a younger man called Tim who was *not* from Egypt indeed. Nor was he my brother! I quickly re-named this Tim of 23 'Ballet Tim' to avoid a confusion of catastrophic proportions, as he would soon become the man to answer all my dreams – well, almost all.

Within a few days of meeting Ballet Tim I was ever so slightly head over heels, and not just in a literal sense when he lifted me expertly in pas de deux. I thought he was the man for me. We even looked alike; sharing the same alienesque proportions of a large head and pointy chin balanced upon a very lean, compact body; though of course he was a much better looking alien than I was. And as if this wasn't enough to prove we were made for each other, Ballet Tim had also started ballet to cure his asthma. This was such a fabulous coincidence that a reporter for *The Sun* newspaper came to write an article on our partnership, titled: 'Asthma Cure: A Ballet Career'. I tried not to wheeze during the interview, as there was no need to mention to the reporter that ballet hadn't completely cured my asthma, as it had cured Ballet Tim's, in case she thought we weren't such a perfect match after all. Besides, it wasn't ballet's fault that I continued to wheeze. That was largely thanks to Babs now keeping her horse-hair covered saddle in our bedroom, as I later worked out.

Miraculously, I wasn't the only one who thought Ballet Tim and I were meant to be together. We quickly became an 'item' in the ballet world, dancing the sexy *Don Quixote* pas de deux at venues all over Sydney, as well as the lead roles, Swanhilda and Franz, in the comic ballet *Coppélia* for the company's

Sydney season at the Regent that year. Sexy *and* funny; what more could a girl want? Not much.

We were invited to dance the *Don Q* pas de deux in the Opera House for the annual Sydney Festival of the Arts, which is about as grand as it gets in Australia. This performance was probably the pinnacle of my brilliant year; dancing the fast and flirtatious *Don Q* pas de deux with Ballet Tim on the Concert Hall stage of the Sydney Opera House – my favourite building – he in his black tights, bare chest and cropped jacket, looking every bit as sexy as a toreador, and me in my red and black tutu and orange-blonde hair stuck with gallons of hairspray to make several stiff Spanish curls around my weak hairline, doing my best to approximate his sexy Spanish lover. It wasn't perfect but it felt perfect, and the packed audience gave us a rousing reception. Even they could see we were meant for each other.

After that performance, we went backstage, sweating and smiling in equal measure, to the plush principal's dressing room we'd been assigned to share, and things promised to get even sexier, as Ballet Tim unhooked my tutu, as usual, and prepared to slip his hands beneath the black velvet bodice around my sweaty, but irresistibly slim waist. Unfortunately, something must have distracted him at that point, because instead of making his move, Ballet Tim said: 'There you go, SJ,' which was what he called me, instinctively knowing I hated my name (I wouldn't have minded *him* using it, but still), before repairing to his side of the room to take his toreador outfit off.

Disappointed as I was that Ballet Tim hadn't seized the moment to take our on-stage relationship off stage, watching him undress out of his toreador tights, while pretending to remove my false eyelashes in one of the twin, well-lit mirrors, was not a bad consolation prize. It seemed to me he knew it didn't take quite that long to remove false eyelashes and took his time about undressing for my benefit. I was encouraged. Then he popped into the ensuite shower and left the door ajar. Was that an invitation? I was inclined to think it was. I ripped off my false eyelashes then faster than you can say false, and the rest of my make-up with a great wad of Vaseline, to sit on the edge of my seat unable to decide if Ballet Tim wanted me to join him in the shower or not, my expertise in such matters being still somewhat limited.

Alas, I did not venture forth into that Opera House ensuite to join Ballet Tim in the shower that day, due to the *slight* possibility that Ballet Tim was gay and so would likely not have wanted me to join him in the shower. Indeed that was the rumour in the company, though I chose flatly not to believe it – well, almost flatly; there was a slight wrinkle of doubt in my denial. Still, Ballet Tim didn't *seem* gay to me and we were, at least as far as the ballet world was concerned, married. Indeed we had been married several times over, in front of thousands of applauding witnesses, during our many performances of *Coppélia*'s third act pas de deux. And if reviews were anything to go by, we made a most convincing couple. We also found every opportunity to laugh like lovers backstage, often while Ballet Tim kindly and uncomplainingly massaged my calf muscles to relieve my leg cramps. What was a girl to think?

And when I had my own dresser for the quick change in the second act, Ballet Tim did not protest that *he* didn't get his own personal dresser. Neither did he offer to be my personal dresser, mind, but that would have been improper, as it was only the second act and we were not yet married. He was again uncomplaining when a reporter from *Cleo* teen magazine came to interview me for their series on 'Sydney girls in the spotlight' and there was no such series for Sydney boys in their twenties. He was even helpful in explaining to me what 'a floating piece of gossamer' was, so I could understand better what was being written about me in that article, but without making me feel stupid, a balance that took special skill.

And again when the legendary comedian Barry Humphries smiled pointedly at me on one occasion as we made our exit through the theatre auditorium after a late dress rehearsal and found him warming-up on stage for his own performance that night, Ballet Tim was not jealous. He said, 'I think he likes you SJ,' and seemed happy for me. It never occurred to me that he was happy for himself, thinking 'If I can get SJ to transfer her affections to Barry Humphries I'll be off the hook. She certainly has more chance with him than she has with me.'

Nor did it occur to me later on when we took *Coppélia* on tour and Ballet Tim and I were featured together in our matrimonial costume for a special colour edition front page of the *Newcastle Herald* that Ballet Tim wasn't as happy as I was to have our union advertised across the entire Hunter region.

And if that was the case, then I guess he wouldn't have been quite as thrilled as I was to discover, as I did recently, that our appearance on national TV to advertise our Sydney season of *Coppélia* survives to this day, and for all days, on YouTube. For in that appearance, fleeting though it is, there can be no doubt that we make a handsome couple indeed, if thanks in large part to Mrs P and the extensive make-up personnel at Channel 7 spending roughly seven hours on my hair and make-up. Still, the camera never lies.

But as thrilled as I was to have Ballet Tim in my life that year, if it did have its confusions and frustrations, my brilliant year was not all about Ballet Tim. While we were touring *Coppélia* in the September of that year I left Ballet Tim behind to fly back to Sydney, with Min, to take part in the 45th City of Sydney Eisteddfod. Carlotta took over for me dancing the lead – with Ballet Tim – which was not ideal; audiences must have been disappointed not to see the advertised perfect couple, but I could not miss the eisteddfod. For at sixteen, I was finally eligible to enter Australia's top ballet competition, the Peter Stuyvesant Cultural Foundation Scholarship (today the McDonald's Cup), worth $4000 to the winner, that was held, including a glittering performance by the finalists in front of a paying audience, at the Opera House. Winning the Senior Championship and SODA were one thing, and dancing with Ballet Tim another, but I had been dreaming of winning the Stuyvesant ever since I gave up Mum's lemonade at the age of ten and committed seriously to becoming a ballerina, after which time I became a regular audience member at these finals.

And since winning the Stuyvesant was probably a slightly more realistic goal than winning Ballet Tim, I could not pass up my chance of competing in it, particularly as Tegan would not be taking part. She had been accepted into the Australian Ballet School that year and moved to Melbourne. Though even if she had still been in Sydney, her mother had never let her enter the Stuyvesant for fear she would win, take the money and run overseas, leaving her all alone (Tegan was an only child). Fortunately, my mother had no such fear.

Entering the Stuyvesant presented another demi-character challenge. My absentminded professor would not do for the

Sydney Opera House; that much was agreed. He had had his day and some. My new classical was even faster than the last, with a *Don Q*-inspired Spanish flavour added to a frantically fast piece of music called 'Peregrine' from *Don Carlos*, by Verdi. To balance the frantic and flirtatious, Mrs P chose the slow and mournful 'Little Match Girl' for my new demi-character dance. I had still been hoping for Tegan's 'Anne Frank', which was still available, but 'the Little Match Girl' was not a bad alternative. And I would not have to dye my hair or wear a wig. But best of all, Mrs P's choice meant she thought I was skinny enough to play a girl who actually starves to death. I had come a long way indeed since the little chub that had first darkened her studio door more than ten years prior.

It helped that I *was* actually half starving to death much of the time by this stage, so that it was no stretch to get into the character of the Little Match Girl. And with the help of Mrs P's choice of music for the dance, the most mournful parts of Vivaldi's *Four Seasons* spliced together, and a saggy, raggedy *brown* dress that hung off my bones, I all but *became* the Little Match Girl that year, begging for my life on the Concert Hall stage of the Sydney Opera House with great ease and conviction, to eventually die on that grand stage, rejected by the rich townsfolk, not persuaded I was worth saving. I had no trouble getting into *that* character at all.

And the Stuyvesant adjudicators seemed to agree. After two days of heats, with around a hundred competitors each performing two dances, I found myself in the select group of twenty semi-finalists chosen. The semi-finals consisted of a Master Class held in the well-appointed Opera House studio in front of the two adjudicators, a gruelling two-hour class that left everyone dripping with sweat and me worried I had not done enough to make it through to the final six or seven. Min had also made it into the semi-finals and after the class we sat together in the Opera House greenroom with the other semi-finalists, anxiously awaiting the adjudicators' decision.

They kept us waiting a long time but for a green-eyed girl like me it wasn't so bad, feeling that in the Opera House greenroom, though not *actually* green, I had truly made it out of the fake forest to those hallowed greener pastures. And when I heard *'That's Sally Jones'* whispered, and turned to see two of the other semi-finalists standing in a close huddle, eyeing me with something approximating awe, I found that for once I didn't mind hearing my dull-as-dishwater name spoken. If you want to like your name, hear it whispered with awe in the Opera House greenroom.

Still, it was a long and agonising wait until the adjudicators' assistant finally emerged with a list and read off the names and numbers of the successful seven. Miraculously, wonderfully, that dishwater name was on the list, as was Min's much less dull one (Cirotto). Mrs P had *two* finalists in the Stuyvesant; one more than any other teacher had. We were to phone her as soon as we got the decision and that's exactly what we did from the greenroom free phone; it was all laid on for the stars (as it should be). She was very pleased indeed and I don't think I've ever been so happy in my life to find myself in Mrs P's good books and the finals of the Stuyvesant. I didn't even care that it was a Saturday and with the finals the next day, dancing as the starving Little Match Girl, I wouldn't be able to eat my usual Saturday night fare.

Mrs P called later to say she wanted more red sequins on

my tutu. The shops were all closed by that time and Dilly was at the mechanics – her second home – all day anyway, so we would have to make a dash on Sunday, to see Mrs Stanton, Northside's tutu seamstress, on our way back into the Opera House. Mrs P also told me to get the Match Girl Christmas lights sorted, as the ones I'd used for the heats that were supposed to light up the tree and evoke a cosy Christmas scene for the Little Match Girl to long for hadn't worked (they were No Frills). So Mum spent her sentimental Saturday night that week testing and re-testing those lights to weed out the dud, rather than admit there was anything wrong with her brand of choice, while Dad did his best to dance the Greek way without her.

But as it turned out on the big night, the plug for the Christmas lights hadn't been connected to the power the first time round, because the stagehand for the finals had to hunt around for an extension cord that he said hadn't been used for a while, and for the finals Mum's No Frills lights lit up the Concert Hall stage without any problem. Mum, sitting in the audience, held her breath, willing those lights to stay on as much for her sake as mine, as afraid of Mrs P's wrath as I was. And when I lay dead on the Concert Hall stage, starved and frozen to death, before any applause rang out among the 1200-strong audience of ballet enthusiasts, there was a hush, as if they were huddled together in the darkness in their shame, convinced, if for a brief moment, that I had in fact died. It was a good sign.

I did not win the Stuyvesant that year, however, but I did come second, the only other prize awarded, which was not bad for my first attempt. A girl from Queensland, a newcomer, with that classic ballet look of dark hair and enviably long, sinewy arms, took the blue ribbon. I accepted my second place red ribbon graciously, depositing my cheque for $500 in my little blue bank book; prize money that was not tied to ballet tuition and could be spent on anything – a deposit on a pool, for example. Better still, Mrs P was particularly pleased, as I was her first Stuyvesant placing. She offered to drive Mum and me home after the 'Finalists' supper' held in a private VIP function room within the Opera House, with the adjudicators and other glitterati of the ballet community. Luckily, Tim (brother not ballet) had his licence by this stage and could drive Dad and Babs home. Although they were invited to the supper too, Dad had by this stage taken about as much ballet as he could – and then some.

There was only a slight let-down in store for me with that otherwise happy event when the report cards were issued the following Monday and showed that my score of 96/100 for Match Girl had been crossed out to 93. I was awarded 97 for my classical. This was disappointing. None of the adjudicators' comments were negative or changed in any way, and there was nothing to indicate what I might have done wrong to prompt the last-minute change in my score; a critical three points that were most likely the difference between winning and not winning, or why else bother to deduct them? I spent a bit of time stewing on this and speculating on what might have caused this last-minute change of heart, and the best reason I could come up with, apart from the other girl's sinewy arms, was that the main adjudicator, a woman by the name of Marilyn Jones, a former principal dancer of the Australian Ballet Company, had decided, on second thoughts, that it wouldn't look too good if a Jones awarded first place to a Jones.

Drat that name! This was just speculation, of course. It was probably those sinewy arms.

But all that dying practice did not go to waste on the Concert Hall stage, because to round off that year of winning and almost winning, Mrs P choreographed a full-length ballet of *The Little Match Girl* and cast me in the lead. The show was to be performed for the Christmastime opening of the Macquarie Shopping Centre in Ryde, then the largest mall in the southern hemisphere, with its own ice rink, no less, a rare feature in Australia indeed.

It wasn't exactly the Opera House, but there was a sort of surreal grandeur in begging for my life on a small stage in the centre of the palatial mall atrium, as shoppers and skaters dashed past, or paused to watch, curious to see a skinny girl dressed in rags trying to sell matches to Vivaldi's mournful music, not the usual jolly Christmas carols. And after the Saturday performance, together with Min, who danced the soloist parts of Frost and lead shadow, two roles instrumental in my death, I lined up at the Southern Hemisphere's Most Massive Ice-cream Shop and prepared to get my reward. There was only a slight glitch in this otherwise fitting conclusion to my week of starvation on and off stage, when standing in the queue for the southern hemisphere's most massive ice-cream I was spotted by a young child who shouted out: 'That's the Little Match Girl, Mummy. She's supposed to be dead,' pointing in my face, clearly disappointed to see me alive and well – and queueing up for a giant ice-cream. I turned away and did my best to pretend to be a regular person, but children are not easily fooled. 'That's the Little Match Girl, Mummy; eating ice-cream!'

Still, our mall season of *The Little Match Girl* was a fitting end to my brilliant year, in which I might not have gained my Higher School Certificate and learnt how to drive, as Tim had done, nor got my periods and a boyfriend (who wasn't gay) as Babs had, but I did get other things, like a permanent seat on the bus to Chatswood and the southern hemisphere's most massive ice-cream.

But never mind all of that. My greatest achievement by far that year was the spectacular, much-awaited arrival of my beginner boobs that showed up well before Christmas, saving me the trouble of singing, once more: 'All I want for Christmas is my two front teats'. A brilliant year indeed.

Chapter 13

Welcome to Wagga Wagga

Alas, my brilliant year came to an abrupt end when three days before Christmas I found I could barely walk, let alone dance. Reluctantly I submitted to a cortisone injection in my left foot, having put it off for months of increasing pain on account of fearing, as we dancers all feared, that the steroid cortisone would cause weight gain. I preferred to put up with the pain than risk the gain, until it got to the point where I could barely walk and the two-week Christmas break presented an opportunity to recover. Cortisone was the price to pay indeed for my brilliant year.

The pain was in a protruding bone on the side of my left foot, the foot that had always been weaker. However in truth, neither of my feet was ideal for ballet. They were strong on pointe, yes, being relatively short, despite that long second toe, but the arch was not as high as it needed to be, especially on my left foot, and the work I did to try to develop the arch put a lot of strain on the muscles, tendons and bones in my feet. Under the strain, my left foot developed this random bone that jutted out a centimetre or more on the inside of the foot. So much for having *no* bones; I had an extra one. When it had started giving me grief some years back, I had gone to see a doctor about it and he had told me that my feet were all wrong for ballet. Although he was not the same doctor who had recommended I do ballet to cure my asthma, he was still a doctor. Pity they couldn't make up their minds. Naturally I had ignored him. Doctors had been wrong about me in the past. Besides, one of my feet was perfectly fine. But a dancer ultimately needs *two* fine feet and the pain in that left bone had only worsened with the increasing amount of dancing, especially pointe work, I was doing every year. Eventually the ray lamps and ice packs were not enough to relieve the pain and more drastic measures were needed.

The cortisone took the pain away altogether, such that the right foot became jealous of the left. For the first time in years I could point my left foot without pain. It was a true Christmas miracle.

After the break I returned with renewed vigour to the studio, only to find that others had been busy making their own Christmas miracles. Busiest of all had been Ballet Tim, who had made a dance video of himself to send to companies overseas and had secured a contract with the Netherlands Dans Theatre – in the Netherlands! He was due to leave in a matter of days. There was barely time to say goodbye. I considered making my own dance video to send immediately to the Netherlands Dans Theatre so I could go with him, but I had no idea how to go about making a video and Ballet Tim assured me that all the contracts for the year were already allocated.

Of course, as everyone in the ballet world knows, contracts

for female dancers are altogether harder to come by than contracts for male dancers, on account of the general shortage of males and oversupply of females. Also, at barely seventeen, I was probably too young to audition for a company on the other side of the world. So altogether it was not feasible for me to follow Ballet Tim to the Netherlands. Facing the fact, but with great sadness and much private melodrama, I said goodbye to Ballet Tim after just one year of knowing him; a year so full to bursting with brilliance, in no small part thanks to him, I had a sinking feeling that once he left it would all come to a crashing end. Fortunately, this was not quite the case.

The Sydney City Ballet show had to go on, as did I, without Ballet Tim. And due to the growing reputation of the company there was going to be even more dancing that year than the one before. The company attracted a very famous patron that year, arguably Australia's most famous ballet dancer ever: Sir Robert Helpmann, the man who had been Margot Fonteyn's first dance partner, no less. Although when he became our patron he wasn't exactly in his prime anymore and was, in fact, almost dead. Also Marilyn Jones, the former Stuyvesant judge, joined the company that year as assistant artistic director to Mrs P, which made for another interesting twist, and got me thinking again about the Stuyvesant decision. Ballet Tim also needed replacing and the whole top tier of the company strengthened so that we didn't have to rely so much on guest artists.

So we hired four experienced soloists and principal dancers: a husband and wife team, formerly of the New Zealand Ballet Company, Rob and Sonia; a male dancer, formerly of the Singaporean Ballet, Kee Juan, pronounced Keeshwan, which we all immediately Australianised, with affection, to Quiche –

like the pie; and Fran, a former soloist in the Australian Ballet Company who was slightly past her ballet prime at the age of 30.

With these experienced dancers added, and Ballet Tim, who was so perfect for me in almost every way, deducted, it did look like my days of dancing lead roles were over before they had barely begun. Rob and Sonia, who were both tall – and married, to each other – seemed like a natural dance partnership, as did Fran and Quiche, who were a physical match too, both dark haired and short. I had to presume that was the plan and suffered a couple of weeks of panic at the start of the year. But this was not how it worked out. *Giselle* was chosen as our new ballet and Mrs P and Marilyn Jones between them decided to cast me as one of the two Giselles, with Fran as the other. I would dance with Quiche, and Fran would dance with Rob, despite their height differences. Sonia would dance the 'Queen of the Wilis', a powerful soloist role in the second act, usually given to a taller dancer. Min would be her alternate.

Everybody was happy. I was ecstatic! I was born to dance Giselle – a young peasant girl who goes mad and dies of a broken heart at the end of the first act. At seventeen I already had a history of going mad and dying on stage with conviction. I could play that in my sleep (and often did). Also, having studied Margot Fonteyn's career so closely I knew that this was the part she made famous, dancing the role with the Royal Ballet Company when she was just seventeen, the youngest ever to do so. *I* was seventeen! Not that it's all about youth with ballet; indeed Fran would dance the role at 30, and Margot Fonteyn herself had made history all over again by dancing the role into her forties, the oldest ever to do so. Altogether I felt I was in very good company and incredibly lucky to be cast as Giselle, the equal youngest ever with Margot Fonteyn and, just incidentally, the age that Giselle is *supposed* to be. And although the Sydney City Ballet was not the Royal Ballet, any more than I was Margot Fonteyn, being cast as Giselle at my age felt like I had joined the ranks of important people who make dance history, which was all I had ever wanted to do. And I would make dance history that year, just not *quite* in the way I had expected to.

After several weeks of rehearsals learning Giselle from scratch, with Marilyn Jones teaching us the female roles and Hassan teaching the male roles – roles they had both had experience of in their respective countries: Australia and Egypt – we were more or less ready to take Giselle on our second tour around the country towns of NSW. Fran and I were set to dance the part of Giselle on alternating nights, with Fran dancing the opening night performance. She and Rob were, technically speaking, the first cast.

When I wasn't dancing Giselle I would be dancing Peasant Pas with Daryn in the first act, and as one of the Wilis – the spirits of jilted women intent upon exacting revenge, by dancing to death the men who betrayed them – in the second. These were challenging roles too, though not nearly as challenging as Giselle, arguably the most technically exacting female lead in the classical ballet repertoire. Also, going mad every night can be draining, even for an expert. I enjoyed dancing the more light-hearted Peasant Pas with Daryn, who I had known now for about two years and got on with well. He was from Yorkshire originally, a Billy Elliot-type character; the first dancer in the family after a series of miners. Some years back his family had moved from Yorkshire to Wagga Wagga in NSW, and there

Daryn had taken up ballet, possibly as a result of culture shock. Wagga was to be the last stop on our tour and his whole family were coming to watch. There were two performances scheduled for Wagga, because it was actually a small city, not a town, and in one of them I would be dancing Peasant Pas with Daryn. This was going to be a highlight of the tour for Daryn, he said, and I was looking forward to it too.

I needn't have been. Our first *Giselle* tour was the best of tours and the worst of tours, you could say, with a *slight* emphasis on the worst. It was the best of tours because I got to make dance history by being the first, and probably the last, dancer to perform 23 Giselles in a row, including 23 mad scenes that became increasingly genuine. It was the worst of tours, because almost everything that could go wrong did go wrong, including Rob dropping Fran during our opening night performance, which closed the show and threatened to end Fran's dance career for good.

There was an omen of things to come of the dropping variety from the get-go. As Dad drove me, at peak hour, into the city in Dilly to catch the tour minibus, while Mum bussed into work, Dilly's hatchback opened in the middle of the busiest road in Northbridge and my hair and make-up 'pin box' fell out. Evidently, Dilly's hatchback boot had not been properly closed by *someone*. But it was not a moment for laying blame. (It wasn't me.)

'Stop the car!' I screamed, feeling the rush of air let in by the open boot and turning to see my faithful pin box, the dimensions and approximate importance to me of a baby, lying on its side in the middle of the busy road. Dad, who did not appreciate distracting noises at the best of times, and who positively despised peak-hour driving, could not have looked more alarmed, as he half turned his head round to yell at me sitting in the back seat: 'I can't stop the car *here*, Sally!'

'I need my pin box. It's fallen out! You *have* to stop the car!' I shot back, with added feeling, so that Dad, who only had one working eye and nerves made of something other than steel, had no choice but to do his best to pull Dilly up on the side of the road as soon as he possibly could. That he managed this without causing a twenty-car pile-up must go down as a best-of-tour moment. Then, drawing on my early experience of crossing dangerous roads, as well as my speed specialty, as Dad stood on the side of the road looking anxious, I dashed across the road during a brief pause in the traffic, seized up my pin box baby and dashed back, with Dad shaking his head and calling all the while: 'Is this absolutely necessary?' It was.

The plastic box was salvageable, though the latch no longer closed and there was a deep crack down one side through which my greasepaint make-up in red, black and beige had fallen out and was now decorating the road, like roadkill. I could tie elastic round the middle to keep the box closed and use some heel tape to bind the crack, but I couldn't manage without my greasepaint. Neither could I rely on the country towns to stock such a specialised product, or the other dancers to lend me a three-and-a-half-weeks' supply. I was Giselle, for heaven's sake! I shouldn't have to scrounge make-up. But where was I going to find replacement greasepaint at 8.30 am in a hurry? The minibus was due to leave at nine. I wasn't sure how to find, from Northbridge, the theatrical shop in the city that I'd bought the greasepaint from, and it probably wasn't open at this early hour anyway. Theatrical people tend to keep odd hours. Meanwhile, the thought of directing Dad through this traffic to look for an out-of-the-way shop that probably wasn't even open presented visions of a wild goose chase of epic proportions that I couldn't face. There was no point asking Dad if he knew of any other shops, his knowledge of shops consisted of Prouds jewellers, various strategically located bottle shops, and the odd florist.

I wracked my brain as I sat in the car next to a subdued Dad, but I could not think what to do. Then Dad suddenly piped up: 'David Jones wouldn't have what you need, I don't suppose?' I had forgotten Dad's knowledge of one other shop. It just might, I thought; it was worth a try. Better still, the city store was on our way and Dad knew exactly how to get there (it being the original David Jones store, once managed by his father). I didn't expect it to be open, but it was; nor did I expect it to have greasepaint, but it did. And Dad insisted on paying, though he wouldn't come into the store, perhaps not wanting to bump into his cousin, Charles junior, who now ran it. But when I returned with the greasepaint, he seemed particularly pleased that I'd found what I needed and insisted I keep the change. I was not inclined to argue.

So that pin box, greasepaint saga ended up as more of a best-of-tour moment too. Just as well, because everything was downhill from there.

* * *

Our opening night performance was in Maitland, a medium-sized town some 160 kilometres north-west of Sydney. I danced Peasant Pas with Daryn, and considering it was at the end of a fairly long day, and the first performance of the tour, I was happy enough with how I danced and was even glad I didn't have to dance Giselle that night, though I had wanted to dance the opening night and couldn't help envying Fran a little. But not for long...

I was standing backstage for the second act in my white tulle Wilis costume, with all the other Wilis in white, waiting for our cue to go on and dance Albrecht (Rob) to death for his beastly betrayal of Giselle. On stage Rob was throwing Fran up in the air, letting her go then catching her on the way down, repeatedly. I knew the sequence well and was impressed and slightly envious of the amount of lift they achieved; Quiche and I didn't do quite so well. Then, I suddenly couldn't believe my eyes when Fran slipped straight through Rob's hands during one of these lifts and landed with a terrible thud on the stage floor, letting out an agonising wail enough to raise the dead.

There was a gasp from the wings and from the audience too, while the music continued, unaware the dancing had stopped and Fran sat where she had landed on the stage, in a pile of white tulle, groaning in pain. Hassan, who doubled as our stage manager, hurried to turn off the music and close the curtain, before our tour manager, Richard, who was watching from the front of house, issued that classic distress call: 'Is there a doctor in the house?' Fortunately there were two. They came rushing up onto the stage, as we all edged out from the wings, standing back to keep out of their way, not believing what we were seeing, with Rob now standing as far back as he could, close to his wife, Sonia, who looked more worried than anyone.

Richard announced that the show was cancelled and the audience on the other side of the curtain began to disperse in a respectful hush. An ambulance was called and Fran was carried across the stage to the wings in the stiff, inelegant position in which she had landed on her bottom, by Hassan and one of the doctors, pointedly not by Rob, her face all the while clenched in a picture of pure agony. After they left, the rumour circulated that Fran may have broken her coccyx bone, in which case she would never dance again. Everyone was in total shock. 'How could this happen? She was dancing Giselle just a minute ago!' As opening nights go, it doesn't get much worse.

The *Maitland Mercury* ran a front page story the following morning on the Sydney City Ballet's 'dramatic' opening night performance. I don't know if ballet had been to Maitland before – many of the towns we toured had not seen ballet before – but the theatre had been full that night and Fran's accident was major news. Fran remained in hospital in a serious condition, still barely able to move, with a badly bruised coccyx bone. But she had not broken her coccyx bone and was expected to make a full recovery in time. Everyone was greatly relieved, not least of all Rob. Fran would not, however, recover in time to be able to dance again on that tour. The *Mercury* reported that her 'young understudy, Sally Jones, has big shoes to fill' in stepping up to take Fran's place, alongside a picture of me looking worried, something Hassan must have supplied. There was no shortage of photos of me looking worried on file.

As pleased as I was to know Fran was going to make a full recovery, my feet in fact were roughly the same size as Fran's and I was *not* her understudy. And despite my relief for her I could not help feeling a bit put out to be reduced to the status of her 'young understudy', when I was the exact age Giselle was *supposed* to be. Reading my dull, distinctly un-Russian name in print didn't help much either.

In truth, as we pulled out of town early that morning, in a much subdued minibus, feeling strange to be leaving Fran behind (to be later collected by her fiancé and taken back to Sydney), I was a little worried about being the only Giselle on the bus and anxious about the challenge of all that dancing ahead, of going mad every night and twice on Saturday for three-and-a-half weeks straight. In particular, I was worried that I would not have enough pointe shoes to last through all those Giselles. Peasant Pas and Wilis combined amounted to about a third of the pointe work that Giselle entailed.

I had four new pairs of pointe shoes with me and two working pairs that I might be able to stretch out for a few more first acts, but not many second acts, which required much standing on pointe; and my long second toes were not going to cope once the tips of my shoes went to mush. I had learnt that the hard way. A new pair of pointes I expected to last for a maximum of four Giselles. The maths wasn't encouraging. Meanwhile, the bone in my left foot was starting to ache again just thinking about all that pointe work. Also, Rob was going to have to carry on dancing Albrecht every other night because he was on a full contract (unlike me and most of the company who were on part contracts). I was going to have to dance with Rob every second night, even though he had just dropped Fran and was too tall for me. There was a fair bit to be worried about.

But when Hassan, having consulted Mrs P and Marilyn Jones by phone, asked me if I was up to the challenge of dancing Giselle every night, I naturally said I was. I wasn't keen to have Carlotta (the actual understudy) step in to take Fran's place, nor totally opposed to the idea of being the only Giselle on the bus, provided I didn't focus too much on the practicalities. My genes were in my favour there. My long second toes would just have to toughen up. Those toes had been a fat lot of use to me so far, I must say. I was beginning to understand Cinderella's stepsisters' treatment of their own too-long toes, a story that had alarmed me as a child. But I couldn't cut my long toes off. It wasn't that simple. (It never is.) Instead I would stuff some extra cotton wool into my toe caps and draw on my high pain threshold. If nothing else, the situation should be grist to the mill for my mad scene.

Then something else was dropped. We were on our way north to a tiny town called Gunnedah after two relatively successful and uneventful performances, when the bag carrying my back-up pointe shoes fell off the back of the sets truck and was left behind on the side of the road. We were a slick operation altogether, we were. When I went to collect my bag off the truck that arrived at our motel shortly after the minibus, carrying the luggage that wouldn't fit on the minibus as well as our sets, my bag and *only* my bag, the star of the darned show, was not to be found. The sets guys turned the truck inside out to no avail. I tried to keep my cool but my long second toes and extra bone were not happy. '*Where is my bag?*' I fairly screamed in a fit of prima-donna panic, such that Hassan came running from the motel reception, with a look of 'What *now?*' on his face, and must have wondered why he'd ever left the peace and tranquillity of Egypt. 'I am *not* dancing Giselle tonight if I don't get my shoes back!' I may have said in a slight pique, followed by a dramatic foot stomp, glaring at Hassan all the while.

Now, I know what you're thinking: this girl doesn't know how to properly secure her things in transit. To lose one thing off the back of a moving vehicle in one week is understandable, but *two*? That's downright reckless. And you'd be right, except for the part that it was my fault. It was not. Being the person who was almost single-handedly keeping the show on the road, I could not also be expected to take responsibility for ensuring all the things on all the vehicles on that road were properly secured. It was too much to ask. Margot Fonteyn would never have put up with the half of it!

But whatever the case, the situation called for high anxiety, threatening to tip into actual madness if my missing pointe shoes could not be found, given the chance of finding replacement pointe shoes in Gunnedah being about as good as finding them on the moon. And I'd been to the moon and I can tell you there's nothing much there. Moreover, pointe shoes are a customised product, with half sizes, numerous varieties of width and vamp lengths, as well as sundry different brands, few of which are made in Australia. And so the chance of finding my *specific* pointe shoes in Gunnedah, given the quirkiness of that long second toe, were even smaller than that. About the same chance as finding pointe shoes in outer galaxies, I should imagine.

Nor could the other dancers lend me their spare shoes, as nobody had feet quite like mine. Indeed it may or may not surprise you to know that the pointe shoes I wore were not made in Australia. I had Russian blood, a Jewish heart and an alien head to body ratio, so it made sense that my feet would come from some place other than Australia. And sure enough, my feet turned out to be Canadian. The pointe shoes I had finally found to suit me, after some trialling of less suitable brands, were called Canadians and made in Canada with an extra-long vamp to accommodate that troublesome toe

(Canadians must be a smart lot). And being a slightly quirky shoe they were only imported into Australia by one shop, and that shop was in Melbourne, approximately 1114 kilometres south of Gunnedah.

As ballet master, Hassan was in charge of dealing with all dance-related disasters on tour, from dropped ballerinas to dropped pointe shoes. And fearing he was in danger of losing a second Giselle, he moved impressively fast to arrange for six brand new pairs of Canadians in my precise size, width and vamp length, to be couriered up from Melbourne by Comet couriers to meet us at our next destination. I was going to have to dance one more Giselle that night on shoes that had already gone to mush in the toes, but at least I would have an extra two pairs of Canadians to last me through the rest of the tour.

As it turned out I had an extra *six* pairs of Canadians, ten in total, to greet me at our next destination, which I think was Dubbo, after Comet duly delivered the ordered six, and some canny detective work tracked the company down to return my lost bag with the original four pairs that had been found on the side of the road and handed into police. So I ended up with rather too many Canadians, but it's better to have too many than too few.

Nothing else of significance fell off or was dropped on the tour after that, though it was not exactly plain sailing. Few of the venues we performed in were adequate to our needs and some were downright dangerous. The venues were organised well in advance by our tour manager Richard, who was not a dancer and didn't seem to quite appreciate even the basic requirements for a company of 22 dancers staging a full-length production of *Giselle*. One stage we performed on was actually a runway, and as Giselle it was my job to dance on the long nose part of the runway while the corps danced somewhere off in the far distance behind me, in a cramped rectangular space. The nose of the runway was only about a metre and a half wide, and with my luck, on *this* tour, I would fall off it while pirouetting *en pointe*, and that would have been the end of the second Giselle. I didn't fall off, miraculously, but I did most of my pirouetting watching the floor, which made balancing a bit difficult.

At least two of the stages we danced on were raked. This was even worse for pirouetting, as the rake threw your centre-weight off, something that takes quite a lot of practice to learn to control and can't easily be adjusted overnight. Under the pressure of dancing on a raked stage one night I forgot my steps in the middle of the difficult second act pas de deux. It was not me, it was the rake! I was dancing with Quiche that night and when I didn't do what I was supposed to do his eyes shot open in a panic as he did his best to steer me right but failed. In ballet the female generally leads, and when she goes rogue there is nothing much her partner can do.

The music ran on and it seemed we might never catch it, as I fluffed about making up steps and Quiche did the same, mouthing '*Arabesque!*' and other cues for me, desperately trying to get me back on track. This, unfortunately, had the opposite effect of distracting me further to the point that I felt I was going to laugh, because he looked so funny in his panic and quite possibly, what with one thing and another, I was becoming just a little bit hysterical by this time, the final week of the tour. I *didn't* laugh, you'll be pleased to know, seeing as I was supposed to be dead and laughter really would have spoilt that illusion, and the music eventually triggered my memory and led me back to where I was supposed to be, the country audience, probably blissfully unaware. But it was a tense moment, to be sure, and I don't think Quiche ever forgave me for it.

But he probably should have, because I really was under a great deal of pressure, one way or another. Not only did I have to go mad at least once a day and pirouette on a hillside or runway, but I was the youngest member of the company, which could be socially isolating at times. The girls of the corps, aged between 20 and 25, were a close-knit group who wore the same costumes every night and danced the same steps. Being the odd one out of this crowd was a touch too reminiscent of my experience with the Toughies of Killarney for comfort. Min was my only friend on tour; we shared a motel room, but sometimes even she, three years my senior, seemed more matey with the other girls than with me. Indeed she once made merciless fun of me in front of the others over a chicken breast. Me: 'Would anyone like my breast?' (I prefer the dark meat) Min: 'What breast?' I was talking about *the chicken*.

But there was another occasion on tour when I took social outcast to new heights of humiliation. I was waiting backstage for the show to start, dressed in my blue Giselle costume, standing behind the dreary back of Giselle's cottage door, while the girls in the corps were waiting in a group further upstage, dressed all alike in their beige and green costumes, chatting together closely. Although the show was due to start any minute, the girls' chatting was making me feel such an outcast I decided, when I heard a curious word mentioned that I hadn't heard before, to leave my cold cottage and brave the social gauntlet to find out what it meant and in the process insinuate myself into the group. That word was 'orgasm'.

'What's "orgasm"?' was my opening line, as I approached the group, wide-eyed and perky with curiosity. After a stunned pause, during which all heads turned my way sharply, with matching expressions of disbelief, the girl who had spoken the word – the ringleader – exclaimed, with far more animation than was surely required and loud enough for the audience gathering in the auditorium to hear: 'You've never had an *orgasm*?' This was not quite what I'd had in mind when I crossed the gauntlet to get in with the in-group. Nor was it a direct answer to my question. But I was used to being a little confused by other people and pressed on, tragically unaware of the size of the social faux pas I had just committed.

'No. What is it?' I responded, an expression of genuine innocence on my face. To Jenny's credit, that was the name of the ringleader, after she had quite finished splitting her sides with laughter, did attempt to explain to me what 'orgasm' was. I won't go into the details of what she said or did by way of this attempted explanation – there simply isn't time – but suffice to say that Giselle returned to her cold cottage none the wiser on that subject and slightly more wary of ever approaching the in-group again.

For the record, and just briefly, I *had* had an orgasm, I just didn't know it. You may not be surprised to hear I achieved orgasm in a rather unconventional fashion (again there isn't time to go into how here), and because of this, I assumed it was an experience entirely unique to me and never imagined there was a name for it. Such a silly name too, if you ask me. But no-one ever did.

* * *

And so it was with a feeling of great relief that I read the 'Welcome to Wagga Wagga' sign on our way into town for the final two performances of that best and worst of tours. It was also good to know that in Wagga we could expect a decent venue, given the size of the town (small city). On the minibus, as we pulled into town, Daryn and I sat together with him massaging my calf muscles, as he had been doing all tour to ease my leg cramps caused from too much pointe work and not enough *plié*, since my former leg massager had escaped to the Netherlands. As we chatted together happily about being in Wagga and his family coming to see him dance, he told me, in his broad Yorkshire accent: 'Me morther is gorna lorve yer' which, considering my social difficulties, was nice to hear. I smiled back and said I was looking forward to meeting her too.

Because of Fran's accident, Daryn and I had not been dancing together on tour after the opening night, so we made up for that on the bus, spending quite a bit of time chatting and massaging. *He* didn't treat me as an outcast indeed. Versed as I wasn't in the language of romance, it never occurred to me that Daryn's increasing offers to massage my legs on the bus and sometimes backstage too, implied anything other than friendship. Apparently it occurred to everyone but me.

The theatre in Wagga was the best we'd had on tour and both the matinee and evening performances went as well as they could. The final performance was a fitting finale to the tour, with Daryn's very vocal extended family giving us an extra rousing send-off – cheering, whistling and calling out 'Well doon, our Daryn!' at curtain call. I turned briefly round from my position slightly in front of Daryn to see him beaming with pride. It was a best-of-tour moment to be sure.

Afterwards I met Daryn's mother at the supper put on for us by the locals, as happened in every country town we toured, and she did seem rather friendly towards me. Unfortunately, because Hassan had arranged a company dinner on the Sunday night to round off the tour, rather than spend our one day off driving back to Sydney, I was saving my one night of eating for the Sunday, so I couldn't eat anything at the supper. 'No wornder there's northin' of yer,' Daryn's mother said in Daryn's exact accent, laughing, as I politely but with difficulty declined her offer of a chocolate caramel slice, which just happened to be my absolute favourite slice. I laughed too, partly because on a normal Saturday I would have eaten half a dozen of those slices and come back for more, and because I liked being called thin. Daryn laughed too, probably because his mother and I seemed to be getting along, which we were – for now.

With the dancing done, Min and I spent a relaxing Sunday hanging out at the motel, wandering around Wagga, enjoying the anticipation of a slap-up dinner at the Chinese restaurant attached to the motel that we were booked to dine at that night, along with the rest of the company, except for Rob and Sonia. They had brought their car on tour and chosen to drive home after the final show, which was possibly just as well, all things considered. Min had been saving herself for the meal too, as Chinese food meant dim sims, which were a mutual favourite of ours and we planned to order extra. As we prepared for the dinner we talked about dim sims and what else we were going to eat that night.

Normally I dressed up so much on stage that I preferred to dress down after hours. Usually this meant a tracksuit or stretch jeans. But this was a special occasion and in anticipation of it

Min and I had gone clothes shopping together in Wagga before the matinee performance and I had bought a skirt. It was a shortish maroon and black-checked skirt, rather more daring than anything I'd ever worn before. I was going to wear it with my black jazz tights and black chiffon blouse. I thought black went rather well with my blonde hair (the orange had finally faded), and with maroon lipstick and black heels, the outfit was complete. When I looked in the mirror, I was pleasantly surprised by the almost grown-up girl who looked back at me.

Then we arrived at the restaurant. 'Sally!' Hassan exclaimed the instant we appeared, a little late. All eyes turned our way, including those of the Chinese staff. 'You so sexy tonight. Look at you!' Hassan continued, in his much too loud, slightly awkward English, standing up and coming round to show me to the seat he'd been saving for me, more or less opposite where he was sitting in the centre of the T-section of tables set up for our group of twenty. Fortunately, there was a spare seat next to mine for Min, because we had planned to sit together to discuss the dim sims. I sat down quickly and Min and I exchanged an awkward look, half laughing with embarrassment, me hoping the restaurant staff didn't speak English and thinking I might have made a mistake with my outfit.

The dim sims and spring rolls soon arrived and all that embarrassment was quickly forgotten as Min and I got stuck in. They were very good dim sims, we agreed, helping ourselves to all of them on the plate delivered to our part of the table; the others could have the spring rolls.

Unfortunately, Hassan wasn't finished: 'Sally!' – there's that wretched name again – 'You know how much Daryn love you?

He *love* you so much! He tell me all the time. He like you so much, Sally; don't you, Daryn?'

The dim sims were ruined. This *wasn't* funny. Hassan must have been drunk because he was yelling all this out for everyone in the restaurant to hear. The girls beside him were telling him to stop, but he wouldn't. I couldn't see Daryn; he must have been sitting behind me and I didn't dare turn around, though I had noticed him when I came in. He had dressed up too and looked very smart in well-fitted, pale grey trousers and crisp white shirt. He was a good-looking guy.

'Come on, Daryn, man. Tell her! Come on!' Hassan would not shut up and now I did turn to locate Daryn and offer a sympathetic smile, but he wasn't at the table; he was hurrying out the restaurant with his friend Nigel following after him. 'No, Daryn. Come back, man!' Hassan tried. But Daryn was gone.

My remaining two dim sims looked up at me from the plate like giant goggle eyes waiting for my decision as to what I was going to do: eat them or go after Daryn. I went after Daryn.

Nigel met me on his way back to the restaurant. 'Daryn doesn't want to speak to anyone,' he said, his face grim, then took off back to the restaurant. 'Surely he wants to talk to *me*!' I thought. I knew nothing.

'Daryn; it's me!' I called out to the orange door with the number 7 on it, just above a whisper, sensitive to the *slight* awkwardness of the situation.

No answer.

I waited and tried again, a little louder. 'Can we talk? Please, Daryn, open the door!'

The night was setting in and the autumn air was fresh.

There was nobody about as it was off-season and I think we were the only ones staying at the motel. Standing there talking to a closed door with a number on it, after what had just happened, with Daryn inside, in the dark, refusing to open the door, was a surprisingly lonely experience, with the rest of the company just across the courtyard eating dim sims.

'Daryn, I want to talk. Please let me in!' I tried for a third time, raising my voice a little more. There was another long silence.

I tried again. I don't know how many times I tried.

Finally I heard Daryn mumble, 'Do yer harv any feelins fer me?' I was so relieved to hear his voice I almost cried out: 'Yes! I do! Let me in for Christ sake!'

Also, I *did* like Daryn. There was not much not to like. He was well built, with lots of thick dark curly hair, a wide smile and bright blue eyes. He was also, not to be forgotten, a nice guy, giving me all those massages and so on. I even liked his mother. But for some reason I didn't like him in *that* way. He was not Ballet Tim, I guess. Still, I did genuinely want to go into the room and talk with him to ease the awkwardness and you never knew what that might have led to. I should have said yes. But as unskilled as I was in all matters of the heart, I didn't put any of this together in the moment, talking to that number seven door, thinking about dim sims between requests to be let in, and felt instead it was important to give Daryn an honest answer. So after much too long a pause, I said: 'I don't *think* so, Daryn. But I like you a great deal as a friend,' or some such rot. More silence ensued.

After trying again – and again – to get Daryn to open that darned door, with my legs now freezing in that stupid short skirt, I eventually gave up and trudged back to the restaurant where I found, not my dim sims waiting for me, as I had hoped, but the meal all but finished and the company moved on to a whole new scandal after Carlotta had been discovered in the toilets bringing up her Chinese – on purpose. There was nothing wrong with the food, I had to presume.

Chapter 14

Laxatives to London

The next day we had to drive 450 kilometres back to Sydney in a minibus. Daryn sat in stony silence in a back corner, his arms folded firmly across his chest and lips clenched, as if to hold himself together and stop himself from screaming – at me – and possibly at Hassan, his head turned pointedly towards the window the whole way. Hassan, meanwhile, sat at the other end of the bus, rather more subdued than usual, probably nursing a hangover and a modicum of regret. Carlotta sat with an empty seat beside her, somewhere in the unpopular middle of the bus, shunned by all the female members of the company for taking the cheat's way out. It was a long ride home. I plugged in my Sony Walkman to listen to *The Man from Snowy River*, my tour soundtrack when I wanted to be alone, or was alone anyway, which I could usually count on to take me far away, transforming the dreary brown countryside into a dramatic, wild landscape of endless possibility. But not on this day; on this day, as I stared out at the dry flat plains dragging past, the *Snowy River* soundtrack seemed to add to the endless bleak brown.

Surprisingly, despite the numerous dramas and difficulties of that first *Giselle* tour, it was a financial success, making $16,000 for the NSW Arts Council; apparently their most profitable venture to date. So with scarcely a month at home to recuperate, and Fran now fully recovered and good to go, we turned the minibus round and headed off again, this time to Queensland and the outback. With Fran dancing Giselle again I was back dancing Peasant Pas with Daryn every second night, alternating with Carlotta. This was fairly awkward. Almost immediately after we returned from Wagga, Daryn took up with Yvette, one of the corps dancers. And while rehearsing Peasant Pas, a pas de deux that required Daryn to hold my hands and waist, he managed to avoid making eye contact. Between rehearsals he would sit with Yvette perched prettily on his lap – for she *was* pretty – the two of them kissing and whispering in such a brazen way that I couldn't help thinking it was partly for my benefit, which made things rather uncomfortable. Yvette, of course, had been in the restaurant that night in Wagga.

Don't get me wrong. I was fine with Daryn having a pretty girlfriend. I was even fine with watching him kiss Yvette at close quarters. I was used to watching people kiss, after all. And I had had my chance to sit on that lap – well, sort of. Daryn had not in so many words invited me onto his lap. I had to take Hassan's word for it. But Daryn's change of heart, if change it was, had been fairly abrupt for a man who was supposed to be head over heels. A week is not long to fall out of love with one and in love with another, is it? I wouldn't know for sure, romance not being my specialty, but it did seem rather quick.

And on one occasion, between kisses, Daryn caught my eye, or I caught his, though I wasn't exactly *watching* them kiss, and the look he gave me seemed to be one of wounded pride, if only for a fleeting second or two before he recovered his composure. But it was enough to make me feel like I was caught in a particularly unfortunate love triangle and all before I had had my first kiss, unless you counted the one with the hand in the tent, which I didn't. I also missed his friendship – and leg massages.

The Queensland tour was a bit of a washout. There was heavy flooding in the flood prone state that year that slowed our transit between towns, kept audiences away and caused the cancellation of two shows. The best you could say for it was that nobody or nothing was dropped, which was indeed a substantial improvement on the previous tour. Nonetheless, one of our stops towards the end of that tour was a personal touring highlight for me, though it didn't start out too well.

The stop was in Lightning Ridge, a small opal-mining town on the NSW-Queensland border, deep in the red-desert outback. There had definitely never been ballet in Lightning Ridge before. And when we arrived there after a long trek through the hot, dusty desert it wasn't difficult to see why. The minibus was hissing and spluttering with the effort of the journey and caked in red dust to boot, after driving most of the day to get there, missing the matinee performance in the process. When we pulled up into the town square the first thing someone said was: 'Where is it?' echoing everyone's thoughts. All there was to see was a rusty XXXX beer sign swinging in the hot breeze from an old tin building that looked like a barn. Hassan, who was the only one not in a gloom about the prospect of dancing in the desert, pointed to the old barn and said: 'There!' Indeed it could be nowhere else.

This pub-barn in the middle of nowhere suggested an all-time low for tour venues, which was really saying something. On top of this, most of us had been told we were going to have to sleep in the bus that night, because the only guesthouse/hotel accommodation in town slept a maximum of six. The more senior members of the company – Hassan, Fran, Quiche, Rob, Sonia and Richard, who doubled as our bus driver and probably deserved a decent bed more than anyone else after that drive – took care of those six beds. The rest of us were sleeping in the bus. Where our audience was supposed to come from I had no idea. There wasn't a soul in sight.

But never mind all of that! A much more pressing concern for me than anything to do with the show or our accommodation for the night was the question of where I was going to find some food, specifically some *cake*. It was Saturday and, on tour as at home only more so, that was my main food and only cake-eating day. More or less every other day on tour I survived on a diet of tinned beans in brine and coleslaw, resisting the cake-based suppers with the virtue of the vain. But on Saturdays I took great pleasure in perusing the town's bakeries before the matinee performance to find the most decadent baked delight on offer.

If there was one thing country towns did well it was

bakeries, and every other day of the week Min had to drag me away from the windows of these bakeries before I left my drool on the glass. That would not have been a good look for Giselle. But on Saturday I got to go *inside* the bakeries and make a purchase. It was practically the highlight of the tour. On *this* Saturday, however, we'd been driving through the desert all day with no stops for cake along the way. So I'd been anticipating arriving in Lightning Ridge for roughly seven hours, chiefly to behold and sample their bakeries. From what I could see from the bus, I'd be lucky to find a crumb, never mind a cake.

I took off from the bus, almost running round the town square, checking the dusty dwellings on the perimeter, on my crazy cake-seeking mission. These buildings looked like ordinary old houses but might be a bakery; you never know. Time was of the essence, as Hassan wanted us back in the barn in half an hour for a warm-up class. It was about a billion degrees in Lightning Ridge, but dancers can't just walk off a bus and onto a stage – even if it is not a proper stage but a barn. I knew I needed a warm-up class regardless, but I needed cake first for my mental-health warm up. A piece of carrot cake would do, though it was not my favourite. My favourite was a toss-up between a matchstick, custard slice, chocolate caramel slice, cream bun or chocolate éclair, depending on the bakery. Cream-filled, multi-tiered gateaux would also do.

These were the cakes that appeared in my mind, more magnificent and mouth-watering by the minute, as I dashed around the dusty square, feeling my hopes of finding so much as a carrot rapidly fading. I was so desperate I almost considered knocking on the doors of the houses to ask: 'Do you have any cake?' No mucking around. Of course I would offer to pay, top dollar if necessary. But time was running out and the houses looked shut up for business, as if everyone inside was either out or asleep – or dead. Eventually I had to admit defeat and return dejected to the pub-barn, which didn't sell cake. I had already checked.

'Gel, you want?' a boy's voice suddenly sprung from the shadows, with one skinny arm outstretched and a selection of colourful lollies balanced on the upturned palm. Where had *he* come from? And how had he sprung like that, I wanted to know, for the boy only had one leg and stood supported by a crutch. It seemed miraculous. He was an Aboriginal boy of maybe fifteen, with a dark brown face, lots of even darker curly hair, and a beaming white smile.

'You want one, gel?' he asked again, with a little more insistence, as I stood in front of him, stupidly stunned and staring at his missing leg and the open palmful of lollies, sensing he had been watching me and even knew what I was looking for. Had I been talking to myself – *again*? I also wanted to know where he got those lollies from. If they sold lollies they might sell cake! But I couldn't exactly ask him; *that* would have been rude. Nor was I comfortable accepting his offer of a lolly, though I had my eye on the yellow Fantale, the biggest of the lollies, which I did very much want. It wasn't cake, but it would do in an emergency, as this definitely was. But in the moment, once again, I didn't have the wherewithal to accept the boy's kind offer and shook my head, saying a much delayed and altogether too formal, 'No, thank you,' before mumbling that I had to go, pointing over his shoulder towards the barn, as if *I* was showing *him* the lay of the land. I moved off in that direction, careful not to hurry in case it seemed I was hurrying to get away from him, or taking rather too much advantage of my two working legs.

Miraculously, I managed to dance Giselle that night without any cake *or* lollies, and the performance in the pub-barn went surprisingly well. Temperatures cooled dramatically with the night and a good-sized audience turned up in a packed bus, just like us, except a proper sized bus, and except for a handful of people, like the boy with the Fantale, who were already there, who also attended the show. It was standing-room only and that boy stood throughout the entire two-and-a-half-hour performance on his one leg. It was a deceptively large barn inside and maybe 200 people were crowded in to watch the performance, a few kids sitting up front on the floor at our feet because there was no actual stage. We were on the floor like everyone else. But the sets guys had managed to lay out our black rubber flooring to demarcate a stage of sorts, as well as to put up Giselle's cottage in one corner by the only door that doubled as our only 'wing'.

All this closeness made for a relaxed, almost intimate atmosphere, which everyone seemed to enjoy, dancers and audience alike. There was some slightly inappropriate cheering, such as during the mad scene when I go crazy with a sword, threatening the townspeople – on stage – before collapsing dead from a broken heart in Hilarion's (Hassan's) arms. Indeed that collapse occasioned a hearty peal of laughter from the corner where a certain boy, standing on one leg, had been seen all night, smiling broadly. And although I was supposed to be dead and broken hearted, I couldn't help smiling too at that inappropriate laughter, as if that boy seemed to know I wasn't actually mad, just hungry – for cake.

Afterwards, in the smaller barn next to the pub, I got to have my cake and eat it too when the locals put on one of the best tour suppers we'd ever had. They must have brought their cake with them in their bus. Perhaps that was an option I could look into for future forays into the outback.

* * *

At seventeen-and-a-half I still hadn't had a period. That sad pair of padded undies that had turned up in my drawer unannounced when I was twelve remained in the back of my drawer, no doubt wondering what they had done to deserve being sent on such a fool's errand. What indeed. But as if my still undeveloped body was trying to do the right thing, to get cracking with puberty in earnest, I was finding it increasingly difficult, especially when not on tour, to keep to my goal end-of-week weight of 39 kilos.

Suppressing puberty is not as easy as it sounds. The breakfast-only, cake-on-Saturday diet I had begun when I was fifteen and continued for more than two years with little variation and few lapses, was becoming harder to stick to, especially at home where there was so much ready food. The worst temptation for me was not the cake but the savoury cooking smells that greeted me when I came home of an evening after a long day in the studio, to nothing but a bottle of TAB diet cola. These alluring smells were becoming an increasing torment for me, especially the rich savoury smell of shepherd's pie on Tuesday nights that made my empty stomach positively curl with hunger.

It was a pity Mum didn't serve shepherd's pie on another

night of the week, as the other problem with Tuesday night was that it was such a long way from the next and the previous Saturday. On Sunday my stomach could still remember Saturday's feast and Monday I was motivated with the start of the new dancing, dieting week. And Wednesday somehow seemed so much closer to Saturday than Tuesday. I also weighed myself every morning, except for Sunday, and the Monday-morning scales after the weekend's eating were usually highly motivating indeed, reading three to four kilos over my goal weight. I really did eat up large on Saturday.

But by Tuesday, everything was different. The Tuesday morning scales, after I'd danced all day Monday and only eaten breakfast, would usually have halved that gain, so the best I could hope for on the Wednesday-morning scale was a slight, often imperceptible nudge of the black wand to the left. Sometimes I had to squint to see it. This was not so motivating. So by Tuesday night, after two days of dancing, with the memory of the previous Saturday's food long gone and the next Saturday three long days and four nights away, my strength and motivation were at their lowest. Put shepherd's pie on top of that, cooling on the kitchen bench as Mum left it, as if waiting for me, the rich brown meat crusting cruelly around the edges of the dish in extra-savoury clumps, and you've got a recipe for dieting disaster waiting to happen. What was a meat addict at heart to do?

To cut a long story short, what I did one Tuesday night, not long after getting back from that Lightning Ridge tour, was crack under the pressure, lunging for the shepherd's pie crust like it was a life raft. I didn't devour all that was left in the dish, which was about two portions of dinner. Instead, telling myself I would just scrape that tastiest bit of crust from the side of the dish, which wasn't really eating, I began cautiously, selecting the smallest teaspoon in the drawer for the delicate task.

That first scraping of crusted, deep brown meat made my stomach and neck glands tingle with a pain almost worse than hunger. The pain of penance, I suppose it was. I wanted to stop there, but once the tingling subsided and all that was left was that sweet savoury taste of rich mince meat in my mouth, the teaspoon still in my hand, I caved in and returned greedily to the pie dish crust again – and again – all the while telling myself that scraping the crust was not really eating.

Then it hit me: 'I'm eating!' I flung the devil spoon out of my hand before it could do any more damage, possessed of a panic even worse than when I realised there was no bakery in Lightning Ridge. I practically wept with the misery of not having an empty stomach, of not feeling that reassuring curling pain in my gut that let me know I was on the right track. In despair I ran for my life to the bathroom and locked the door on that devil spoon and evil pie crust. The rusty metallic scales, almost more familiar to me than my own face, glared up at me from beneath the vanity drawers where they lived, like a troll under a bridge, lying in wait to pounce the following morning with an off-the-scale reading. I couldn't face that. Then I remembered the laxatives...

For a couple of years a box of herbal laxatives had lived in the back of my top drawer, keeping those padded undies a strange sort of company, the legacy of a suggestion made to all the full-time students by our jazz teacher a couple of years prior. She had suggested we try these herbal laxatives as a weight loss aid, telling us they were quite harmless because they were herbal. I didn't need to lose any weight at the time, but I am one of those people who will try anything once (at least). The herbal laxatives she recommended were called Colon Care, and after swallowing several spoonfuls of the dried herbs that tasted like BO and refused to dissolve in water, gagging all the way, I vowed never again. I'd rather starve. But that was then. I didn't know if they would still be active, but I was ready to try. I retrieved the box from the back of the drawer in a hurry, tucked it under my top, and returned to lock myself in the bathroom with the troll scales to force down as many BO-smelling herbs as I could.

It was all downhill from there. I was hooked on Colon Care, despite the aftermath of a night spent repeatedly dashing dangerously backwards down a clanking metal bunk ladder, waking Babs, but never mind, *she* didn't need her beauty sleep, to make it to the bathroom before it was too late. This was *not* pleasant, nor particularly careful of my colon, but it had a quiet thrill to it nonetheless, as I emptied myself inside out and rested on the toilet, in the calm after the storm, staring down those troll scales with renewed confidence. Welcome, my new addiction.

As soon as I could, I hurried up to the health food shop at Arndale to buy a fresh box of Colon Care, as well as the heavier-duty black senna powder and a box of laxative pills that came with a warning on the side to seek medical advice if constipation persists. I was fairly confident it wouldn't. After that, Tuesday nights and some other nights as well became regular pie and laxative feasts, delivering pleasure and pain in approximately equal measure.

The thick senna powder mixed with water was almost exactly like drinking mud and tar combined and was the hardest laxative to swallow but the most effective. The pills were the easiest to take but the least effective, and the herbs were somewhere in between. So every time I broke my breakfast-only diet from that June Tuesday on, I had to decide what combination of laxatives and in what quantities I was going to take, while locked in the bathroom, the rest of the family watching TV unawares, except for Dad, who was drying up dishes, unawares.

Before long I was returning to the health food shop up at Arndale, then the one in Chatswood, after the Chinese man in the Arndale shop said I was too young to take so many laxatives and refused to sell them to me a second time. Never mind; I was not as young as I looked. I became familiar with all the health food shops on my way into the city and worked out a satisfactory combination of all three laxatives that I could take without too much difficulty if I closed my eyes, blocked my nose and thought of Eeengland. Laxatives felt like the answer to all my problems; a much needed release in the dieting pressure valve, but not so much that I felt like Carlotta the cheat. Making yourself sick was cheating; making yourself poo by drinking a truckload of tar and BO-smelling herbs, that was finding a more creative way to suffer for your art.

But laxatives were not quite the solution to all my problems. In the July of that year I missed out on the $2000 RAD Bursary, possibly due to a loss of stamina and sleep as a consequence of taking laxatives. Alternatively, it might have been that the other girl competing for the Bursary was the Elle Macpherson of ballet – slightly shorter, but with better ballet feet. She was stunning. We had both been invited to compete for the Bursary on the strength of our high RAD grade averages. But when the other girl, Kathy-someone, who was from that problematic state, Queensland, turned up for the Bursary class, I pretty much knew the game was up before the first *plié*. Whether laxatives affected the outcome we will never know. But I'd bet she wasn't on them – her legs were long enough to accommodate an entire shepherd's pie each without sacrificing their slimness.

But never mind. I would get another chance to show this Elle of the ballet world what I was made of in London. A talent scout had come to Australia from London the previous year to find dancers to compete in the top ballet competitions in England and Europe: the Adeline Genée in London and the Prix de Lausanne in Switzerland, and she had selected both of us. I believe we were the first Australians to be invited to enter these competitions; numerous Australians have entered them since. So it seems the talent scout, who went by the slightly terrifying name of Herrida May, with a posh accent and personality to match, must have been a pioneer of sorts. And I suppose we were her guinea pigs, though anyone less like a guinea pig to look at than that Kathy-someone would be hard to imagine. Me, not so much.

After seeing me dance in the Stuyvesant that year, 1982, Herrida had approached Mrs P to make the suggestion that I be sent abroad to compete in these competitions in the January of the following year. When Mrs P mentioned this to me I was not inclined to argue. Europe had proper forests, after all, and of course I had been dreaming of going to Eeengland to follow in my idol's footsteps for a very long time. But, and this was a big *but*, I wanted to win the Stuyvesant first. Indeed I didn't want much. And when Herrida May first made the suggestion I was a also bit young to be taking myself off to Europe on my own, and there were insufficient funds in the Jones coffers, drained by a large horse, for Mum to escort me over there, as Kathy's mum was escorting her. So I would have to go on my own the following year when I was a bit older and hopefully had accumulated the necessary funds, namely the $4000 Stuyvesant first place scholarship money. By mid-1983 this was roughly the plan. All I had to do was to win the Stuyvesant.

* * *

In the August of that year, with the 46th City of Sydney Eisteddfod Stuyvesant just a few weeks away, the Sydney City Ballet found itself in dire financial straits. We had branched out in our Sydney season at the Regent that year to more contemporary ballets, boldly encroaching on the Sydney Dance Company's territory. The contemporary ballet *Symphony in C*, by the famous American choreographer George Balanchine was one of the ballets we staged that season; the other was *Ballet Egyptien*, by the somewhat less famous choreographer Hassan Sheva.

Hassan's older brother, Reda, a principal dancer in the Egyptian Ballet Company, came out to Sydney to appear as our guest artist for both ballets. Because he was tall, and Balanchine choreographed for tall dancers, Min and Sonia were cast in the lead female role for *Symphony in C*, and the dark-haired Fran, with another dark-haired dancer, Leanne, were cast in the lead for *Ballet Egyptien*, not because they were tall, which they weren't, but because they were passably Egyptian. Not being either tall or passably Egyptian I wasn't cast in *Ballet Egyptien* at all and only given a secondary soloist role in *Symphony in C*. I think this casting might also have had something to do with my lapse into laxatives, but I wouldn't like to say for sure. I wouldn't like to blame *others* for my actions.

Similarly, I don't know if my lesser role in this Sydney season was a contributing factor to its box office failure, but that season at the Regent broke the ballet bank and some of our dancers on full contract had to be let go, or asked to stay on without pay on the promise of future earnings. Fran and Quiche stayed; Rob and Sonia left.

'The Sydney City Ballet Fights Back' was the cover page story for that quarter's edition of *Dance Australia* magazine. The picture of Hassan and Fran, dressed for *Ballet Egyptien*, with Hassan's bare brown chest on impressive display and Fran with a fabulous foot extension and back bend over Hassan's knee, amply demonstrating her full recovery, struck a sensational cover pose. I was a tiny bit jealous.

It was quite something to be on the cover of *Dance Australia*. I was pictured inside with Mrs P, Marilyn Jones and the rest of the company, laughing my head off for some reason not entirely clear or befitting the occasion of the company's financial collapse. To be fair, everyone else is laughing too, but they had more reason to laugh than I did, because *how* the company was going to 'fight back' was by going on tour again, this time to Tasmania, at the invitation of the Tasmanian government, and on a plane instead of a minibus. The tour was planned for the exact two-week period of the Stuyvesant. I was given the choice to go, but for me there was really no choice. I had a date with destiny with the Stuyvesant that year and no state government or exciting airplane ride was going to tempt me to change it.

Still, when the company took off for Tasmania a few weeks later, full of excitement and without any obvious sense that my absence was breaking anyone's heart, I felt a little like I'd been abandoned by my family. Left in the studio on my own, as I prepared my two new dances in the week leading up to the Stuyvesant, without a teacher, as Mrs P was using the time to focus on training up her new batch of full-time students back in Belrose, was a little lonely. Earlier that year, the company had moved its city studio from the Institute of Technology building, which had a concrete floor that was giving everyone shin splints, to a studio on the fourth floor of the original Museum of Applied Arts and Sciences in Ultimo, an old brownstone building dating from the late 18th century, so one of Australia's first buildings. So I had nothing to object to on the building front. But on my own, with scarcely anyone else in the entire building, which was rather run down and under-occupied at that point, it could be a little eerie, especially first thing in the morning.

My morning journey into 'the museum' as we called our new studio, was a bit of a gauntlet. Without the other dancers to keep me company I had to walk the Ultimo Tunnel from Central Station alone, a half-mile long, poorly lit, narrow tunnel, occupied by various 'street' people taking shelter in crumpled heaps either side that occasionally came alive unexpectedly. With my hair pinned up and make-up on I felt even more the odd one out than usual when these crumpled people stared at me with curious worn faces. I tried not to walk too fast or stare back. But it was a little unnerving.

Fortunately, my new demi-character dance for this Stuyvesant was Ophelia, which required me to get in touch with my mad side, just for something completely different. It seemed to have been decided that madness was my new specialty. So at least one of my two dances came along well in those empty weeks with the rest of the company away in Tasmania. And with the Stuyvesant looming, my motivation to stay off the shepherd's pie – laxative combo improved, which translated into renewed stamina for that fast Spanish classical that Mrs P had made even faster this year by adding extra tricks and turns. When I went to Belrose two days prior to the first Stuyvesant heat to show Mrs P my dances, she said it was the best she had ever seen me dance them and if I danced like that on the day I had 'every chance of winning', which was gratifying coming from her, who rarely dished out direct praise. And I felt ready; as ready as I was ever going to be.

* * *

The prize-giving ceremony for the 46th City of Sydney Eisteddfod Stuyvesant took place on the Concert Hall stage of the Sydney Opera House, the best stage, in the best building in the world – or so I thought then, as I stood proudly upon it. To be standing on that stage meant I had made it through to the finals once more. Indeed I had not only made it through to the finals but was the frontrunner to win the competition. The principal adjudicator, Dame Margaret Scott, the Director of the Australian Ballet School, had singled me out in the semi-finals Master Class, asking me to demonstrate a triple *entrechat*: a fast change of the feet mid-air. 'That's how it's done!' she had said emphatically, leaving the other semi-finalists to stand and stare in silent awe. Nobody else was singled out. It was a very good sign.

Then, in the finals, after I had finished my fast Spanish classical, landing a split *jeté* on one knee, hitting the last note with emphatic emphasis, the 1200-strong audience had fairly raised the high ceiling of that Concert Hall theatre with their applause. And when I left the stage after an extended curtsey, the Director of the Queensland School of Dance, who had been watching my dance on the backstage monitor, said: 'Congratulations. You've got it with that! Well done. How does it feel?' which was big of her, as her own finalist was standing right beside her at the time. She didn't get an answer because I was doubled over, still barely able to breathe from the speed of that dance, but I was gratified all the same.

Mrs P wasn't backstage, she was watching from the audience, as she preferred to do. Once again she had two finalists in the competition. But in place of Min, who was in Tasmania, there was a very pretty, beautifully built blonde sixteen-year-old girl called Kelly Donovan, who was one of her new full-time students. Being a somewhat more seasoned dancer than Kelly, I had helped her space out her dances on the stage earlier after she had asked for my assistance.

The wait on stage through the many speeches that had to be gotten through before the prize-giving itself, was the most exquisite agony I've ever felt, feeling extremely confident I was going to win but not quite being able to celebrate yet. The seven finalists stood in a row of nervous tutus across the centre of the stage, in our number order. I was second from the right. We all stood, as we were expected to stand, with one foot placed neatly behind the other in *coup de pied* position, which put pressure on one long second toe that went entirely numb, squashed inside a cold Canadian pointe shoe, but never mind; it was a small price to pay for winning the Stuyvesant. I could have changed feet but I didn't want to look fidgety.

The trophy table in the opposite front corner (downstage left) shone under the bright stage lights. I was mesmerised by the winner's wide blue and gold ribbon hanging tantalisingly over the edge of the table, and had to repeatedly force my eyes to look away and face the audience, seated in an immense darkness beyond the speaker. It wouldn't do for me to be staring with my tongue hanging out at the trophies. But how *right* that wide blue and gold ribbon was going to look draped over my black and red tutu! The vision was so vivid it was almost terrifying.

A man in a suit was talking into the microphone at the front of the stage while the two female adjudicators stood elegantly poised over by the trophy table. I stared at them too, especially Dame Margaret, whose face I was hoping would turn my way so I could get confirmation of my win. The slightest turn, the slightest smile or glint in her eye would have done it, but she was giving nothing away. Her face remained sternly focused throughout on the speaker, like a statue. I felt a tiny bit uneasy about this, as she might have put me out of my misery with a quick glance, but remembering the triple *entrechat* I drew a deep breath and told myself to remain calm.

Easier said than done. My nerves were shot. Words cannot describe the feeling in my stomach as I stood there in that tense line of tutus. The speaker droned on and my palms melted with a cold clammy sweat, while my heart thumped like it was about to leap out of its tutu.

When Dame Margaret finally stood at the microphone ready to announce the winners, second place first, as always, I was practically weeping with nervous anticipation. All I could do to stop from losing it and running up to seize my first place ribbon and trophy before it was announced, was to meditate on the back of Dame Margaret's bouffant grey head, and try not to think at all. If she didn't hurry up and announce the second-place winner I would not be responsible for my actions.

At last her introductory speech about the 'exceptionally high standard', the standard speech, was concluded, and she began to introduce second place. 'This dancer is a formidable technician,' I heard her begin and gulped, my heart beating so loudly now I thought surely everyone could hear it. 'She has extraordinary stamina and remarkable footwork, and her dancing altogether is a delight to watch.' Please God, no. 'Her dramatic ability ...'

* * *

I will surely combust with grief. I cannot bear it. Second place *twice* is worse than coming last. It is worse than dying. I go limp with shock and misery as I am made to walk the gauntlet from that line of tutus to the front of stage to collect my dull red ribbon, smaller trophy and much smaller cheque from Dame Margaret, that traitor most treacherous. How I manage this, unsmiling and un-curtseying, like a lifeless zombie, I don't know, but the thick black tears are already running down my face before I get there and I can't face Dame Margaret's eyes. Back in the line – the firing line – of tutus, my head is spinning with grief and I think seriously about running off the stage there and then. I am about to start sobbing. I look longingly towards the exit and almost do run for my life, for standing through the announcement of the winner will surely kill me.

And when it is Kelly Donovan, the youngest and technically weakest of the finalists, who I didn't even consider serious competition, and who will give Mrs P her first Stuyvesant winner, I truly think I will dissolve with grief. Surely I cannot be made to watch as she accepts her trophy and blue ribbon; *my* trophy, *my* ribbon, and yet I am made to watch – the brightness of that blue, her stunned, smiling joy, the applause, so cruel, like mocking laughter – all the most miserable kind of torture.

At the first opportunity, ahead of the others, I bolt for the exit, overtaking the girl to my right then sweeping past the people backstage, who I can feel staring at me and my molten black-red-green eyes, one of them that premature woman from Queensland who stands aside to let me pass, looking uncomfortable. Good. Not good. Nothing is good or ever will be again.

Backstage of the Opera House is a rabbit warren of corridors. I must find the farthest, darkest corner to drop down into and never come out of.

Somehow Lana is crouching down beside me; I don't know from where or how she came. She must have talked her way beyond the stage door security, normally reserved for finalists, their parents and teachers. She has become more of a friend since giving up ballet herself and taking an interest in my career. But I didn't even know she was in the audience. Her rage at the decision is almost a comfort, but there is no comfort. She tells me, after a while, that Mrs P wants to see me in the studio for a photo with Kelly. 'You shouldn't have to go. She's such a bitch,' Lana says, with real anger on her face. 'I wouldn't go if I were you.' I stare at her, unable to respond, my eyes stinging like acid, my body wracked with stupid sobs that won't stop. I'm half grateful she is there but unable to express my gratitude or properly even feel it. I just stare at her blankly.

I am in shock. Lana looks genuinely worried and puts an arm round my shoulders, as we sit together on the carpet up against a cold wall, in the darkest corner of the Opera House, my expensive tutu squashed beyond repair.

There is some small satisfaction in keeping Mrs P waiting. I don't intend on going for the photo, but then I do go, despite myself, too weak to make the harder decision. I stand without speaking to walk and then run towards the studio, wanting this over with. Lana hurries to keep up.

The brightly mirrored studio stings my already burning eyes, the energetic buzz of the group surrounding Kelly stings my ears while anger and shame sting my sorry soul as I catch a glimpse of Mrs P, and she gives me a brief impatient look before returning to Kelly and her beaming blue-ribbon smile. My red-rimmed, snake-green eyes are worse than I imagined and I almost give myself a fright when I look in the mirror. Is that Mrs P talking to Lana? There are too many mirrors in here. Lana passes me some tissues for my face. I will not, cannot smile for the photo. Mrs P and Kelly are smiling enough for the three of us. I do not speak.

Lana comes with me as I charge back out the heavy door and along the corridors to the dressing room that I'm sharing, of course, with Kelly. Suddenly all that matters is that I am packed up and out of there before she returns. I cannot see that golden stolen smile again. It is the same dressing room I shared with Ballet Tim that magical time we danced the *Don Q* pas de deux. Except that it is not the same at all, it is changed beyond recognition forever. Kelly (Dame Margaret) has taken that too. Lana helps me shove all my ballet bits and pieces into messy bags. Ballet can be such a prissy art; it's what she hates about it. I hate it too now. I want to leave the red ribbon for Kelly to find and know what she's done. I don't need *two* Stuyvesant reds. But Lana shoves it in a bag and I don't have the strength to take it out.

We meet Mum and Dad beyond the stage door. Lana has come in her own car. We hug and part company. The pain – and shame – feels even worse in front of Mum and Dad (especially Dad). Mum gives me a sympathetic smile that doesn't help: 'Come on now, it's not that bad, eh Sal?' she says, looking on the bright side as ever. What would *she* know? It *is* that bad. Dad is a bit more understanding; he knows something about losing, even if my loss is kind of his win, proving him right about ballet's excessive 'focus on appearances'. Thankfully, he's above gloating. 'It's tough, Sal. It must be very upsetting for you. I can see that,' he says gently, with a sympathetic stutter, offering to help with my bags, looking older than ever as he tries to help but can't manage much. I'd rather take the full burden myself anyway, and can't help resenting how much more he has to say to me when I lose than when I win. Still, he is trying.

I almost leave him and Mum behind as I rush for the exit, towards those sweeping Cinderella stairs out the front of the Opera House, past the VIP room, already humming with finalists – there will be no Finalists' supper for me tonight – and outside into the night, like Cinderella at midnight, returned to life as an ordinary, unremarkable girl.

* * *

The next morning, Mum is woken by a phone call at 6.45 am that begins: 'We was robbed!' as she notes in her diary. It is Mavis Sykes, an elderly dance teacher we barely know. She says all the teachers are up in arms about the decision (not quite *all* of them), and that the consensus is that Dame Margaret knew I was heading overseas and wanted Kelly for her school. The decision was already made, even before that damned *entrechat*. In fact the *entrechat* was probably a consolation prize. As it's not possible to feel any worse, or any better, I receive this information without emotion. I am trying to get it together to go with Mrs P at ten o'clock that morning to drive two hours to Gosford to help her audition dancers for her full-time school. It's a prior arrangement that I don't have the strength to get out of.

I have no memory of this trip and only know it happened because of Mum's diary entries. Monday, September 19: 'Sal arrived back from Gosford 7.30, quite exhausted and sick. Went to bed fully clothed. I gave her aspirins and cold packs.' And the next day: 'Sal stayed home (woke 10.30). Not feeling too good'; and the day after that the same.

The company returned from Tasmania a few days later and I make myself go in to meet them in the studio. They are buzzing with the success of the tour; the best ever, they all agreed, which doesn't exactly help. But it does help to have the studio alive again. 'You don't look too good,' someone tells me, and I shrug. I don't feel too good. The September–November edition of *Dance Australia* comes out with a full-page article and photo of Kelly, still wearing that stolen smile, her arms laden with her winner's bounty of flowers, trophy and hefty cheque. There are a few words dedicated to the 'runner up'. Dame Margaret's phrase 'formidable technician' is repeated. I hate that phrase with a passion. It makes me sound like a machine. Machines don't faint with fury or ache with envy. Nor do they dance from the heart, as I most definitely do. Machines don't cry. The article concludes by announcing that Kelly is off to the Australian Ballet School next year.

The Sydney City Ballet must keep on dancing to stay afloat, and so, somehow, must I. Another production of *The Nutcracker* to be performed for schools by day and the general public by night is planned for late November, early December, to finish a few days before I leave. I am going to London despite the Stuyvesant loss – and because of it, in a way. I have enough saved in my little blue bank book for a one-way ticket and after the Stuyvesant I have no more doubts about leaving, possibly never to return. Australia can kiss my formidable arse.

The Genée and Prix are both held in January. I'll have three weeks to recover from jetlag before the Genée. In the meantime, between rehearsals for *The Nutcracker*, for which I am dancing the part of Clara, a lead role, but not the long-coveted Sugar Plum Fairy, which Fran and Carlotta are cast in, I must learn the two Genée variations from a video and manual. This is a gruelling process undertaken awkwardly with Mrs P's help in the smaller studio next to the one in which Hassan runs rehearsals of the second act, which doesn't involve Clara much. The piano accompaniment for the Genée dances is clunky and uninspiring next to Tchaikovsky's passionate *Nutcracker* score, and the steps are so technical that I can't muster much enthusiasm for them. They are the sort of steps that should suit a formidable technician, but they don't suit me.

My confidence and stamina are shot. The dancers on the video are intimidating in their technical brilliance, and the truth of the matter is that I am not as fit as I was for the Stuyvesant. In just a few weeks I have lost condition, returning to abusing laxatives on an ever more regular basis, and extending my binges beyond a few spoonfuls of pie. On my way home from the studio one evening, the custard cannoli in the window of the Italian bakery at Central Station that I have successfully resisted for approximately 700 days finally wins out and I don't stop there.

That night the laxatives don't work, possibly because my body is getting used to them, or perhaps laxatives don't work on custard cannoli. Whatever the case, waking up with all those cloying calories weighing me down the next morning is more depressing than losing the Stuyvesant – almost. I starve myself the next day, not even eating breakfast, and again the following day, then break out with another binge the day after that.

And so the vicious cycle begins and continues until one day Mrs P, taking me through my Genée variations, tells me I have put on weight and need to lose it before the Genée. She leads me to the mirror and says: 'Here,' pinching the fat on my upper arm, 'and here,' pinching my upper inner thigh, which is not the first time she has touched that part of me – ballet teachers have a free pass to the *whole* body – but it is the first time she has done it for the purpose of finding fat. I have finally failed the pinch test.

I am a miserable wreck. I charge headlong into a carrot-and-TAB-only diet that I intend to stay on for the remaining weeks till I leave for London. It lasts precisely three long days; not quite long enough for Mrs P to notice any improvement or say anything if she does, but long enough that I'm so ravenous I could eat an entire Italian bakery – and almost do. My battalion of laxatives comes out in full force that night and this time they do work. By the time I get into the studio the next morning, I am light-headed and dizzy from a very draining night. And it's not over yet. After another visit to the studio bathrooms I collapse unconscious on the floor – fortunately just beyond the toilet cubicle.

When I come to, I am being carried through the streets of Sydney in Daryn's arms. Later on I find out that he insisted on being the one to carry me to the hospital, although Hassan, a much bigger man, offered.

I spent that day after collapsing in the museum bathrooms in intensive care at Sydney Hospital being tested for drugs and diseases, questioned by a psychiatrist (I admitted nothing), given a sedative and finally diagnosed with anorexia 'in its early stages'. I was deeply ashamed of those 'early stages'. I had always taken inspiration from Karen Carpenter's battle with anorexia, even if she had just died of the disease earlier in the year, but 'early stages' anorexia feels like being 'runner up' in the Stuyvesant.

But the show must go on. I was out of intensive care and onto the stage dancing the role of Clara quicker than you could say *Nutcracker*. Three days after my collapse, we opened at the Capitol Theatre (the Regent being prepared for demolition by that stage), with the dress rehearsal the very next day. And although I had missed out once again, and forever, on dancing the Sugar Plum Fairy, Clara turned out to be a fitting farewell of sorts. For Clara is the central character of the ballet, the Sugar Plum Fairy a product of her imagination. In the second act, after occupying the spotlight in the first, Clara commands everyone to dance for her from a candy and jewel-encrusted throne, in a fairyland of her own creation, being treated like royalty, which is all I ever wanted, really.

And the icing on that royal cake? One of those sweets is Kelly Barden, dressed as a red-and-white-striped candy cane, one of a group of a dozen or so candy canes, all dressed the same. And although I do know that the Stuyvesant was not Kelly's fault, and bear her no lasting ill will, it doesn't hurt to see her reduced to a candy cane from my elevated throne.

Three weeks later I am on the plane to London. And it is this goal that saves me, I think, as well as my brief stay in intensive care, which was a bit of a wake-up call. After that, I put away the laxatives and got back to my much more balanced breakfast-only, no-cannoli diet. By the end of those three weeks I was down to 41 kilograms, roughly my goal weight, and felt more or less recovered. I could lose those last two kilos in London.

More cautious parents may well have wanted to keep their *slightly* unstable, recently hospitalised teen at home for a while longer before sending her off to the other side of the world unsupervised. So it was just as well that my parents were not the cautious type. In fact, in those three weeks Mum and Dad had once more taken themselves off to their favourite guesthouse in Bowral where Mum, according to her diary, 'sank a 20-foot putt', and Dad bought her an eternity ring to celebrate twenty years of marriage, while waiting to hear back from Oxford University Press who had sent him some encouraging letters on his book. Nana, 97, did not come to French's Forest to supervise us while they were away. We didn't need supervision anymore – clearly – and she wasn't quite up to it, though she was still going strong in her Queenscliff unit, catching the bus into Manly once a week, being extra careful not to fall off. She always said she never wanted to live to 100; just as well for me, perhaps not so well for her, she didn't get her wish.

And Tim and Babs were getting on with their lives too. Tim had successfully completed his first year of university and achieved a surprising level of competency on his surfboard, while Babs had left school to take up an apprenticeship with one of Sydney's top jockeys, her story and photo appearing in the *Telegraph* newspaper.

So, sitting on the plane, pointed towards Eeengland, that Narnia-like land of proper forests, cute critters and chirruping birds, I am more or less content. I plug in *The Man from Snowy River* (in my ears) for a bit of premature nostalgia as the plane clears that vast brown continent of fake forests and improbable fruits, heading north over the bright blushing blue sea. A box of Colon Care is tucked safely in the hold – just in case. They might not have laxatives in Narnia...

Epilogue

Local Warming

As I sit here now looking out the window of the room that was once Babs' and mine, the spine of Dad's book *The Economic Problem in the Poorer Countries* standing tall on the shelf, having the last word for all eternity, all I can see is green. The pipe that Mum persuaded the Council to paint all those years ago remains a deep dark, forest green, the lawn locker she won on *Temptation* in '71 is a paler, somewhat mouldy green, and even the fruit on the orange tree next to it are a bright lime green, as if the tree is somewhat confused about which sort of fruit it is supposed to bear – a confusion I can relate to. But the deepest, most confusing green of all is the grass on the back lawn. It looks like it has been freshly painted in the greenest of greens. Perhaps Mum had the Council paint that too. But no; I've checked. It seems real enough. Besides, the grass is not the Council's to paint. So what happened? What happened to all the brown? It's a mystery of global proportions.

Of course, I've returned to the fake forest many times since my laxative-fuelled escape in '83, an adventure that taught me a thing or two about green grass indeed (that's another story), but never before has it welcomed me back with such luminous, lush green arms. It's almost as if it were trying to make a fool of me, which wouldn't be right – if it wouldn't be difficult either – because *some* things never change. But if that's the case, then it's making a pretty thorough job of it. Because even the birds seem to have found their chirrup and the critters their frolic, if the chirrup is rather stuck on the one note suggesting that it might be a recording of a chirruping bird, and the bandicoots that now frolic at large about the fake forest, digging holes all over our back lawn, challenge anyone's definition of cute – although they do give the Christmas cricketers something to think about. And the screeching cockatoos, like white-winged Dementors, still patrol the place from dawn till dusk, while the cocky Kookaburras still want the last – and the first – laugh: 'Mwa-ha-ha-haaaa!' But somehow I find myself thinking even so, 'What kind of forest is it without a few screeching demented cocks?' A dreary forest indeed.

So when I returned to the fake forest this Christmas from my long-term residence in exile with my non-Russian (Kiwi) husband and three, somewhat dislocated children, to squeeze, as ever only more so, into our modest living room with the much expanded family of Dad's father's fourth wife, and the giant power pylon outside took a direct hit from a lightning bolt that lit up the house like a nuclear explosion or meteor strike, I did *not* run for the hills, next stop Russia. The cat did, mind, and is yet to return. But I stayed bravely put, only partly because I thought the end of the world had come and there was nowhere left to run to.

And when the blinding light cleared and sonic boom faded to be followed by a dramatic drum-roll thunder and river of rain that sent the next generation of Christmas cricketers stampeding inside like a herd of wild Snowy River brumbies full of loudness and life and 'Did you see *that*!', I realised we were not at the *end* of the world but somewhere smack bang in the middle of it, here in this big, brash and bountiful, if ever so slightly barking mad, bush.

Acknowledgments

My sincere and hearty thanks to everyone involved in getting this book published, in particular my publishing manager Samantha Miles for her spookily astute editing and, for the later edition, my cover designer Nikki Davies for helping me bring an old miniature photo back to large and lovely life. Also many thanks to my brother and sister; without you, childhood would have been much too easy – and much less fun. And to two fine writerly chaps, Drs. Jack Ross and David Haywood (neither are proper doctors); thanks for convincing me I could and should write, and for helping me to do so with your insightful guidance. Thanks too to 'Ballet Tim', the best dance partner a girl could ask for (almost), and to the many dancers at Northside and the Sydney City Ballet, lively and unforgettable characters one and all. Finally, but mostly, thanks to my long-suffering (non-Russian) husband and our three hybrid Aussie-Kiwi children who told me to hurry up already with this book. I would not be here without you – I would have been a whole lot quicker about it – but it would not have been half as much fun in the journeying. And a last note to everyone else who found their way into the pages of this book, named or renamed – some names were changed to better ones – I hope you are happy to be immortalised here. If not, feel free to send your complaints to Middle-earth, addressed to Saliana Jonoptonova. If they don't find me, blame the Russians – or, better still, the Kiwis...

About the Author

Sacha Jones spent her first twenty years focused on her physical fitness, becoming a soloist for the Sydney City Ballet at sixteen. The second twenty years were focused on improving her mental fitness, studying and tutoring at university, to finally graduate with a PhD in feminist politics at the age of forty-two. She then moved laterally to creative writing and stand-up comedy to try and find a better mind/body balance, all the while taking charge of the raising of her daughter and two sons. Today she lives in Auckland with her husband, cat and (occasional) kid while writing, performing comedy and campaigning for a world where XX and XY humans are more fairly valued for their respective strengths rather than pitted against each other to everyone's cost. Her favourite food is *still* cake.

umbilicalbooks@gmail.com
facebook.com/sachajoneswritercomedian

Other Books by the Author

The notion of 'body positivity' is widely promoted in the modern West as a feminist ideal empowering women to reject the unhealthy pressures of the thin body-beauty standard. But is it really as empowering as it sounds?

In *The Fatter Sex*, former ballerina Sacha Jones brings a fresh perspective to this contentious issue by highlighting the extra weight management challenges that modern female humans face as the sex programmed to store surplus body fat in our age of Big Food, fat activism and thin fashion. Drawing on her own long battle with eating disorders and weight obsession/denial, as well as the hard lessons she learned trying to raise her daughter to have a healthy and happy relationship with food, Sacha exposes the increasing challenges women and girls face as a result of these conflicting pressures with insight, honesty and some much needed humour.

Through a range of celebrity case studies, Sacha reveals the extent of the modern female 'body battle' and the limits of both 'diet culture' and 'body positivity' activism to effectively fight it. Her eight-course 'feisty feast' of a battle plan is outlined as an alternative approach, with the ultimate aim of empowering women of all sizes, not least the mothers and daughters, to recognise and find strength in their common cause.

facebook.com/sachajoneswritercomedian